Here's what the ground-breaking psychology of fishing, *Pavlov's Trout: The Incompleat Psychology of Everyday Fishing* ...

It was only a matter of time before someone wrote a book-length study of what goes on inside anglers' noggins — quite a bit, we were pleased to learn. ... Pavlov's Trout is a lot more fun to read than many of the psychology texts we remember from college.
— **American Angler magazine**

Fishing is his vehicle, but behavior — yours and mine — is his subject, and Quinnett dissects it with insight and wry humor.
— **The (Tacoma) News Tribune, Tacoma, Wash.**

Dr. Quinnett's unique blend and presentation of disciplines will benefit all fishaholics, and the bewildered family members seeking to understand them.
— **Trout magazine**

Sheds some light into the darkest recesses of every fisherman's mental tackle box ...
—**The Martha's Vineyard Times**

Every fisherman knows that a day spent fishing is not subtracted from your life. Fish every day, then, and live forever. And, as Spokane psychologist Paul Quinnett proves here, "It is much better to fish hopefully than to catch fish." This is a lighthearted cast through the murkier waters of 'fishaholism.'
— **The Oregonian, Portland, Ore.**

Great good humor and insight ... Dr. Quinnett explores 'the essence of sport fishing and why we all love it so.'
— **Sporting Classics magazine**

This is a light-hearted and often insightful book that comes from still another perspective to address the question, 'why fish?'
— **Fly Rod & Reel magazine**

This wonderful little book ... explains how to cease being a 'human doing' — driven and defined by constant activity — and relax back into a 'human being.' Quinnett maintains a light touch throughout, even while angling for life's most elusive secrets.
— **CC Small Press Review**

Pavlov's Trout *has cast a new mold for fishing literature.*
— **The Spokesman-Review, Spokane, Wash.**

Darwin's Bass

The evolutionary psychology of fishing man

Paul Quinnett

Keokee Co.

PUBLISHING

SANDPOINT, IDAHO

Published by:
Keokee Co. Publishing, Inc.
P.O. Box 722
Sandpoint, ID 83864
Phone: 208/263-3573

ISBN 1-879628-11-2

 Printed on recycled paper

Printed in the United States of America

Publisher's Cataloging-in-Publication Data
Quinnett, Paul
Darwin's bass : the evolutionary psychology of fishing man/Paul Quinnett
1. Fishing — Psychological Aspects. 2. Psychology, Applied. I Title
SH456.Q56   1996
799.02
ISBN 1-879628-11-2   Softcover

Contents

Author's Note

Today is the opening day of the general trout season where I live. It is a good day to begin the adventure of writing a new book. That I am writing this morning instead of trout fishing attests not to any sense of self-sacrifice to my readers, but to the wisdom one eventually acquires after witnessing enough opening days. Not to worry, I'm going fishing this evening, well after the madness has waned and the wounded have been removed to the hospital.

Allow me to make a short cast.

The author's note is like a first cast to waters filled with hungry readers. The author's note is a lure. With a flashy note you hope to get a take so that you can, with a swift lift of the rod tip, drive the barb well and deep so as to hook the poor reader.

Then, if played well, the reader will be brought to net in the last chapter, spent but satisfied. Not to worry, this is a catch-and-release book.

My hope is to lure you, hook you and keep you for a time.

Now, let's see if I can tempt a strike.

Charles Darwin was a fisherman. Like most fishermen, he

was a curious man, and it was his profound sense of curiosity, perhaps more than anything else, that enabled him to see things in ways others had never seen them. As he said of his own makeup, "I am not apt to follow blindly the lead of other men."

The result? A long and productive life, many books and researches, and the publication of *The Origin of Species* in 1857. This book contained the single most dangerous idea presented to the world since Copernicus suggested the sun did not revolve around the Earth, but just the reverse was true. Where Copernicus moved man from the center of the universe to its outskirts, Charles Darwin moved him from the head of the class to a seat in the third row. In their time, each move was unsettling.

As an earthquake unsettles a familiar landscape, so the theory of evolution unsettled many of mankind's favorite myths. The tremors from that quake are still being felt. Like night crawlers spilled from a bait can tipped over from an aftershock, whole new sciences can be seen wriggling away from the evolutionary epicenter: genetics, molecular biology, ecology, ethology, neurobiology and sociobiology to name a few. Hardly exempt, the fields of sociology, psychology, psychiatry, ethics and even general medicine are being powerfully influenced by a better understanding of how and why we came to be what we are.

Almost daily these natural sciences speed to the same final frontier and intersection of understanding: the human brain. The most complex thing in the known universe, the human brain produces the least understood thing in that universe: the human mind.

We stand, just now, at the portals of the 21st century. We have solved many mysteries, but even greater mysteries lie ahead of us. And of these, our greatest challenge will be to understand how something we call a brain produces something we call a mind. The answer, if we find it, will change mankind like no other discovery in the history of the world. No Richter scale will be able to measure the shaking.

Only 150 years ago, Mr. Darwin wrote of natural law, "Everything in nature is the result of fixed laws." No more. We are now in charge of natural law, or almost so. Our power is growing exponentially. Leapfrogging over the slow pace of natural selection, we already play god with the fishes. Tiger muskies and albino trout are child's play compared to the new transgenic fishes being spliced together in today's biology labs. From a fish's-eye view, man-the-gill netter, man-the-dam-builder, man-the-hatchery-operator, man-the-gene-splicer is already a god, complete with all the powers of life and death and even creation.

In Darwin's time human behavior was not well-understood. Man and the mind of man was not even a fit subject for scientific inquiry. The behavior of fishermen was best explained by philosophers, men of God, bumps on the head, or the shape of one's nose. It was widely believed in the 19th century that a man's character could be read by the shape of his head. Phrenology, or the slang "bumpology," was the only available psychology, pop or otherwise.

Today we find such primitive thinking amusing. But consider that when he applied to sail as a naturalist on the *Beagle*, Darwin had to receive permission from the captain, who had to first undertake a careful study of the scientist's nose. It was on this voyage that Darwin's thinking about evolution matured.

Captain Fitzroy applied the latest scientific methods in examining young Darwin's nose, found it satisfactory, and thus determined their personalities were compatible and that a five-year voyage together would be possible. That such bad science could launch such a great scientist is a splendid irony.

This book is devoted not to Darwin's nose, but to his curiosity as a young fisherman and the float he so intently watched.

It is under the fisherman's float where the mysteries of the fishes and life and imagination swim.

It is under the fisherman's float that we see the shadows of our ancient beginnings and the flashes of our possible futures.

It is under the fisherman's float that we are drawn, not so much to see the fish, but to learn what we do not know.

It is under the fisherman's float that we may, one day, find that final understanding of the fishes and ourselves.

Darwin fished with worms. Later he fly fished with his college friends. A tender and thoughtful man, he studied earth-worms intensively and wrote a definitive book about them. As a young fisherman, he was told by another angler that spitting on the worm might kill it. He later wrote, " ... and from that day I never spitted a living worm, though at the expense, probably, of some loss of success."

One of the greatest scientists in history, young Darwin began his magnificent search for truth with a fishing rod in one hand and a collecting net in the other. A modest man with a rare kind of self honesty and humility, Darwin wrote to a friend about how publishing *The Origin of Species* may have helped launch something new in this world, "Well it is a beginning, and that is something. ... "

And so is this.

Paul Quinnett
Cheney, Washington

I had a strong taste for angling, and would sit for any number of hours on the bank of a river or pond watching the float.

— Charles Darwin, 1809-82

All things ... linked are,
That thou canst not stir a flower,
Without troubling of a star.
                    — Francis Thompson

A Strike in the Night

The sun starts down. The wind dies. The quiet time has come. If you listen closely, you can hear the song of mosquito wings. Against autumn's bright blue sky, dragonflies and nighthawks swoop to take the singers. Somewhere beyond the cliffs a pack of coyotes howls. In the lily pads ahead of me, a bass swirls. Hope soars.

I cast a surface popper between the pads and wait for the rings to smooth away. I like to think of this wait between splashdown and first twitch as wind-up time. I like to think I am winding up the predatory springs inside a black bass, just as a good cast to promising water winds up the predatory springs in me.

For a bass to strike with force and certitude, it must first orient to its prey, then coil energy inside itself, loading tension and power into its muscles and sinew. Locked onto its target for the killing strike, the twitch of the lure is the trigger. Oh, how I love to pull the trigger.

This relationship between the bass and me is an ancient one, too ancient to even understand. Some say predators have been killing prey for at least 500 million years. At the level of microscopic life forms, perhaps much longer than that. We go back a long time together, the bass and me. We share a common ancestor. The bass may not care about our shared history, or our being blood cousins, but I do. He may not need me, but I most certainly need him.

If there is a largemouth oriented to my black-and-green popper just now, and that bass thinks like bass must think, then the bass believes he is about to have a frog supper. He will be wrong, but then that is the trick, isn't it? The fishing life is laced with deceptions: I deceive the bass with a phony frog just as the bass deceives the osprey with its camouflaged green back.

The frog is to the bass what I am to the mosquitos: a source of nourishment. The dragonflies and nighthawks are to the mosquitos what I am to the bass: a bigger predator. The coyotes beyond the cliffs are to voles what the voles are to the grubs: They, in their turn, hunt a meal. In this quiet, peaceful time of twilight there is, in this great circle of life, an awful lot of hunting and fishing and catching and killing and dying and eating going on all around me. As the old fisherman said, "That's the way it is with life. Sometimes you eat well; sometimes you are well-eaten."

All the creatures here with me tonight around, above and in this lake, have made what the anthropologist Loren Eiseley called, *The Immense Journey*. It is the great journey of life from its beginnings to now. We have all made it, each by our own devices; some clever, some strong, some better deceivers than others, some eating their neighbors, some being eaten but able to keep up with the losses through great reproductive engines. Of the millions upon millions of species that have come and gone in the great journey of life, those of us still here are the lucky ones.

We are, all of us, still on the great journey. We have won a sort of lottery, and we are in on the winnings together — fishermen, fish, predator, prey, plant and plankton — all of us moving through space and time on this little out-of-the way planet tucked away in a distant corner of a small galaxy. Some call the journey of life a miracle; others call it luck.

The rings have smoothed away.

If my popper's splash between the pads has wound up a bass, the wind-up works both ways. Tonight, I am a predator. Tomorrow, I will be a psychologist, a mostly civilized one, but one with a constant yearning to stalk water side by side with the great blue heron.

Tonight, as I slowly take the slack from the line for the twitch, I feel especially predatory. At once tense and relaxed, I am totally focused, alert, wound tight and ready.

It is hard to wait for the strike when the light is failing and the tick of the ten-second countdown passes slowly. And yet, there is this delicious tension — this tension that fills the body with hope and anticipation. It is an ancient excitement, and it answers one of the whys of angling. The tension in a fishing line runs both ways.

I twitch the popper, then strip it toward me in short, quick jerks, but no strike comes. I make ready for another cast.

Rotating away from the sun as I cast, the dark will soon replace the light. I did not remember to bring a lantern, and a choice lies before me: Should I quit now and row back to the boathouse, or fish on into the coming night?

A little night fishing? What is wrong with a little night fishing? As the philosopher Lao-tzu said: "Yet mystery and manifestation arise from the same source. This source is called darkness. ... Darkness within darkness, the gateway to all understanding."

A Little Night Fishing

Theologians say man has something called free will. Being a man, I should therefore be able to choose between staying on to fish into the coming night or going home. Gifted with this touch of the divine, I am supposedly capable of such choices. The courts hold me so endowed. So do my friends, family and colleagues. And yet, do I really have free will? Are my choices really free choices? Or am I just a more complicated animal whose behavior, because it is more difficult to predict, is easier to explain by something called a will?

If I have willpower, where do I keep it? In my mind? No

one has ever seen a mind, or put one on a scale to weigh it, or held it under a microscope for inspection. Since no one can find the mind, or even define consciousness, it is hard to tell just where the will is kept. And if it is kept in something called a mind, no one yet knows how to power it up or power it down. After all these centuries of search, many of us cannot even say if our minds rule our bodies, if it is the other way around, or if the two are so intertwined that the question is too stupid to ask.

What is the will anyway? Why do some of us seem to have more than others? Why does my willpower wilt when the bass really to start to hit and I'm supposed to be somewhere else?

Do the fishes have willpower? Can they use it to refuse something phony with a hook in it? If the fishes can use willpower to not strike, then what sort of fly or bribe or bait or presentation or retrieve does it take to dissolve a fish's willpower? If fish have willpower, do they keep it in a mind?

Failing light, a perfect evening, bass swirling in the pads; these are the ingredients that cause restive thoughts. For example, if I am a man and made in the image of God and have the good sense and decorum that comes of civilized people, then why do I feel this powerful, primitive urge to fool and catch a predator like me?

Should a 5-pounder explode on my popper right now, and if I can set the hook, it will be a fight so fundamental and so wild and natural and instinctive that, for the duration of the battle, I might as well be the bass.

And maybe I am. We both have backbones, hearts, eyes, brains. We both chase fish and are taken in by bass plugs. We share the same ancient biological ancestor. From a human perspective, I dress a little better, but I wear bass T-shirts. I dine in restaurants, go to the theater and sometimes even church, but under all the linen and manners, we two are more alike than not. The bass may object to the similarities I draw between us, but Mr. Bass is not writing this book.

I am willing to accept that pulling the trigger on a surface popper and setting steel in the jaw of big fish is what life is truly all about. At least for me. Perhaps I'm what those who know me well have long suspicioned: a genetic throwback to a more primitive type — a knuckle-dragger with long reachers and a fly rod. If this means I get to fish more because I have less willpower or because I have a smaller mind and can't help what I am, then hey, "I yam what I yam."

Fortunately, I am not expected anywhere this evening; no church, school, family, theater or social obligations. I can do as I please. I can go home, or I can stay, fish and search for the iron key that opens the golden door to one of Lao-tzu's understandings.

Back in the lily pads against the lava cliffs, another bass swirls. Time required to make one of those considered, free will decisions with this ephemeral, indefinable, immeasurable mind: one nanosecond.

And yet, night is coming. I like night fishing, even though there is a molecule of terror in it. Maybe it is that tiny bit of terror that I relish, that going mano a mano with another predator in the dark. I know it is not entirely civilized, but there is nothing to compare with the sizzle of fear except, perhaps, the rush of being feared. Either condition confirms you are alive.

I lay out another cast, this one close to a bone white log floating in tea-colored water.

Surrounded by wonderful life by day, we humans experience too little of the life that fills the night. As children we fear the dark. Some of us never come to relish it. When night falls, we think of home. Our eyes widen to gather more light. Our vigilance machinery kicks in, and we go on general alert. It is as if we are entering an unfamiliar world, one where we are not entirely welcome, even as fishermen.

And yet, it is to those long nights of our evolutionary past that we owe our large, light-gathering eyes and any ability to fish after the sun goes down. Our kind, the mammals, began in the dark. We knew the stars before we knew the sun.

A quick, noisy retrieve uncoils no bass. Making a couple of false casts, I let the popper down hard next to the end of a log and study the coming night sky as I count down for the first twitch.

There, a first star. Or is it Venus? Our ancient ancestors knew the difference instantly, as did all humans only a few centuries ago. We measured our lives by the steady beat of the seasons and by the journey of the stars.

Given my rudimentary knowledge of the heavens, this bright orb could be an approaching asteroid some astronomer failed to pick up and warn us about. I never used to worry about stars turning into approaching asteroids until all that fuss up on Jupiter in the summer of 1994. As if we didn't have enough to worry about, now we have to be reminded that the time allotted the human race could be shortened up considerably by a single, direct hit.

If this bright spot in the heavens is an incoming asteroid, and if it is headed directly into Chapman Lake with the bass and me, then I'd better get busy casting; that, or get busy praying.

Asteroids, Faith, Fishing and the Future of Mankind

If that bright light is an asteroid steaming directly at me and my fishing boat, I won't have much time to get any real repenting done anyway. In the few minutes remaining before impact, I couldn't make a nickel payment on what must be a million dollar debt. So, I might as well strip in this fly and make another cast. In the religion of fishing, a cast is a prayer. As a devout angler, I try to do as much praying as possible.

Ahhh, it is growing darker. I always think best in the dark.

Man has always been afraid of the dark. Or maybe what is in the dark. He's not very fond of his dark side either. Our self-knowledge is incomplete, and what we don't understand has the potential to disturb us. Our distant past, for example. Our relationship to other creatures, and especially other primates, for another. Our lust. Our greed. Our jealously. Our predatory nature. Our proven ability to extinguish entire populations of our own kind, let alone other species. As a species, most of us are slow to explore our capacity for anger, rage or violence.

With many experiencing a crisis of faith these days, and what is worth believing in, our most urgent problems are social, psychological, religious, political and environmental, not finding food and shelter. But between us and the solutions we seek hangs the dark veil of ignorance and human denial. As said in *Peanuts*, "There's no problem so big you can't run away from it."

Maybe there is something about the how-and-why we came to be humans that could help us move beyond our present level of self-understanding. The explanations might not be charitable. They could even embarrass us. We might find that we are rather more like black bass than shining gods, and for some this just wouldn't do.

So, maybe it is better to just keep to the well-lighted paths and ignore that part of fishing man's nature which might account for my undeniable predatory behavior tonight. Better to buy my bass in a supermarket, cut and wrapped, than to admit I have a great and powerful need to see my cousin, the largemouth bass, explode on my frog popper.

If you are a true fishermen, you hunger for explanations. You gladly accept directions to the honey hole of truth. I know few thoughtful anglers who are not amateur philosophers, and fewer still who do not seek a deeper understanding of themselves and the fishes and the water.

For me, I want to learn as much as I can about how and why and by what paths we — the bass, the nighthawks, the mosquitos and me — all arrived here together tonight, at this same time and in this same place. Too much of what I know about such things is shallow, even superficial.

I know a little of how these bass, here in the lake with me tonight, got to this lake: They rode in water barrels lashed to the sides of covered wagons as American pioneers brought their fishes with them from St. Louis in the 1870s. Me, I got here by way of riding west in the gene pool of my great grandparents over the same hundred or so years, and because I remembered to gas up my Chevy pickup before I left town this afternoon.

I make another cast. It settles, sending out concentric spreading rings.

The real mysteries of our much longer journey together is what I thirst for. Sliding past the middle of my life just now, I have come to believe that ignorance is never bliss. Ignorance is dangerous. Very dangerous. Free will, choice, playing gods to the fishes and ferns without perfect knowledge is the great tragedy unfolding before our eyes late in this 20th century. But most cannot see it. Without more complete knowledge of what we do because of what we are, we are pathetic and simple-minded — like a child with a loaded pistol — dangerous to ourselves and a public health menace to every living thing around us.

As I look up at Venus shining low in the sky, I am reminded of how ignorant we humans were only a few years ago. I don't know about you, but I am very grateful to Sir Isaac Newton for describing the natural laws of gravity and motion that oblige Venus to move in an orderly fashion around our sun instead of falling into Chapman Lake while I'm trying to catch a bass. I'm also grateful that I don't have to strain my eyes to see the angel that, for centuries and centuries, people believed pushed Venus across the night sky. An angel, after all, could get called away on a new assignment, and then where would we be? The world must have been a scary place for fishermen before the basic laws of gravity got worked out and you could really begin to count on things like planets to stay in their orbits.

One hundred years ago, no human being believed we could go to the moon. Fifty years ago, perhaps ten percent of the people believed we could go to the moon. By the early 1960s half the people thought we could get to the moon. Today, 100 percent of all living humans believe we can go to the moon, and most couldn't care less. Thus does scientific knowledge move us forward and set us free to seek yet more knowledge.

Stardust Melody

Standing in this old rowboat in the night as the moon begins to rise over the far lava cliff reminds me of what we are made. We, the bass and me, are both made up of itty bitty molecules of this and that. Atoms. Photons. Quarks. And even smaller than the quark but yet to be discovered, something one physicist calls the God particle. Stars, moons, Earth, fish, fishermen, ferns and the Firehole River are all made of the same stuff. All are one.

Experts say the universe is 11 billion or 12 billion years old and that all life on Earth began only a few billion years ago, and that it will all surely come to an end again somewhere, sometime. Others say the universe is as it has always been: constant, unchanging forever and ever. The first version of the universe ends in death and disaster for all life. In this universe you want to fish hard and die young. In the second version you want to pace yourself and keep hope alive. Personally, I prefer the constant, never-changing universe and choose to postpone any pessimism until the all data are in.

What cosmology finally best explains our universe and how the stars and black holes and galaxies hang together is interesting enough, but it is the journey of life down here on planet Earth, from the very beginning to the next hookup, that most fascinates me.

From stardust to contemplating stardust is the greatest story imaginable. Lucky us, we humans are the only known creatures in the only known universe able to grasp the scope of such a journey. With a better understanding, who knows what we might yet become — that is, if a stray asteroid doesn't take us out before we have a chance to evolve into something more admirable than we've accomplished thus far.

Not long ago I heard a story about a 4-year-old boy who, when asked why God made him, replied, "I guess he was tired of making dinosaurs."

If you believe in God, and that God directs the flight of asteroids, then the boy was right. But even if you don't believe in God and another big asteroid happens to land in your zip code you will, at least for those few seconds before impact, believe in asteroids. Either way, we don't want God or mindless meteors to get tired of making humans. Now is our time. Now is our chance to become something better than we've been and to bring new hope into the world.

The history of asteroids smacking planet Earth is older than life itself. Mother Earth has been taking hits for billions of years. The good news is that, thanks to the great asteroid that knocked off the dinosaurs 65 million years ago, we mammals got a chance to grow up and get bigger and smarter. Except for that asteroid, we would still be nothing more than small, warm-blooded, burrowing creatures whose only niche in the great panoply of life was to sneak out after sunset in search of food and sex — a lifestyle, I might add, still quite characteristic of New Yorkers.

The bad news is that the last asteroid has not struck Earth. As I like to remind myself when I'm out fishing, no living thing owns the land or the water or the sky. We are all renters, just camping out for the weekend. Man thinking he has permanent property rights is just another symptom of hominid arrogance. Compared to all the creatures that ever camped on this little planet before us, our species and our mammalian cousins are Johnny-come-very-very-very-latelies.

When dinosaurs did all the major fishing back in the Jurassic, we mammals were no more than appetizers. Small, defenseless, jumpy, our primary mode of travel was the scurry. We lived in burrows and caves and hollow trees. Anything that went bump in the night could eat us, probably in one bite. If we ventured out during the day when all the big scaly guys were up and feeding, we ran a very good chance of leaving the gene pool on a cracker. We can, all of us, thank not our lucky star, but our lucky asteroid.

Reminded of snacks and small, furry, night-traveling mammals, I'm going to snip off this frog and tie on a deer hair mouse. Cousin Bass is very fond of Cousin Mouse and will go to great lengths to slurp one. Since bass were feeding in the lily pads during the time of the dinosaurs and no doubt gobbled up some of my direct ancestors, I'll sharpen this hook a bit, and remind any bass listening, à la Schwarzenegger, "What goes around comes around, baby."

Glancing up, the bright object in the sky grows no larger, so I cast, think, cast, think and, per chance, dream to pull the trigger. There, the mouse with the backbone of steel splashes down.

Ten, nine, eight, seven, six, five, four, three, two, one.

Take a deep breath and twitch the popper.

KERSPLASH!!!

The tea-black water erupts into a white fountain. The mouse disappears in a black whirlpool. I set the steel. I feel the raw energy of a big bass, its head-shaking power as it rips fly line through the pads and pulls me into a strange and wonderful place.

Suddenly it is a million years ago. The stars above are the same. The lake is the same. The lava cliffs and Venus are the same. We, the bass and I, are newcomers to this ancient place. On the clock of life, we only just arrived.

And yet, we found each other in the night and dark water and are now locked, predator to predator, in a struggle as old as life itself. In the black of night, on this little lake, on this little planet tucked away in the corner of the cosmos, my rod arches, my heart pounds and my hope is answered.

The initial mystery that surrounds any jour-
ney is: How did the traveler reach his starting
point in the first place?
— Louise Bogan, **Journey Around My Room**

Darwin's Bass

Casting for bass in that old wooden boat many years ago, I had only begun to wonder at our origins and evolution as human beings. Evolution explained the evidence of paleontology and why we have so many variations of finches and fish, but social Darwinism had earned a black eye earlier in this century and you didn't hear much about it after the Nazis and racists and bloodless capitalists had finished twisting the theory to their own ends.

Until recently, evolution is what happens to moths and radishes, not human beings. But the science of biology has begun to flex its considerable muscle and focus its attention through the long lens of evolutionary theory, and the result is about to force massive changes in the social sciences, including psychology and the psychology of fishing.

There are only a handful of evolutionary psychologists as of this writing, and most social scientists haven't a clue about what's happening, and is about to happen. They don't know it yet, but some of their pet theories are like the passenger pigeon: doomed to extinction. New directions in research are emerging. Since psychology has never enjoyed a general theory of human behavior from which to organize and prioritize its goals and research, evolutionary biology and findings from allied sciences are about to shake our customary beliefs and prejudices to their very foundations.

Less than 100 years old, psychiatry and psychology have bristled with hundreds of theories, dozens of schools to defend those theories, and too many ideological traditions, fads and foolishness to count. When you get right down to the question, "What makes people tick?", what you hear is the discordant din of tiny swords clashing. There's a standard gag in my field: Ask three psychologists for an opinion and you'll get five answers.

I'm not sure where an evolutionary, biological and adaptation theory of fishing man will eventually lead, but one thing is now clear: While the answer to who we are lies in the past, the answer to what we will become has never been more in our own hands.

Pond Scum on the Old Fishing Hole

I doubt if Charles Darwin understood that when he handed science his theory of evolution he gave us the most powerful weapon against ignorance ever imagined. Judging from his letters and autobiography, he had an inkling of its explanatory powers, but my guess is he never dreamed where his ideas would lead us these 150 years later. To pond scum, for example.

Pond scum is important to fishermen. Too much pond scum, and the fish in the pond will die for lack of oxygenated water. Too little pond scum, and the food chain is endangered. No pond scum means no microorganisms, no food chain, no fish and no fishermen. This formula is true for your stock pond bass and, in the ocean, for everything from blue crabs to bluefin tuna. Perhaps pond scum is a good place to begin our grand journey to understand how we Homo sapiens, though we are "neither fish, flesh nor good red herring," ended up inventing such clever things as barbed fishhooks and graphite rods.

People who study evolution generally look for changes. Paleontologists look for changing fossils that link ancient organisms with modern. Fish biologists examining the results of stocking programs look for wild fish that change from one generation to the next. Chemists and molecular biologists look into test tube brews to study evidence that something old and familiar is changing into something new and different. When such changes are documented, we see evolution in action. Evolution is occurring each and every second of each and every day. What is not so well understood is why some organisms don't change, and therefore don't seem to evolve.

Every angler is familiar with that blue-green pond scum (cyanobacteria) that forms on your favorite bluegill lake. A living film on stagnant water, it comes and goes with the weather. But pond scum is a fascinating life form that helps us understand why some living forms change and some don't.

According to J. William Schopf, a paleobiologist at the University of California, blue-green pond scum has not changed all that much in the last 1 billion years. It may have been different before that, but the billion-year-old fossil forms of blue-green bacteria are essentially a perfect template for the modern pond scum on my bird watering pools. Imagine that. A life form so perfectly adapted to all its possible habitats that, according to selection theory, few requirements to change have ever occurred.

Sharks and turtles share lengthy unchanged evolutionary histories, but pond scum has been trucking along in a straight line for at least five times as long as these creatures. If pond scum enjoys politics, it probably votes conservative.

According to the fossil record, most species of creatures last no more than 8 million years, so holding on for a billion years ought to win some kind of "Lifetime Fitness" award. The vast majority of new species like us appear, find a home, exploit a niche and then, when the environment changes and our local adaptation fails, we die off and become extinct. The number of failed life forms that once filled specialized niches is astronomical. Victory belongs to the generalists.

The blue-greens go on and on and on and on. They live in hot springs, on snow fields, under rocks, in acidic environments, in the salt seas, desert water holes and on the insides of rocks, clocks, wallets and watches. They can survive with or without oxygen. Some can live for long periods without the sunlight necessary to turn their engines of photosynthesis. They've been doing the same asexual reproductive dance for eons and eons and eons, and it has only been in the last 500-or-so million years that newer, more competitive organisms have finally forced the blue-greens into less hospitable environments.

The blue-greens account for a large portion of the primary food production of the seas today, providing the first rung in the food chain of life that leads eventually to bluefish, bluefish hookups and bluefish fish stories. Next time you're out at the old bluegill hole, tip your hat to the pond scum, because without it you wouldn't be all that much.

On the Origins of Life

In Darwin's time, scientists put things like pond scum under crude microscopes to search for the fundamental elements of life. They didn't have very good microscopes, so they didn't find much. Because they had not yet been discovered, they could not know about what goes into things like pond scum: atoms, cells, genes, chromosomes, DNA and such. They could only guess at what accounted for the quickness of life. After long and careful study, the scientists of Darwin's day concluded that pond scum was not even alive.

At the bottom of all evolutionary research, well below the level of pond scum, lies the plausible premise that increasingly complex life evolved from lower, unicellular forms. The progressive fossil record is mostly complete. The story is a straightforward one based on stratified, datable, hard evidence: More complex life forms evolved from less complex forms. Common ancestry with earlier life forms is linked not only to our shared anatomical features, but to our DNA codes.

Complex life forms like bass and bass fishermen took much more than a week to make, or a year, or even all the time since the day of creation back on October 23, 4004 B.C.

In his day, Darwin was stuck with trying to explain the great journey of life found in the fossil record, in something under 6,000 years. He needed a much older Earth to make his theory work. He didn't have one. Now, posthumously, he does. Our size 12 evolutionary theory now has a pair of size 12 shoes or, to be more precise, an Earth 4.5 billion or so years old.

Darwin's prime thesis on the evolution of species no longer excites much debate. Exactly how life first began, however, still fuels arguments, research and campfire discussions.

Did life emerge randomly? Was evolution accidental? Did God plant a seed and start the process? Or did some space-traveling fishermen stop off here for a lunch break and leave a half-eaten tuna fish sandwich and its associated microbes on a lifeless planet?

A thesis to explain life's beginnings is emerging, a thesis worth springing on some hapless fishing pal around your next campfire. Here it is.

Given the mix of lifeless chemicals available under the primordial atmospheric conditions believed to be present when the show began, what if the origin of life was not an accident at all? What if it was a perfectly ordered, highly determined and quite predictable consequence of the laws of physics and chemistry?

Back in 1953 Stanley L. Miller and Harold C. Urey pioneered the origin-of-life research at the University of Chicago, basically showing that amino acids could be formed out of complex molecules under the right blend of primordial conditions. In a word, the building blocks of life could be replicated in a laboratory. But exactly which chemical components first appeared in the prebiotic soup, and in what order, still loom large in biochemical research today.

Just a few years later in 1958, researchers Sidney W. Fox and Kaoru Harada showed that under original primordial conditions, amino acids can assemble themselves into simple proteins that serve as the core structural components for living cells. Nowadays, Fox continues his work at the University of South Alabama in Mobile, where he and his colleagues found that these proteins can make themselves into tiny cell-like objects called protein microspheres.

It is only a small step from these cell-like protein microspheres — able to join together into electrically communicating networks when stimulated by light — to the possibility that these cells may have provided the necessary safe environment for the emergence of nucleic acids. It is the nucleic acids that ultimately gave rise to DNA, RNA, self-sustaining cellular life, pond scum and dry fly purists.

This new research has an interesting twist; it may explain not only the how of life, but the why. It is the whys our minds truly hunger for; the hows are only the salt and pepper.

If it can be shown that life was somehow inevitable, then it might be a little easier for us to accept ourselves and our place in nature. We couldn't help how we all got here, so why all the fuss? Why argue about who we are? Or how we're special? Why not just go with the flow of our biological roots and honor our natural origins as we come to know them?

If you're the kind of person who simply must know your birthright and, with it, the exact location of where life first began, I will give you what the researchers gave me: All life began at the edge of a warm, sandy beach. The sun was shining. It was probably the middle of July, and the zip code was 00000.

There, now you know.

Or, perhaps life didn't start here at all. Perhaps we are all descendants of something extraterrestrial. Studies of meteorites and asteroids from outer space show they, too, contain amino acids, the building blocks of life. The mathematician Chandra Wickramasinghe and Sir Frederick Hole, the British astronomer who came up with the term "Big Bang," hold that organic microbes are regularly deposited on the Earth by comets and other such extraterrestrial visitors. If these scientists are correct, our creation myths may need a little tinkering.

At least for me, there is a great deal of comfort in the notion that down at the chemical, electrical and amino acid level somewhere long ago and far away on a warm, sandy beach at the water's edge, a gradual, lawful, completely necessary series of events took place that eventually changed non-living molecules into self-assembling, genetically endowed, replicating systems that, inexorably and with great luck, led to the bass, the butterfly and me. I mean, what a trip.

Here's a footnote.

If the process described by these scientists makes sense scientifically, and if the processes they describe led to the conditions necessary for life, and if life then lawfully occurred, it only stands to reason that since our planet is no different than other planets scattered throughout our universe, the same natural process, following the same laws of physics and chemistry applied to the same elements, has taken place elsewhere. Which means there is very likely other life in the universe, and which means that when our first starships travel to those distant, watery places, we'd better pack travel rods.

Horseshoe Crabs, Coelacanth Fish and the Sea Inside Us

All living things had a watery beginning in the salty sea. Some of us, like the horseshoe crab, remain in the sea, while others of us roam the land or fly above it. Wherever we are, wherever we go, we bring the ocean with us. The sea is still inside us. Our blood is salty. When we weep, we weep salty tears. We need a saline solution to soothe our eyes. If God is angry enough, he can simply remove our water content and turn us — as with Lot's wife— into a pillar of salt.

While the oceans teemed with life for 3.5 billion years, the continents remained as sterile as the surface of the moon for the first 2.5 billion years. The oldest-known land fossils are you guessed it, the blue-greens, perhaps other yet-undiscovered bacteria, or even fungi. Only a micrometer or two in length and less than one-tenth the thickness of human hair, these were the earliest living colonists to invade the sterile soils of the continents from the briny deep.

As every angler knows, you need bait to catch fish, and it appears the bait invaded the land first. The fish, naturally, followed the bait.

One theory, which I especially like, is that the first fishes to try breathing air and hunting land worms came out of the sea to avoid predation in a dangerous, fish-eat-fish world. Called *Hynerpeton bassetti*, these earliest-known landwalkers lacked the tough body and huge teeth so prevalent among the bad boys of the swamps some 365 million years ago.

A kind of weeny in a watery world where every competitor

was bigger, meaner, faster, tougher, and more deadly, old H. bassetti pioneered the land with a set of lungs and limbs capable of a fast crawl, thus making it one of the first vertebrates to conquer the continents. Even the amphibians came much later, no doubt to find they had escaped the sea only to meet Mr. Bassetti and his gang of thugs.

H. Bassetti was a tetrapod, or four-legged. He had robust, well-muscled shoulders capable of moving up and down in a very unfish like manner. His general type shows up in the fossil record all over the world including, most recently, Pennsylvania. Unlike the cartoon where a single fish has one front fin up on a beach and is holding a little flag in the other that reads "First Fish Landing!", it appears fishes of all sorts were evolving into land dwellers over most of the known equatorial world. They still are.

Not Everybody is a Land Lubber

The first true vertebrates, some fishes tried the land and, for reasons we may never know, said "To hell with it!" and returned to the sea. Cousin Coelacanth is one such fish.

I have never caught a Coelacanth, but someday I might like to try. It would be a great hoot to catch a fish that man thought had become extinct some 60 million years ago. A kind of mystery fish with stalky, lobe-like fins, this creature caused quite a stir back in 1938 when the first one was caught off the South African coast.

With several species in hand now and carefully examined by scientists, it appears these fishes have remained virtually unchanged for over 200 million years, which puts them on par with that survivalist turtle you sometimes meet at the old bluegill hole. That old turtle you look down on for being so slow and stupid, by the way, has done nothing but survive since the Triassic, which means that Cousin Turtle enjoyed tea and crumpets and watched — from their box-seat shells — the entire rise and fall of the dinosaurs.

Coelacanths have long, curious fins on wristlike stalks used for creeping along the ocean floor, not swimming. They live at depths of 500 to 900 feet, which probably accounts for why no one has ever caught one on the dry fly.

Coelacanths are not small fish. Some weigh over 100 pounds, and the largest caught thus far weighed in at 160 pounds. They have a robust and heavy body, degenerate lungs, are closely related to the lungfish, and probably walked around on dry earth before returning to the deep in search of food or to avoid predation on land. Voracious, active, and the same in fossil form as when caught today, coelacanths preceded the whales, porpoises and seals back to the briny. Except for a couple of gill-sprouting, badly addicted surf fishermen I know, humans are unlikely to return to the sea except in boats and waders.

Natural Selection is Natural Enough

The process of natural selection is not something you have to read about to understand. Every time you go fishing you can witness natural selection at work. The mayfly that lingers a moment longer than the mayfly next to him on the surface of the stream is sipped out of the gene pool by a rising trout. The crawfish that zigs when he should have zagged is swallowed by the young bass. The young bass that swims close to the surface above the school is taken by the osprey and leaves no offspring.

It is the other young bass, the one swimming deeper, below the school that avoids the osprey's talons and becomes "Darwin's Bass." Darwin's Bass takes cover a little quicker at the approaching shadow of a bird of prey. Darwin's Bass swims a little faster. Because of a lucky draw among the mutated genes of his brothers and sisters, Darwin's Bass enjoys a bit better camouflage, thus escaping detection.

Or, perhaps Darwin's Bass fights a little harder and breaks free from the predator's beak and claw and hook to make it to the warm, spring spawning waters. Perhaps Darwin's Bass can tell a live frog from a rubber one with a hook in it better than his brother or sister. Whatever it does, however it succeeds, however it adapts, it survives, and it is this survival machine that is Darwin's bass.

Natural selection does not work on groups, it works on individuals. Big bass and big fish generally get away to spawn again precisely because, as individuals, they are *big fish*. The reason Darwin's Bass is big is because it has already won a thousand battles, caught a thousand meals, avoided a thousand deaths and otherwise outlasted the vast majority of those bass fry who hatched with him. A warrior, a battler, a tested and proven survivor, the big one often gets away. It's supposed to. That's why I never feel all that bad when it does.

Darwin's Bass is any fish, bird, deer, worm, oak, rose or blade of grass still among the living. The story of life is the story of natural selection, of surviving long enough to reproduce, long enough to protect your young until they too reach maturity, reproduce, and carry on the species.

Imagine for a moment that of the 50 billion species of plants and animals that appeared on the great stage of life, only 50 million are still here. Because we are still here, and still doing well, we too are Darwin's Bass.

Fishing in a bayou in Venezuela a few years ago, I watched evolution in action for part of a morning. Schools of peacock bass were chasing bait in the shallows of a remote jungle lagoon. The bait would swim ahead of the bass and, when rushed for the kill, some of the small escaping fish ended up on shore. Some would lay quietly while others would immediately flop around and end up back in the water where the bass were waiting to nail them.

Those little fishes who stayed out of the water a few seconds longer than their brothers and sisters, and thereby avoided being eaten, gained some small survival advantage. Not much, but enough for another hour, another day, or another spawning season. They lived through one more peacock feeding rampage. Those that survive the peacocks of the world become Darwin's Bass.

Stay out of the water for longer and longer moments, put a big mean predator at your back, the safety of the beach to your front, and a worm on that beach and you have, with a couple of million years to work out the travel arrangements, a reasonably good story about how we — and I mean the land-walking cat fishes, little white rats and college sophomores — all came ashore.

Sitting there in the jungle resting my casting arm that

morning, it was plain to see that one way to win the arms race in the water is to get out of it. There is nothing harder on the future of your genes than to get yourself killed before you reproduce. As the old fisherman once remarked, "Sometimes the best way to win a fight is to just skip it."

First campfire question: Is this how we all got started, trying to outrun hungry bass?

Answer: Probably.

Second campfire question: Does this mean we humans evolved from a cowardly, worm-eating fish?

Answer: Well, of course we did.

Third campfire question: Which came first, the worm, the fish, or the fisherman?

Answer: We all came in the same car, but the worm drove.

Go down the dark stairway out of which the race has ascended. Find yourself at last on the bottommost steps of time, slipping, sliding and wallowing by scale and fin down into the muck and ooze out of which you arose.
— Loren Eiseley

A Fishy Story

Question: What is the principal difference between a bullhead and a politician? Answer: One is a scum-sucking bottom-dweller, while the other is a catfish.

Question: Is there another difference between a scum-sucking bottom-dweller and a catfish?

Answer: Only one can catch and eat the other.

Hold it one minute.

What about a giant catfish?

Just when you think you're starting to understand this wide, wonderful world of fishing and how it works, you get a news flash. Here's a late one.

According to a recent newspaper story, Malaysian officials conducted a frantic search for a huge catfish after it had gobbled up two dogs struggling in the swollen floodwater of River Endau on the Malay Peninsula. Officials were determined to catch the giant catfish before it caught small children adrift in the flood. The catfish was thought to be about 10 feet long, complete with sharp, poisonous spines capable of paralyzing even a full grown politician. The story did not report what sort of bait, hook, rod, reel or assault rifle was used in the search. As the story did not say they caught it, apparently this big one got away again.

Man eats fish is not a story; fish eats man is. Jonah made the first headlines in this category. *Jaws*, Peter Benchley's book and film about a great white shark, made more recent worldwide headlines. When a fish eats a man, we humans make a big deal out of it. With no capacity for irony, the fishes couldn't care less.

No fish can appreciate that swallowing a man is a felony offense — unless that man is a lawyer, in which case it is only a misdemeanor. I have a lawyer friend who assured me he is never in danger of shark attack while wading for bonefish.

"Why?" I asked.

"Professional courtesy," he grinned.

Because it has no mind as we know it, no fish can appreciate its relationship to man, let alone its immense evolutionary history, its possible future, or even its next meal. A fish's vision is as short as a floating worm, a drifting mayfly or a darting minnow. And no fish can appreciate the fact that there are more different kinds of fishes than all the other vertebrates that have ever lived on this planet.

By comparison to all other life forms, fish have ruled the world. More than half of all things with backbones that have ever lived have been and are fish. There have been jawless fish, armored fish, spiny fish, and fish larger and longer than a locomotive. All these, including what would have been the greatest tackle busters of all time, are now extinct. The *Chondrichthyes*, sharks and ratfish, and the bony fishes, the *Osteichthyes*, are still with us. These are fish we angle for.

Fishing Man, or Fish-Man?

Since fish were the first vertebrates to colonize dry land some 350 million years ago, all mammals, reptiles, raptors, demigods and Democrats can glance down the family tree to a fish. Some of us are more adapted to the land than others. Fishermen, sailors, swimmers and such, never seem entirely happy when removed so far from water they can't see it, smell it, hear it, or get in or over it. Personally, if I go more than a few days without getting close to fishy water, to my ancestral beginnings, my soul begins to dry out, crack and peel.

Our common ancestry with fishes begins with an ocean-loving, 1-inch long creature called, *Pikaia gracilens*. *Pikaia* had the first proto-spinal cord. *Pikaia* is evident in fossil form from the shales of the Canadian Rockies and was named after Mt. Pika by the man who found it among the debris from the floor of an ancient Cambrian sea. Our phylum, Chordata, descends directly from *Pikaia*, through the first swimmers, through the fishes, and right up to the fellow casting a three-piece rod.

We humans are inordinately proud of having arrived as vertebrates with spinal cords rather than, say, arthropods with an exoskeleton. We don't consciously think of ourselves as biological cousin to the fishes, but I will submit to you that part of our identity as humans rests squarely on the fact that our spinal cords are encased in bone.

To be a fisherman of good character, one needs "backbone." From my handy-dandy synonym finder, here's the short list for backbone: integrity, soundness, manhood, quality, principles, firmness, resolve, endurance, fortitude, valor, metal and courage.

To properly insult a fisherman from the *Chordata* phylum, simply remove his backbone. Try, "You spineless bastard!" Or, "You jellyfish!" Or, "You cockroach!" Or, "You worm!" Want to slam someone to a station even lower than a worm, try, "You slime ball!" You can't get much lower on the complexity-of-life scale than blue-green algae.

Between us and *Pikaia* is not Cousin Monkey of our 19th century fear and ignorance about human ancestry, but a long chain of life forms that include crawlers, burrowers, climbers and, most importantly, swimmers. I don't know about other fishermen, but it is easier for me to accept being descended from a fish than from a monkey, which is not to say I have anything against monkeys except they are not as much fun to catch. One day when I was backcasting a huge bass fly and snagging it in the Amazon jungle behind me, my Indian guide asked, "Are you fishing for *el mono?*"

"*El mono?*"

"Monkey."

Where the tribolites, dinosaurs, great marine reptiles and billions of other plants and animals did not make it this far in the journey of life, we and the fishes shot through the narrowing gap of the great die-offs and mass extinctions. And it's a good thing the fishes made it with us, because without them the fishing wouldn't be much worth a damn.

When Uncle Lobe-fin finally came ashore in search of angle worms or to keep ahead of whatever was after him, he made all us vertebrates one big family with Brother Bass, Cousin Trout and Sister Salmon. This is the kind of family I always wanted.

Spawning Runs, Then and Now

Comparative psychology is mostly about comparing us to other warm-blooded mammals, and especially those who look like us. The research in ethnology, primatology, physical anthropology, and the cognitive sciences have been targeted toward chimpanzees and apes, apparently on the hope that while we know we are pretty close cousins with one another, we are not *all that close!*

Everyone knows our minds set us apart from all the others. This gulf between us is wide, not narrow, so wide that it allows us the use of not only language, tools, and the ability to think about problems, but to ask ourselves such curious questions as, "How should I now think about the problem before me?" Einstein did most of his problem-solving in this manner, simply by thinking.

Unlike other creatures who must test the environment with a new behavior and perhaps die, we can test the environment in our head, see in advance that we will get ourselves killed, and take another path. Such capacities for imagination have given us a huge survival advantage, as well as certain, moral responsibilities — to which I will return once I have made several more false casts.

As a psychology student in the late 1950s, I was taught that man was mostly mind and intelligence and language and has no trustworthy instincts like the salmon's spawning run to count on for what to do next. Even when confronted with a problem as important as finding a mate and reproducing, you pretty much had to figure out how to do it on your own, or have someone show you. Being human, you don't automatically know what to say or what goes where. Nowadays, of course, this problem has been solved by daytime talk television and afternoon soap operas.

In the 1950s I was also taught that if you have strong, deep feelings boiling up out of your loins and blotting out rational thought, you should try not to pay attention to them. These were dangerous animalistic instincts. They could overtake you. To combat them, reciting the multiplication tables was recommended. Or cold showers. Or prayer. Unlike the fishes, you were supposed to overpower such feelings with the power of the mind. No thinking with your glands, we were told.

I knew these recommendations for mind control to be true and workable because my teachers told me they were true and workable. Unless you were a salmon, glands were not to be trusted. Glands were installed to test you. Fail the test and you end up in trouble. Until you're married. Then glands are okay. Of all the glands that gave me trouble as a youth, testes topped the list.

I grew up before something called sex education was invented. As a teenager I couldn't tell a gonad from a grapefruit. Married before the sexual revolution, neither my wife, Ann, nor I had any sex education, which accounts for why we had three children before we figured out what was causing them.

Then I grew up a little and, by the late 1960s, I was teaching Psychology 101, including comparative psychology, at the college level. I told my students pretty much what my professors had told me; that while man had a few built-in needs, he is not like other creatures, and certainly no relative of the fishes.

I told students that man had no instinctual, hard-wired, direction-finding, automatic on-off, highly tuned machinery for such important functions as, say, sex — despite the fact when I was young and dumb and full of testosterone, I seemed to have just that.

Cursed with testes troubles, too, my pals and I, just like mature buck salmon loaded with milt, experienced a powerful urgency to head upstream. In the 1950s we never failed to run up the mountains to Big Bear Lake every summer to see if any beautiful girls were hanging around the public, Saturday night dances. Saturday night would roll around and, like pods of anadromous fish scenting fresh water, we'd climb in a Chevrolet and make a mad run up the mountain.

If that mad dash up the hill wasn't a summer spawning run, the cement dance floor wasn't a hardened spawning gravel, and those beautiful, perfumed, alluring, egg-laden, fertile young women swaying to and fro to the rhythmic strains of Glen Miller's "In the Mood" were not our other half in that ancient reproductive dance that started way back in the warm waters of our birth as chordates, then the parallel is certainly close enough for a book entitled *Darwin's Bass*.

Of course I realize that speculation of this kind about any similarities between the reproductive habits of humans and fish is highly irresponsible from a scientific point of view. I know humans don't go on spawning runs. I know we don't meet, make eyes at each other, touch fin to fin, and try to mate. On the other hand, if you believe breeding in warm shallow water is strictly for the fishes, you haven't tried it in a hot tub.

The Brightest of all the Fishes

Although we and fishes are all of the same ancestry, we are now responsible for them. As land-adapted fishes, we are the brightest. Blessed with an inner world of thought and reason and the ability to think, we have become not only the most intelligent, but the only moral animal, the only animal capable of compassion. This makes us responsible for the rest.

We didn't ask for this responsibility, but we have it all the same. Of all the billions of species that have come and gone before us, and that are still with us today, we humans hold the first wild card in all of evolutionary history: intelligence. This card has more power, offers more danger and more opportunity, than any of us yet realizes.

Because fish have been selected for something other than brains, and because we have been selected for brains, the fishes must now rely on our outsized brains to save them — not from each other, but from us.

While many of us engage in mindless, routine behaviors day in and day out, like going to work and watching television, when we choose to engage our minds to solve an important problem, our eyes take on a clever glint and, quite suddenly, we transform ourselves into the most cunning creature ever to appear in the history of life.

Not only are our brains loaded with built-in survival devices from a billion years of successful evolution, but each us is filled with vast memories from personal experience and, some argue, an even more vast collective unconscious inherited from our ancestors. More, we have access to and are connected with all other human intelligences, past and present, through books, the media, and now the Internet. *Homo sapiens* are quickly becoming one vast, planetary cognitive system whose powers are limited only by the next bright idea, which is only a few nanoseconds away.

If information and use of language is power, and deliberate planning is the measure of intelligence, then let us please grasp the scope of our moral responsibilities — not to ourselves, but to all living things.

No other creature is going to replace us in the near future and assume this responsibility. You don't see apes sitting around campfires discussing the diminishing salmon population. Apes haven't even mastered the cigarette lighter, let alone how to gather dry wood, make kindling, and keep and carry a flame. You won't see chimpanzees putting guides on their fishing rods because, while some of the chimps know how to fish for termites with a fishing twig, no chimp has written a how-to article on the finer points of termite fishing and published it in *The Chimp's Guide to Better Termite Angling.*

Like it or not, we are the masters of the animal kingdom. As kings and queens we have responsibilities well beyond just looking out for ourselves, a kind of *noblesse oblige* which requires us to move forward only with the utmost care, caution and deliberate speed.

How Shall We Shepherd the Fishes?

Cattle were domesticated over time as roving bands of hunter-gatherers tracked and killed the weakest from great herds of big, slow-moving animals. Driving them into box canyons or out onto spits of land surrounded by water, early man eventually came to fence them, feed them, and make this special deal with them: If you won't run away, we won't kill all of you.

When this deal was struck with wild sheep, we called ourselves shepherds. And now that we are making similar deals with the fishes, maybe we should call ourselves "fisherds."

Fisherds in the Laboratory of Life

Darwin drew much of his data and knowledge about the variation of species from animal breeders. He knew that breeders of horses and pigs and sheep were engaged in unnatural selection, somehow mixing various manifestations of species types with one another to produce even more variations, eventually manipulating outcomes until the offspring met the desired configuration. Fatter pigs, for example.

There was no science of genetics in Darwin's day. Something like genes were suspected, but an understanding of the mode of transmission for hereditary characteristics would not be learned until the 20th century. Now, the science of genetics is leaping ahead of itself. Our methodologies for creating variations on species are improving daily. Each week we learn more and more about which pieces to manipulate, which to splice together. In a matter of a few more months and a few more years, our technology will allow us to put together just about any old kind of fish we want.

Consider, then, a transgenic fish. Unlike a cross-bred, sterile fish like the tiger trout whose mother is a brown and whose daddy is a brookie, a transgenic fish can be engineered to reproduce. Created first in the mind of man and then in a petri dish, coho salmon that average 1,100 percent faster growth than normal are being produced by research scientists in Canada's Department of Fisheries and Oceans. One experimental fish grew thirty-seven times faster than normal.

Transgenics involves moving genetic material from one animal to another. In this case DNA from growth hormones taken from a sockeye salmon were tinkered with, copied and injected into fertilized coho eggs. These sockeye-coho grow to weigh 8 or 9 pounds, instead of the normal 4 or 5 pounds, over the same two-year period.

Growth acceleration has been achieved in Chinook salmon, Atlantic salmon, rainbow and cutthroat trout. But this is the first time genes from one species of fish were used to speed up growth in another. These fish are not yet released into wild stocks, but since they are fertile and can reproduce, imagine their potential impact on ordinary salmon.

And if this isn't enough, other transgenic fish are on the drawing table in other labs. How about a transgenic halibut and catfish? Or, if you like steak and lobster, why not order up a lobsteak?

Is that you, Dr. Frankenstein?

At first this idea of producing creatures to our own specifications sounds pretty good. We humans say we have always wanted this kind of personal power, if not so much to fool around with designer humanoids, then at least to fool around with designer pigs, pigeons and trouts. The genetic engineers have already produced strains of albino trout, partly to convince fishermen in heavily fished areas that there are, since you can see them, still plenty of fish in the stream.

I've seen these trout. With a high, pearl-white finish, they practically glow in the dark. Catching them is easy, you just cast to the well-lighted holes.

But imagine that you are one of these genetically engineered rainbows. There isn't much color in your rainbow. You can't hide. You can't run. You can't blend in. Compared to the other fish in the stream, you look like a free sample at the predator's supermarket. True, you were not engineered to grow old and spawn, but your very existence raises moral questions.

Do we fishermen really want to play god? Do we really want to be able build the fish of our dreams? Perch with dull spines? Ten-pound crappies? Dumber largemouth? Steelhead that take only the dry fly? With transgenics, we will soon be able to build the fish of even our wildest dreams.

Remember what the old fisherman said, "Be careful what you ask for; you just might get it."

Scientists from the University of California at Davis have mixed the genes from two different species to come up with a "geep." A geep is a cross between a sheep and goat and looks something like a floppy-eared llama in wool knickers. Like the tiger muskie, the geep doesn't get many dates and remains sterile, but the transgenic coho is fertile and, if released into the wild, will probably get a lot of dates — and I don't mean just for coffee.

Sooner or later we animals with the super brains are going to have to ask ourselves the question, "Is there a good place around here to stop all this fooling around and think things through?"

Another question has occurred to me, "Are we too damned smart for our own good?"

What if we get so damned smart we outsmart ourselves? What if we keep jiggling this, jostling that, tinkering with that over there, adjusting everything from river flows to the color of trout and end up, some day, blowing ourselves up in our suits? Wisdom is rare. Just between you and me, I worry there might be too many kids in the lab without adult supervision.

How to Make Dumb Fish

Able to override the oldest laws of nature, we in the Northwest United States are making up for the threatened steelhead runs by propagating millions of hatchery steelhead. We do this by trapping a few big spawners, ensuring fertilized eggs, and protecting the fry until they are able to start to the sea. If there are too many government-built, hydroelectric dams between these fish and their future in the ocean, we barge them around the obstructions. Any natural selection of a year's class of these lab fish is strictly unintended.

By nature's standards, and except for their inherited wits and instinctive resources, these sea-going trout are pampered, spoiled, overindulged. Absent a natural developmental history in their birth stream and the subsequent, danger-filled swim to the ocean, these fish can never be street smart, clever, wary, or strong because they never had to live by nature's rules. Nature's survival rule is this: First you get by the predators, then you get to reproduce.

Hatchery steelhead are not naturally selected by nature, but unnaturally selected by man. By fisherds. If these human-reared fish have stupid genes, we will never know it. Until it is too late. A hatchery steelhead is what you get when you let the Corps of Engineers set you up on a blind date.

Since government-issued steelhead compete with and threaten the few remaining wild steelhead we haven't figured out how to finally kill off, the whole gene pool could end up as dumb as posts. Worse, we could end up with uniform, genetically defective stocks. Should a new virus find them, and their autoimmune response fail because they were never tested in the wild, an entire fishery could be lost.

Mucking around with Mother Nature to achieve what we believe today to be good cost-benefit ratios is not only dangerous, but stupid. As Albert Einstein said, "Only two things are infinite, the universe and human stupidity, and I'm not sure about the former."

While I try to never confuse sincerity with stupidity at the Corps of Engineers, I would like them to consider that there are some problems in the lives of fishes and men that cannot be fixed through the proper application of high-powered explosives.

An Evolutionary Approach to Caring for Fishes

A Darwinian approach to the fishes that we love has much to recommend it. As good fisherds, it might be helpful if we humans understood more about the evolutionary explanations for the things that pester us. Like diseases.

Both fishes and humans have bodily defenses to invading microbes, too much sun and injury. Both must fight off bacteria and viruses who consider us meals. Both are engaged in nothing less than an arms race with these bugs. Bugs are sophisticated opponents. The bugs can, do and are evolving faster than we are, thus challenging our autoimmune systems and our modern medicines on a daily basis. This is all-out war.

Further, we and the fish are faced with unnatural environments; the wild steelhead trapped in a still-water pool behind a dam that wasn't there when his ancestors evolved faces a new enemy, as do I when I am trapped in an office that wasn't there when my ancestors evolved. Neither of us fits all that well into the brave new world we humans are refitting for ourselves, and neither of us is likely to change fast enough to catch up.

It is probably too late to rewind the last 100 years and run the tape forward to a different ending. We're in it now and there is no backing up. We cannot, as Blanche does in *A Streetcar Named Desire* rely on the kindness of strangers. We are it. All that is left to discuss is who gets to decide what we do next.

Question: Who among us knows a better law than natural law?

(Respectful pause.)

I didn't think so.

So, what shall we do about bending natural law into unnatural acts? The moral, religious, ethical, social and political implications of designer fish is just the tip of the iceberg.

As a fisherman, it has always been easy for me to accept the idea of tampering a bit with the evolution of fishes. Albino trout are kind of novel. Now I'm not so sure. When I think about the wild westslope cutthroat I dearly love, the thought of fooling around with their genes, their water, their habitat, their spawning gravels, and their watersheds, suddenly is an anathema. The wild cutthroat trout has remained unchanged for centuries and centuries and centuries and centuries. It is a successful fish. How could I or any other human being, or committee of human beings, no matter how big our collective brains might be, do anything but see to their safety and security? Is not the goal of the Good Fisherd to protect what is?

The Brave New World

Science does not run on opinion, science runs on ideas, followed by observations, followed by research, followed by facts. Now that the light of science has been cast back over the old path of our evolutionary history, it will be hard to turn away from what is lighted up. There will be no safety in dogma. Pretending we are special gets harder and harder. As we confront ourselves anew, we might even find the journey of self-discovery less than merry.

The fact that scientific research leads us closer and closer to our blood ties in the animal kingdom is simply an artifact of the research, not an indictment of our origins. Unless you can reach in and rearrange your DNA, you must admit to a whole new set of relatives, including Cousin Bass and Sister Salmon.

But since you *can* reach in and rearrange your DNA, splice things together, mix and match genes, you can also turn yourself into something never seen before, and at least as strange as a geep or a sockcoho. If the idea of designer fish doesn't get your attention, the idea of designer humans should. Unless a large asteroid takes us out and gives the insects their chance at running the place, the next 100 years should prove verrrry interesting. One day in the next century, when transgenic humans are commonplace, we might wake up to the following headline during the Olympics, "400 Meter Winner Swims Like a Fish Because He is a Fish." And the lead sentence begins, "Olympic swimmer Jacques Cousteau IX was disqualified after gene count shows he is more salmon than man."

How, then, shall we care for the fishes? Because we humans sit atop the food chain of life, we are now responsible for that food chain, from top to bottom. Our sense of kinship with the fishes needs to be stronger, not weaker. It is not us against them. It is us *with* them.

Some trout fishermen kiss a trout they've caught before releasing it. Some bass anglers thank their bass and then release it. Many anglers talk to the fish they're fighting. If we eat them, we ought to thank the Great Spirit, or God, or the god of the fishes, or the fishing gods, or some higher power for the privilege.

The more we see ourselves as cousins of the fishes, and all those creatures with whom we share this great journey of life, the easier it will be to see their lives and our lives as one.

Therefore, my vote is to accept our blood ties with the chimps, the trouts and the chickens — well, maybe not the chickens — honor these, and get on with the job of learning about ourselves and how to fit into the world, not fit the world to us.

Not long ago, I talked to a serious, deep sea sport fisherman who said that a blue marlin knows, somehow, whether or not you intend to kill it. At the end of the battle, and as the great fish is pulled alongside the boat to be offed or released, it locks eyes with the fisherman. Well-hooked and exhausted, the great fish is either doomed, or about to be set free. "Somehow," the fisherman said, "it knows. Because if you are not going to kill it, it stops struggling and lets you release it."

This man had landed many marlin and swore that these fighters could read his intentions. Entirely sincere, he added, with a bit of love and mystery in his voice, "After the release, they always swim back to the boat for one more look, as if to say 'Goodbye.' "

Whenever I hook a big fish my throat gets dry
— not because I give a damn if I lose it but
because I need desperately to see it before I
might lose it. For me, the worst blow in fish-
ing is losing an unseen big fish. I am haunted
by hundreds of them.

— Ted Williams

The Angler's Eye

As a psychology graduate student many years ago, I conducted some terribly important research on the human eye. Unfortunately, this work was overlooked by my major professors and although you may find this hard to believe, not a single one of them thought to nominate me for a Nobel Prize.

"Please think twice before you undertake anything like this again," sighed my advisor at the end of the project. Pouring himself another double bourbon, he then fixed me with the studied gaze of an inebriated full professor. "Paul, you are *not* a researcher. I beg you, please find something else to do."

Able to tease the subtlest meanings from complex communications, I took this to mean that perhaps my talents as a psychologist lay elsewhere. After all, not everyone is suited to teach white rats algebra equations or to train college sophomores to turn left in T-mazes. Or is it the other way around?

The fact is that I never much liked psychological research in the first place. Research takes time, patience, careful attention to detail and grant money. Lots of grant money. You have to be clear thinking, logical, fussy and a good money grubber to be a good researcher. You also have to be able write in *Lingua researcha*, a form of scientific English so narcotic that only a handful doctoral candidates, full professors and amphetamine addicts are able to remain awake after reading a single paragraph. Then, too, it seemed to me that 90 percent of the studies I was obliged to memorize were of such weight that they could be favorably compared to throwing size 18 trout flies into the Grand Canyon and then listening for them to hit bottom.

Still, I would be nothing as a psychologist but for the hard work of researchers. Psychology without research is little more than conjecture. Perhaps, in my case anyway, I read too many rat studies and suffered from an overdose of triviality. Because for a time there I began to wonder if all the animal studies I was required to learn were preparing me for a field other than psychology. I recall one time in graduate school when a fishing pal consulted me about a personal matter. "I'd have a lot of advice for you, Norm," I responded, "if you were a white rat."

No doubt my attitude and general incompetence as a man of science accounts for why no one ever nominated me for a prestigious research position at, say, Harvard. Oh well, the fishing isn't very good around Cambridge anyway.

But for a year or so I did my level best to understand something of how science works and how science might explain the human eye, especially how it functions in relationship to emotions. The why of the human eye is a question only evolutionary biologists might answer, and while I have always been more interested in answers to why questions, I was in the wrong field to expect a good answer. So I tried to study how the eye works. Here were the questions to which I sought answers:

Is the eye, as the poets have offered, the window to the soul? Can you look into someone's eye and tell what is going on in their mind or body or both? If so, how accurate is your reading?

Less concerned with the photochemistry of one of nature's most sensitive light detectors, I didn't much care how the eye converts light falling on the retina into the images we call vision, but rather how the involuntary response of the pupil itself might be used as a diagnostic tool.

Why, as my question was framed, does the pupil open up, or dilate, when it is presented with a pleasing stimulus, say the photograph of beautiful girl in shorts and hip waders? And why does the pupil constrict when presented with an unpleasant stimulus, say an expensive rod smashed in a power window? By watching a pupil open and close, could an astute observer learn something about what a person was thinking or feeling?

Could you, I asked in *Lingua researcha*, watch the pupillary response in your lover's eyes while you kiss him or her and tell whether or not he or she is in the mood for a spawning run? Because the pupillary response is not under voluntary control and cannot lie, could my research lead to a new and painless lie detector? Had a suspect robbed a bank? Cheated on his taxes? On a more practical level, could a study of the storyteller's eyes determine if he was lying about the size of his fish?

These and other monumental questions fired the imagination of this young researcher. With a fevered brow, I threw myself into the work; reading, researching, building the technical equipment necessary to study how eyeballs respond to psychological stimuli, rounding up hapless subjects in the hospital where I worked and, as result, missing out on several good fishing trips with my friends that summer.

The mysteries surrounding the psychophysiological functions of the human eye tormented me, sometimes for up to several seconds at a time. Graduate school, in case you've missed the pleasure, is not so much a place to enjoy books and learning as it is a place where the word "thesis" or "dissertation" can make your food go down in lumps. Anxiety rules. Depression is king. Exams haunt you. The work is tedious, endless and costly. You must learn to ignore the inflated egos of young professors and avoid giving them groin kicks for arrogance. The best advice I ever got about attending graduate school was from the chair of our department, Dr. James Elder. He said, "The most important thing to get out of graduate school is you."

The Angler's Eye

When you look into a mirror, that double, fixed gaze you see is the gaze of a predator. If you are cottontail rabbit and you suddenly feel that human gaze, you freeze. If you are brook trout and feel that human gaze, you flee. If you are a law-breaking, over-the-limit fisherman and a game warden fixes you with that gaze, you sweat; such are the powers of the human stare.

All great predators have this power, this ability to fix prey and cause terror. All predators have their eyes mounted in front of their heads, thus allowing them to find, fix, focus, track and attack prey in three dimensional space.

In many ways, the predator's eye is the centerpiece of evolution. It is hard to imagine how the great diversity of life might have developed had we creatures never been able to see each other.

We predators are famous for our accuracy. We seldom miss what we intend to hit or strike or grab. We eat well because of our vision. Most fish eat well because of their vision. After fixing their meal in space, a few predatory fish like the shark lose their targeting ability in the final millisecond of attack. In the recent case of a huge northern pike from northern Alberta, Canada, that missed my surface popper by 6 inches (thus causing a momentary coronary arrest followed by severe shaking in the extremities) I can personally attest that northerns sometime miss their targets, too. Rainbow trout, so the research finds, miss their floating mayflies as much as half the time. Still, predators have terrific eyes.

Prey tend to evolve camouflage since they must survive in sufficient numbers in order for the predator to survive. In turn, predators with better and better vision are favored. Salmon, trout and other fishes have dark backsides. If you are unlucky enough to be born with a light backside, some large predatory bird like an eagle, with eight times the visual acuity of man, will have you for lunch before you are old enough to date.

As an aside, I recently read about an all-white, damsel fly pattern which, according to the author, works extremely well on all sorts of trout. And why wouldn't it? As the prey creatures out there in nature know, "No camo, no future."

As with our cousins the owl, the hawk, the largemouth bass and the mountain lion, the best predator can fix a meal in space *without* moving its head, thus allowing an even greater survival advantage by not giving away one's ambush position while computing the distance, range and timing of the attack.

The most advanced visual systems require binocular, stereoscopic vision that not only automatically adjusts for movement of the target, but continuously feeds this movement information to the brain so that the appropriate vector can be calculated and executed. At least in humans, the more complicated the calculations and the more challenging the vectors, the more rewarding the hit seems to be.

Casting a fly or plug to a visually spotted, cruising fish so that the lure intercepts the fish in that very narrow window of opportunity — in between where the fish is and where it will be when the lure lands — is such a wonderfully complex mental and physical operation that we anglers feel god-like when it happens and the fish strikes.

The perfect cast is angling's sweet spot. The sweet spot, as most everyone knows, is that place on a baseball bat where hits are most effective at making the ball sail out of the park. Whether golfer, tennis player or lure caster, the entire human psychomotor world is on a quest for such sweet spots, sometimes the only spot that makes any sense in this crazy old world.

The Visual Angler

Fishermen are heavily dependent on vision, and especially on binocular, stereoscopic vision improved by polarized sunglasses. By removing the glare from the surface of water, the shaded, bespectacled human predator is now ten-fold the fish hunter he was just a few years ago. The single best thing some fishes evolved to help them escape detection, camouflage, was rendered ineffective with the invention of polarized lenses. If they could get them, kingfishers would be wearing them.

Compared to predators, prey have eyes on the sides of their heads so that they can see what's sneaking up behind them. Personally, I much prefer my predator eyes right where they are on the front of my face; it helps in spotting fish, distance casting, and tying trout flies. But once in a while I wish they were mounted farther back, like when I was raising kids. Or, when caught across town one night in New York City, I had to hike through Central Park after dark to get to my son's apartment. Walking at a brisk clip, I remember wishing my eyes were mounted in back so I could see if the muggers were gaining on me. With our city streets overflowing with eyes-to-the-front human predators these days, is it any wonder they call it a jungle out there?

The angler's eye is a wondrous tool, and perhaps 70 percent of all sensory information that reaches the brain passes first through the eye. So reliant on understanding the world visually, it is hard to imagine how we humans would amount to much, let alone be the top fishermen, if God's first command had not been, "Let there be light."

He must have known we needed light first, if only to see where to cast, because without light — and without the visual organs necessary to interpret light and what is lit — it would have been very difficult to carry out the later command to gain "dominion over the fishes." Nothing so distinguishes the evolution of the human brain as the eye. Nothing provides so much information to the brain. And nothing has caused so much controversy about evolution as the eye.

A highly complex organ consisting of a lens, retina, rods, cones, a viscous fluid and, connected to the brain in the most complex ways, the eye may be best thought of as part of the brain, rather than a separate organ. The eye is so often equated with the rational assessment of the truth that when we doubt some guy who claims to have a 12-pound walleye in the cooler in his boat, we say, "Oh yeah! Show me!" And he, grinning, says, "Seeing is believing." Then, when we repeat this fish story and someone challenges us about its veracity, we say, "I saw it with my own eyes!"

In the *Show Me!* state of Missouri, an entire population of fishermen do not believe any fish story unless they were an eyewitness.

All eyes — yours, mine, predator's and prey's — evolved from a few light-sensitive cells in some ancient, sea-dwelling organism several billion years ago. The first creature to experience even the slightest ability to distinguish light from dark must have gained a tremendous survival advantage over its competitors, as in the old saying, "In the land of the blind, the one-eyed man is king." Without the gift of vision, a single candle cannot light a darkened room; nor the sun light a world.

Fishing walleyes against the shoreline the other night with only starlight to steer by, I had forgotten my flashlight, but I didn't need it. Reflecting off the water, the moon and stars gave off enough light to fish by. Keeping company with Caesar, who said of Gaul, "I came, I saw, I conquered," I hooked and landed several nice walls and one 6-pounder.

The Guide's Eyes

Several years ago I was fishing off Mexico's Baja coast with a man named Jon Cave. Jon is a flyfishing expert who guides, teaches and writes about the sport, and mostly fishes Florida salt water. He has what I call "guide's eyes." Guides eyes are different than ordinary eyes, not in structure, but in function. A guide sees things the average sport fisherman does not see.

"There," says Jon, pointing to the far horizon. "Dorado!"

Our Mexican guide follows Jon's pointing finger, nodding and smiling.

I study the sea. I study it some more. Manuel, our guide, turns the bow of the panga, an open fishing boat, in the direction they are both now looking. At least two people in the boat know what the hell is going on.

I stand and study that part of the Pacific Ocean to which we are now headed at a high rate of speed. I not only can't see fish, I can't see a damned thing. Finally, I ask Jon, "What gives?"

"There," he says, pointing again. "See that little black speck?"

I squint. Then I see it. "Yes," I say, "I see it."

"That's a bird diving on bait. Bait means fish. Dorado chase bait to the surface and the birds dive on the schools."

"But that must be two miles away."

Jon shrugs.

Sure enough, a few minutes later as we close in on the birds, Jon points to a long, iridescent green streak in the blue water. "There! Cast ahead of him!"

I stand, lay out a long cast that lands in angling's sweet

spot just ahead of the cruising fish and strip the big, white fly twice. Hitting like a runaway train, a huge dorado jerks my arms out of their sockets and drags fly, rod, reel, hands, wrists and limbs far out to sea. Fortunately, we are able to retrieve my detached anatomical parts and gear in about twenty minutes and get back on the school; otherwise, I might have to had to be taken to the hospital to be fitted with prosthetic appendages and a new fly rod and reel.

Find this yarn stretched a bit? Well, I guess this is one of those fish stories you had *see* to believe.

It was, however, spotting the bird that made all the difference. Mind you, just like Jon and Manuel, my retinas received the image of the bird the first time I looked at the horizon. What the brain could not do was to perceive that a tiny black speck means bird, which then translates to fish.

Perception is different than vision. Perception is making sense of the visual information that strikes the retina and ends up at the cortex for interpretation. Off the Baja Coast that morning, we all had the same visual information striking the retina. But to me, the tiny black speck on the far horizon could have been anything from a stray aircraft to one of those annoying dust balls that float around in your field of vision when you're trying to see something else.

All successful anglers must move from seeing water to "reading" water. Reading water means to interpret and understand water and how the fishes fit into it. As fish foragers and hunters, we must learn what animal psychologists call useful "search images." For Jon that day on Sea of Cortez, the search image was diving birds represented by tiny moving specs low over far horizons. For the chalk stream trout angler, the search image may be trout rises, or the way a streams curves, dips and rushes through structures and how the surface hydraulics create likely trout lies.

A friend of mine who is a world authority on flyfishing salmon in salt water can read tides, upwelling water, surface slicks, gulls and the mix of fresh water and salt water in the blender of an estuary like a scholar reads ancient Greek. Just as the radiologist is taught to look at an x-ray to spot a hairline fracture with a practiced search image, so the fishermen learns to *see* a body of water, to spot subtle rise forms, the cutting fin of a permit, the subsurface flash of trout taking nymphs, diving birds or the shadow of a lemon shark on the flats.

This journey from vision to perception to productive search images is the angler's great journey. To arrive at that place where you can with confidence sit on a river bank and study the fish below the veil of moving water and know — and I mean *know* — that what you see is not illusion, but truth, is to arrive in that far and wondrous place where angler and fish become one.

Fishual Arousal

"Fishual" arousal is just like human sexual arousal except without all the problems. Let me explain.

We fishermen like our eyes big, not only on our bass plugs and salmon flies, but on the fish we catch. We want to dilate the pupils of the fish we fish for, just as they are dilating ours. Ours is a kind of "Mutual Arousal Association."

We build plugs and flies with big eyes because — just as Cleopatra used a little eye shadow to catch Mark Antony — surely a little more eye shadow on our fishing lures will help us catch more fish. And it does, as I will explain later in the chapter on the psychology of deception.

As measured by the pupillary response, human arousal, fishual arousal and sexual arousal are all pretty much the same thing — which may account for why some fishermen favorably compare hooking a trophy fish to sexual excitement. There may be some merit to this comparison from a physiological point of view, but I do not recommend making such comparisons in mixed company, meaning where non-fishermen are present.

For example, I once made this regrettable error at a dinner party one evening within earshot of my wife. From the male anglers assembled at our end of the dining room, I got many nods of agreement when I favorably compared hooking a steelhead to a sexual encounter.

"I ask you," I said, "is not getting one on in the river as good as getting one on in the bedroom?"

The men erupted in a cheer of approval not unlike that heard in the British House of Commons the day Winston Churchill marched the English language into war against the Nazis.

Just then I turned to see Ann staring a hole through me. Her pupils were considerably smaller than the heads of pins. I instantly realized that there are certain downside risks to making such offhand scientific observations. Moreover, I can personally attest that there is, despite heartfelt apologies and expensive gifts, a great deal of truth to the old adage that women and elephants never forget an injury.

Which leads me to yet another observation about eyes and light and the wonder of how we see what we see and know what we know.

How, I ask you, did I know to turn to see my wife staring at me?

How did I sense she was staring?

How did I know exactly where to look to perfectly intercept her stiletto stare?

Since she was clearly using her most terrorizing predator gaze, did I feel this on the back of my neck?

Can you, can a fish, *feel* a predator's gaze?

Do we all, predator and prey, have some sixth or seventh or eighth sense of which we know nothing scientifically?

Maybe you, like me, have had one those parapsychological experiences out in the woods or while walking along a darkened boulevard when, suddenly but unmistakably, you sensed something was looking at you. The hair tingles on the back of your neck. Someone, or some thing, is watching.

Suddenly, you turn and there he, she or it is, staring you straight in the eye. When you turn to look for the looker, you do not have to search or scan; you instantly come eyeball to eyeball with the watcher.

How do we explain this phenomenon?

Having once had a large shark swim up behind me while I was snorkeling in Mexico, I remember feeling something was behind me, staring at me. When you're a puny mammal in a big ocean, this is not a good feeling. Turning to see the shark cruising just behind me and gazing at me with one of its large, dark orbs — which was still not nearly so frightening as my wife's gaze — I realized I was being examined for the menu. Since it was his pond, and he had a couple hundred pounds on me and was a bit better swimmer, I backed away, made shore and changed shorts.

The Angler's Eye in the Back of the Head

From an evolutionary point of view, having an eye in the back of your head, or a sixth sense, makes sense. Those creatures who experienced arousal and acted defensively on a hunch, or an unexplainable inkling of being hunted ought to — over the eons of time — have a better rate of survival than those who ignored such subtle cues. Unless you're the CIA, the response cost for checking out your suspicions is usually low, so why not check? Checkers would avert the occasional attack and thereby have a better chance of becoming Darwin's Bass. As we psychologists sometimes crack, "Just because you're paranoid doesn't mean they aren't after you."

Such "paranoid genes" would then get passed along to future generations. Paranoid genes are very useful to humans in places like grizzly-infested Alaskan rivers basins, urban centers and the Balkans, if only because a heightened state of vigilance allows you to better anticipate potentially fatal outcomes in a dangerous environment.

Fishermen need to be a little paranoid and pay attention to their sixth sense these days, especially now that mountain lions are losing their fear of us. Mountain lion attacks are up, especially in the West. Because we don't hunt and kill them in some areas anymore, some lions no longer need fear us. We've become safe food. Unfortunately, mountain lions don't practice catch-and-release.

Interestingly, all big cats attack their prey animals, including fishermen, in the same way: a silent stalk, a quick charge, and a bite to the back of the neck. A study of lion attacks worldwide suggests that the attack is often triggered when the human kneels to, say, tie a shoelace or, in the case of fishermen, to land a fish.

Crouched in a low profile, looking away from the cat, and with the back of the neck exposed — well, I guess it's just too much of a green light for a hungry pussycat.

One last story. While you may not think of a fishing rod as a defensive weapon, a young fly rod company representative told me a story about California angler who claims to have driven off an attacking mountain lion with a 2-weight. The man described sensing something behind him on the trail and, turning to see a large cat loping toward him from not twenty paces away, whipped his fly rod into the face of the oncoming cat.

The lion swatted the rod, broke it, and kept coming. Our hero parried and thrust. The jagged graphite proved an able rapier and, jabbing the blade into the attacker's nose and eyes soon caused the lion to yield and retreat back down the trail. Touché!

"Did you repair the rod at no cost," I asked the salesman, "or did you figure this one for another tall tale?"

"Of course, we fixed it for free," said the young man. "No one could make up a fishing story like that."

Clearly this young salesmen doesn't know anglers. Whether or not this how-I-broke-my-fishing-rod yarn has any truth to it is beside the point; the yarn has enough of a ring of truth that I intend to use it myself the next time I slam a car door on a rod.

So we don't start losing fishermen to mountain lions, let's all accept that we have some sort of eyes in the back our heads, pay attention to the hairs on the back of our necks and look over our shoulders once in awhile. A little checking behavior could pay a big dividend.

The experts say, by the way, that the best way to stall an attacking mountain lion is not to turn your fishing rod into a sword or run, but to simply turn and face the animal, stand tall, puff out your chest, fix the kitty with your most determined, terror-inducing, predator gaze, and shout. I'm told prayers work well, although I'm partial to obscenities.

The Eyes Have It

Fishermen lust for visual contact with the fishes. We love their bright colors. We love their dark eyes. We love to watch them jump. We love to watch them swim. We study the water endlessly, looking for swirling fins, wrinkles, sips and shadows. We love to stalk fish in the shallows, catch them off guard, or see them shoot away from our boat as we approach. We love to be near water, the light, the ...

But now I'm crowding into the subject of the next chapter, so let me return to answer the question I tried to answer as a young research psychologist.

Is the eye really the window to the soul? Can you, by watching the pupil open up or narrow down, know what a fisherman might be thinking and feeling?

Well, of course you can.

What other, more diligent and skilled researchers have now proven is that anything which arouses your autonomic nervous system also causes your pupils to flare — thus letting in more light so that you can more clearly see the object of your desire. Whether or not the pupil narrows down to negative stimuli is less clear.

But as an adaptation to enhanced survival, an expanding pupil not only lets in more light by which to find and fix prey, but a larger pupil permits more lateral vision. You need more lateral vision when you're jogging through Central Park at midnight, hiking in mountain lion country, or if you hope to see trout rising far to your left or right out of the so-called "corners of your eyes."

Wonder if your lover loves you? Watch the pupil as you move in for a kiss. Provided you are not blocking the light with your bean — which will cause the pupil to expand to accommodate to less available light — the pupil should change size as you close in. If it opens up, it means positive arousal; if it narrows down to the size of a pin hole, check yourself for bad breath. Or perhaps your attitude. If this is an attempted make-up kiss after the fight you won last night, maybe you didn't win the fight after all. (But don't make too much of a narrowing pupil; remember, I didn't get the Nobel for this work.)

Research has shown that if a woman's pupils are large, she is perceived to be more sexy, alluring and attractive. In ancient Rome, women used the drug belladonna, meaning beautiful eyes, to dilate their pupils while trolling for men. Enlarged pupils are one of the sure signs of sexual arousal, and it explains why that branch of the cosmetics industry has been such a roaring success for at least 4,000 years. Just why tackle manufacturers have enjoyed such roaring success with big-eyed lures will be dealt with in another chapter.

Finally, as the retina picks up visual stimuli, it fires this information into the cortex where the brain, clever instrument that it is, attempts to recognize the object. If that object is recognized as desirable, wanted and lusted for, then the pupil will dilate in a happy expansion and tell all. If that object is the face of your true love, and he or she is smiling with one those big-pupil, I'm-hot-for-you gazes, then *your* pupils will dilate, too, and another pair of spawners will be off and running.

If you are, on the other hand, just a simple fisherman and the object of your desire is, say, a huge brown trout steadily rising for mayflies, you will get exactly the same hot, wide-eyed, big-pupil, automatic, pleasure-pounding, fish-aroused, autonomic-nervous-system response when that big brown finally rises from its lie and slurps in your dun. Smoking afterward is optional.

To live is not necessary. To fish is necessary.
          — **Latin inscription**

Why Fish?

"You know what it's all about?" asks the stranger.
"What's what all about?" I say, surprised by the voice behind me. I had not seen the old man approach through the tall grass above the dark river.

"Fishing," smiles the stranger, waving his rod tip toward the river. He is carrying a fly rod, a chrome shotgun for bears and a big grin. Standing tall and dark in his yellow slicker, rain drips steadily from his wide brimmed hat. He seems to be waiting for an answer.

I stop casting to a pool filled with silver salmon and study the man in the rain.

"Well ... " I start to reply.

"The grab," he interrupts. "It's all about the grab."

"The grab?"

"The grab. When I was just a boy forty years ago, an old fisherman like me approached me out of the rain like I am you right now and asked me what I thought fishing was all about. Before I could answer, he said, 'The grab! Think about it.' And then the old man turned and walked away, just like I'm going to walk away from you right now. You think about it, too."

And with that, the stranger turns, climbs the bank to the trail in tall grass and quickly steps away.

For a time I stop casting to watch him hike toward a row of dark timber and the estuary where new pods of bright fish are riding the surf to share fresh water and passion. A man with only a few years on me, he showed all the signs of late stage fishaholism: patched waders, weathered hands, battered rod, fish-chewed flies tucked in the sheepskin ring around a well-worn 5X beaver Stetson, and the sparkling eyes of an angler still lusting for the thrill.

What had he called it? The grab?

I make another cast as the stranger disappears into the gray rain and black trees.

I have spent more than a few hours thinking about the nature of fishing and why we anglers love it so. The stranger's query started me thinking yet again.

The grab? Surely the stranger meant the hit, the strike, the bite, the tug, the stop, the rise and a dozen other active verbs that describe how a fish takes a lure. Hummmm, I had not thought much about the grab. Is the grab at the top of the list of all the reasons we so love to fish?

Of all the things predatory creatures do to survive, grabbing comes first. No grab, no food. No food, no sex. No sex, no offspring. For there to be eaglets, eagles must grab fish. For their to be cubs, bears must grab salmon. Bass must grab crawfish. Crawfish must grab minnows. Minnows must grab bugs. Bugs must grab smaller bugs. Having just tailed a 12-pound salmon, fishermen must grab fish.

In nature, bad grabbers don't make it. Successful grabbers dine well, enjoy sex and reproduce. If my fish-as-ancestor notion is correct, we come from a long line of good grabbers. Perhaps our angler's lust is really a holy quest for the grab.

And it is a holy quest. A friend of mine flew to New Guinea last year to take a New Guinea bass. But only on the surface. While others caught fish underwater, he stayed with top water lures the whole trip, hooking only a handful of bass. Why? "Because you don't fly 10,000 miles to catch them underwater," was his reply.

Just then I feel my line stop. I am using a heavy shooting head, a steelhead swing with a single mend, and a fluorescent green and Krystal Flash fly, laying the works across the narrow head of the pool, mending it once, and letting the color sweep down and through the rows of layered silvers. A "stop" under such conditions is the grab.

The line stops. I set the hook with a swift lift of the rod.

Unaccustomed to handling 15-pound fish in tight quarters, this one, as with too many others on this trip, beats me up. A strong fish, it shoots upstream, corners high, turns on a dime and bolts downstream in a headlong lunge that pulls the fly free. Finally exhaling, I check the hook for sharpness and begin casting again, hoping for another ... what did the old man say? Grab.

While a stop will do, it is not the same thing as a hit. A hit is harder. You can feel a good hit in your vest pocket. A stop is what a steelheader mostly prays for. I like a stop on a moving lure as well as the next angler, but what I really want is something more.

What more? A surface smash? A chase I can see? The kind of grab used by the old bass that chased our ancient prototypes up onto the beach?

Personally, I love those attacks through shallow water where, with the fish knifing toward your lure, you can see the whole show. You cast and pull the fly or plug away from the shoreline and cause a commotion. Then, you rest the trick until the rings subside. Then, you give it a single twitch. From an ambush site, water begins to move.

To see a big fish shouldering away water in a quickening V toward your lure is to suck your heart into your throat. These torpedo takes go with spawning largemouth, shallowed-up June northerns and billfish following the teaser. An angler could specialize in thin water, torpedo takers alone.

Trouters who fish dry flies have built a religion around the grab. They study rise forms and worship accordingly. They adjust their flies and tippets to the sip, the swirl, the splash or the leap for the escaping mayfly. True believers read their favorite trout like a book with big print. Some eschew all nymphs, all subsurface takers, even though this is mostly where trout dine.

When the trout fishing is very, very good I will stay with a dry fly even though a nymph would catch more fish. Why? Because I want the surface grab, the one I can see. The feel of the grab is not enough. A trout seen making the grab is a sensory banquet, whereas just feeling the tug on a nymph is but a ham sandwich — which is why I love the clear rivers of the Rockies where I can watch the bright fish push off from the bottom and rise perfectly to my hackled duns. Seeing leads to testimony.

Another drift through the hole produces no takers. I move downstream two steps, loft the long line and lay the shooting head down in a noisy splash. Throwing a mend, I wait for the stop.

A Grab Bag of Grabs

And there are other grabs, whole worlds of grabs. There is something the walleye does which I cannot name, but when a walleye takes a wormed-tipped jig in deep water, there is but a slight surge against the line. It is not a hit, but rather a slight resistance in the line compared to the weight of a free jig. Sometimes you get a distinct *tap*, but mostly you don't. You must learn this delicate grab and how to set the hook with a sweeping lift of the rod.

When fishing at night for landlocked kokanee salmon in the Pacific Northwest, the preferred bait is a glow hook tipped with a maggot or kernel of shoe-peg corn. Fished on 4-pound test from a wand-like rod, the bait is lowered into deep holes under Coleman lanterns where the salmon gather to chase plankton. The take of the silver is so light and slight that only a handful of anglers ever develop what they call "the touch." One of my sons developed the touch and, outfishing his grandfather and me ten fish to one, it seemed he was using some kind of parapsychological extrasensory perception to detect the grab.

Compare this to the arm-jolting, even dangerous, grab of saltwater fishes. If you cast a fly to the sargasso, or gulfweed, and strip quickly into a school of feeding dorado, you had better be ready to instantly drop your line and spread your arms at the grab, because if you get tangled in your own line, you may become the victim of a hot fish instead of the other way around. Line burned hands are a specialty with saltwater species.

Once a dorado sees the target, it powers up to full speed *on the way to the fly*. The hit is so hard, a 15-pound fish requires a 40-pound shock tippet, lest you break him off before the fight begins, or snap a rod or ruin a finger. You have to admire a fish that can send you and your reel to the hospital for repairs.

How Old is the Grab?

This business of the grab is as old as life itself, some say at least 550 million years old. The first predators in the Precambrian seas perfected the grab; darting, chasing, catching, crunching, eating. The game fishes we anglers chase the world over are far and away the greatest practitioners of the grab.

The ecology of predator feeding behavior suggests there are three ways to grab food in this world: Go find it, wait for it to amble by, or find a place from which to ambush, and then wait. Some ambushing fish use lures to attract prey, some don't. Barracuda go find it, black bass wait for it. With some exceptions, all fishes tend to fall into one camp or the other, chasers or ambushers. And so do fishermen.

In my neck of the woods, some steelheaders use shrimp tails on black marabou jigs fished under stationary bobbers. These anglers wait in ambush for steelhead to swim by. Another equally hard-core bunch cast their arms off throwing spoons or flies while they hike up and down riverbanks in search of fish.

Drift boaters chase; ice fishermen ambush. Fly fishermen are necessarily chasers. Lure casters who hunt shorelines for largemouth bass are chasers. I've wondered if the type of angler you are, ambusher or chaser, says something about your personality and what it is that turns your motor. No one, so far as I know, has done this research — and if they ever do, they better not use tax dollars.

I prefer hunting water and chasing fish, not waiting for fish to swim by. Even better, I like hunting individual fish and casting to a fish I can see. Like all predators, I have what I have already noted as a "search image." If I can, I want to see my mark, cast to it, and watch the grab. Nymphing for trout, I have caught many dozens of them by watching the white lip on their lower jaw open and close in the general vicinity of my fly.

Of the best takes I've known, the grab of the peacock bass ranks high. Peacocks live mostly in shallow water. Their hide-outs and watery lairs are predictable and perfectly fishable from small boats. They take the fly if it is big and noisy enough. Like other ambush predators, they lay in hiding or, if chasing bait with their fellows, push schools of smaller fish into the shallows. If you listen closely in a still jungle morning, you can hear the boiling slashes of peacocks at breakfast.

The peacock grab is heart stopping. A big fly is cast, settles and is stripped. A V-wake erupts from the corner of your eye, cuts instantly across the tea-colored water and, engulfing your fly, the bass makes a U-turn while still at full speed. The erup-tion of water at the U-turn strike produces a booming geyser not unlike the sound of a bowling ball being dropped into a pond from ten stories up.

Even if the bass misses the fly, or if you miss the bass, such grabs are the stuff of memories. Whether ever hooked, fought,or landed, simply witnessing such grabs are worth great journeys.

V's of silvers cut upstream through the shallow water. The fish are just visible along the far bank. The rains have kept the fish moving. I keep casting to them. Hope is at the heart of angling, and a grab is hope affirmed. I make a cast to intercept a streaking salmon.

No luck with the cast, so I cast again.

Today I am both a kind of chaser and ambusher; the fish are coming to me, and I am trying to intercept and entice them.

I am not alone in this strategy of chase and wait. Alligator turtles move about in search of food and then use their tongues to lure passing minnows into the grabber. A deep sea anglerfish uses a lighted bait in its mouth for identical purposes. On hot, sunny days, a blue heron will spread its wings to form an umbrella over its head, thus providing shade for the hapless minnows who then swim into range of the heron's grab. Everybody has got an angle on angling.

Perhaps, as much as anything, it is the grab we anglers are truly after. Like the old stranger said, the fight is good, but the grab is better. Especially if we can see it. Since I don't eat game fish much anymore, I would rather take one rainbow on the surface than three underneath. This is not snobbery, just preference. Since we humans are such visual creatures, perhaps what I'm hoping for is the memory of the take, not the taking.

The Next Step in Angler Evolution?

Barry Thornton, a Canadian friend of mine and well-known steelhead and salmon author and expert, told me of a recent development up his way: steelhead fly fishers fishing not just barbless, but hookless. Yes, hookless.

A small band just now, these anglers snip off the hooking part of the fly and fish only the shank. They entice the rise and the stop, feel the grab, and then it is over. Sometimes the fish will hold the hookless fly in its mouth and even make a run before letting go, but the fish can never be landed. All these fishermen want is the grab.

"Just think," said Barry with a grin, "you don't even have to bother fighting and unhooking them anymore."

Is this the next step in the evolution of angling: fishing for the grab, not the fish?

Fifty years ago no one had imagined catch-and-release. Fifty years from now who can say how our concept of fair chase will have evolved. Being humans, and being able to override our biological imperatives with brain power, the choice is up to us.

A fishing guide once told me about a young eagle that dropped down from a tree and grabbed a 50-pound Chinook salmon in the back as it passed through a shallow braid in a coastal river. With talons locked in its back, the big salmon bolted from the shallows and disappeared into the depths of the river, taking the adolescent eagle with it. Eventually the eagle surfaced, floated downstream and made shore, where it flapped its wet wings and then held them out to dry. Sometimes fishing can be too much of a good thing.

The evolutionary biological imperative for eagles requires that when an eagle grabs a salmon in its talons it cannot, for a few seconds, let go. The forces of natural selection resulted in this positive, fish-grabbing, talon-locking system, and it has worked for millions of years.

But unlike the eagle, we can change our minds about the things we've grabbed. We can let go of a fish too big. By pointing our rod tip straight at a foul-hooked fish, we can choose to break it off and set it free from an unfair fight. We can do this because we have a mind, something that can override our biological imperatives or genetic histories.

Too many people these days want to believe in a simple kind of sociobiology that says what we humans do is the direct result of our genetic history, instinctual imperatives and biological machinery. We are only a little fancier mammal than the wolf or the chimp and cannot be counted to rise above our mammalian history. The perfect excuse is that none of us can help being what we are or doing what we do.

I disagree entirely. If we can let go of our grab of things, like love and money and trophy fish, then we will always be much more than our biology. The reason fishermen have such huge cerebral cortexes is so that, if they grab a fish big enough to tip the boat over, they can cut the line instead of going down with the boat.

Only anglers who rely on their ancient, angry, reason-free, pea-sized reptilian brain go down with the boat. One Captain Ahab comes to mind, as does the skipper in *Jaws*. As the old fisherman said, "Never get in a bitin' contest with a shark."

If we catch a fish we don't need, we can override our instinct to hold, kill and eat it, and just let it swim free. The wonder of being human is not just knowing how and what to grab, but having the wisdom to know what and when to let go. From anger, to insults, to old lovers, to bad whiskey and wild trout, learning to let go is one of life's great secrets, and one of the only sure signs of wisdom.

A fresh pod of silvers slips into the tail of the pool. Their V's are visible as they broach the shallow riffle and plunge into the darker, deeper water. I step quickly down the bank and lay out a long, quartering cast to these new arrivals. The fly sinks briefly, and I begin to strip line. From beneath the overhanging grass along the far bank, a large V streaks toward where my fly should be. There is a swirl, a surge and an explosion of water.

With a tight line between us we have, in our own ways, grabbed life.

Sometimes a man hits upon a place to which he mysteriously feels that he belongs. Here is the home he sought, and he will settle amid scenes that he has never seen before, among men he has never known, as though they were familiar to him from his birth. Here at least he finds rest.

> — W. Somerset Maugham
> *The Moon and Sixpence,* 1919

The Curious Psychology of Home Waters

Several years ago an old editor friend asked if I would write a piece for a book he was putting together. The book would be titled "Home Waters" and the basic idea was to enlist a number of fishing writers to contribute a piece about their home waters. Given that home waters are difficult to define and highly personal, the editor said we could decide for ourselves what home waters are. The pay was in the high two figures, so I jumped at the chance.

According to Gary Soucie, home waters could be the creek behind the house, the lake of your childhood, or some mystical river in Argentina that remains, like Bali Ha'i, a destination you only dream to fish. Gary didn't care. Interestingly, while Gary has fished the world over, his voice sounded a bit like a lost child when he said, "I'm not sure where my home waters are." In his introduction to the book, he wrote, "Home is where the heart is, in fishing as well as in homily."

At first I thought the assignment would be a breeze; I'd just knock out a few thousand words and join the ranks of such great fishing writers as John Gierach, Roderick L. Haig-Brown and Nick Lyons, among others. But no sooner had I begun a draft than I ran into trouble. Emotional trouble. Here is how the story about Rock Lake begins:

It is not easy to write about your home waters. I'm not sure why. Maybe words alone won't do it justice. The word favorite, for example, is too puny to do the work. Chosen, preferred, ideal — none of these is strong enough either. What is strong enough? Read my will.

Of course there was some consternation about my desire to have my ashes spread over Rock Lake during a June mayfly hatch. But those who love me know there will be hell to pay if I don't get my way on this. I made the decision a long time ago and, although I was probably a little drunk at the time, it still stands. Cold sober I feel the same way. No eternity in a pine box for me; just toss me, as the Ames Brothers used to sing, "Smack-dab in the middle."

That was the title of the piece, "Smack-dab in the Middle of the Rock." Seeing the story in print a couple of years later confirmed it wasn't all that great a piece. If you're a writer, reading your old stories reminds you of why someone once quipped that there's a special hell for writers: They force you to read your old stuff out loud to strangers. But, it turns out I was right; words alone can't do home waters justice.

Maybe this is because once you find that special place on the water where you finally feel you belong, everything seems to come together. The universe is no longer chaotic. Or psychotic. There is an audible click as the pieces fall together.

Things smooth out. The water shimmers, and the trees stand still. All things begin to connect. Mysteries are solved, and a calm settles in the center of your being.

Rock Lake is that place for me. More from the piece:

To get an idea of what Rock means to me, you have to understand that all my life I've been shading life's major decisions toward the perfect fishing spot: where I went to college, where I went to graduate school, the profession I chose (psychology — a job you can do most anywhere because, as it turns out, there are troubled people everywhere), and where, finally, I found a job, built a house, and raised a family. That place: eastern Washington, southwest of

Spokane.

As W. Somerset Maugham says, "Sometimes a man hits upon a place to which he mysteriously feels he belongs." Always a lucky bastard, I found that place.

So what gives? What is it about a place — a particular stream or river or pond or lake or shoreline or far shoal on the high seas — that makes us feel at one with the world?

Are home waters just good fishing waters, or are they something more? Is there something about being near water that brings on a tonic effect? Is there something in the air or under foot or in and around home waters that makes them special?

Perhaps home waters are the place where, if you cast your lure, you stand to catch not just a fine fish, but a fond memory. Home waters abound in fond memories, fine fish and fine friends, so perhaps we fishermen fall in love not only with people, but places.

Yes, places. I think we fall in love with places. I may love only one woman, but I love many places, and one does not suffer at the expense of the other. In loving places, there seems to be enough to go around. So, let's turn over a few stones to see what we might learn about this business of loving places and home waters.

Fishing and Optimality Theory

"Optimality theory," a theory that attempts to explain why certain fishing traits and practices evolve over time in ours and other species, suggests that only those fishing traits and practices whose benefits exceed their costs, compared to all other possible alternatives, will be selected for in subsequent generations.

If the above sentence didn't make much sense on the first reading, it is because I wrote it in *Lingua researcha.* This is just the sort of scientific writing that accounts for why so few people read it. It is precise, but boring. If I tried to write any more such sentences, I'd fall asleep myself.

Here's a rewrite. Optimality theory explains that the best fishers with the best equipment catch the first, most and biggest fish. Thus, they become Darwin's Bass, have more babies who carry their traits, and keep their more successful replicas in the only pool worth swimming in: the gene pool. Now, that wasn't so difficult, was it?

There are also optimal fishing sites. Optimal fishing sites have existed in nature for millions of years. They include the base of waterfalls, weedy bays, estuaries, ocean drop-offs and any habitat around which fish congregate. Except for billfish and tuna, all marine fishes are what fish biologists call "nearshore dependent," meaning they require inshore habitat to spawn or find food. Fish have home waters, too.

All fishing creatures either learn to exploit these sites of high fish concentration, or go the way of the woolly mammoth. Other things being equal, home waters are most likely optimal fishing sites, for us and for other fish predators and for fish who prey on their own kind.

Optimality theory was not developed to explain fishing sites, but to explain the evolution of successful food finding and catching methods. The evolution of the eagle's fish-holding talon-lock must, therefore, be the optimal grab for modern eagles. The heron's long beak is currently of optimum dimensions for the heron's fish-grabbing requirements. The shark, as a feeder on other fishes, is one of the optimum designs for catching fish under the waves.

On the human side, gill nets work better than spears, barbed hooks work better than barbless ones, and graphite rods are pretty much evolving into the optimal fishing rod. Natural selection is a constant force, the result of which is more and more efficiency.

Are home waters simply optimal fishing waters?

Perhaps, but it depends on your motives.

Optimality theory is targeted toward food gathering efficiency. This formula holds up for eagles and black bass and barracuda, but human sportfishing is something more than efficient food gathering. A great deal more. Except for those knuckle-dragging, throw-back anglers from the Pleistocene who kill more fish than they need, or more than the fishery can stand, sport fishermen seldom fish for food alone, at which point optimality theory begins to break down.

Optimality theory predicts that creatures always forage to maximize the rate of energy gain per unit of time spent searching. Research has shown that successful predators select the most profitable prey species from all others available, focus their search behavior in those areas where these prey are abundant, and then search in a manner that produces the highest rate of predator-prey contact. Predators will, by the way, engage in territorial fighting over such productive areas.

If you think fishermen are not just a better dressed predator willing to quarrel over who gets first grab at a hot run of new fish, then you haven't seen Alaska's Kenai River in July, or a thousand other honey holes the world over when the bite is on.

Humans are highly territorial creatures; otherwise, we would enjoy fewer boundary disputes, fewer border wars, fewer hot tempers around the old fishing hole, and a lot less bickering over who's on whose side of the bed. As every angler knows, the most exquisite disappointment is to arrive on your home waters to find a stranger already fishing them.

High-speed bass boats, fish-finding electronics, and fast casting with the most likely lures in the most likely places are all examples of optimality theory in practice. Where things break down with the theory is that you could never possibly catch enough bass to pay for your boat, let alone the motor, trailer, rods, reels or even a tenth of all the plugs you own, unless you think fishing is more than food gathering — which, of course, it is.

Commercial fishing is another story. Commercial fishing is all about return on investment. When your home waters pay for your home and feed your kids, you already know all about optimality theory and the importance of rapid prey location and a good grab. Commercial fishermen who do not detect and capture fish in a highly cost-effective and efficient manner soon go by another name: broke.

The dramatic collapse of high seas fisheries around the globe in recent years can be laid at least two doorsteps: too many fishermen from too many countries consider the same waters home waters, and too many fishermen from too many countries know too well how to take too many fish.

But home waters for the sport fishermen are more than foraging habitats. Most sport fishermen consider taking fish home a bonus, not a requirement. For catch-and-release fishermen, optimality theory breaks down completely, since a good caloric return on investment is a powerfully negative number. On the other hand, I will confess that when I want a few crappies for a fishwich, I know the precise location of a sunken tree in my home waters where, without fail, I can take several nice slabs without half trying. I suppose that's why I call it the "meat tree."

Going Home to Home Waters

The sport fisherman's home waters are as wide as they are deep. More psychological, more emotional, and more like a comfortable old fishing vest and a favorite hat, home waters are also a place where the spirit dwells.

You can travel to home waters in your mind. You can travel to home waters in your heart. And, yes, while you've caught fish there, you must confess that there were days when the bite was poor but the fishing was still good.

Perhaps what is homey about home waters is its familiarity and predictability. Like an old neighborhood, it's nice to know your way around. We catch a trout from behind a rock, release it, and when we return a week or a month or a year or ten years later, we know, expect, dream, that that same trout rests their still. Only now he is bigger.

But is he?

The other night I was giving a talk about sex, hope and the psychology of fishing to a group of wildlife law enforcement personnel and, upon concluding my remarks, I asked for questions. An older, retired gentleman asked, "How come when you are a child a day seems as a year, and when you are my age a year seems as a day?"

This was a very good question, and I would have loved to have had a very good answer. But I didn't have one. However, being a psychologist, I quickly made one up.

The answer I gave may not have been on the mark for this

gentleman's question, but it was close enough for horseshoes and government work. It has to do with why, when we fishermen return to the home waters of our childhood, we are often disappointed.

Some ten years ago my older brother and I were on a pleasure trip to Southern California and, on a lark, we rented a car in Los Angeles and drove out to our hometown near San Bernardino and then up into the mountains to the trout stream of our youth. Finding the pool over which we once quarreled over for first casting rights, our hearts were broken.

The place felt odd, hostile even, to our memories. Beer cans littered the bottom of the pool. Lying next to an old log, we found bottle caps and a spent syringe. The once beautiful home waters of our childhood had become a place to get loaded and shoot up. Curiously, the trout pool of our boyhood seemed small, shallow and devoid of life.

Thomas Wolfe said you can't go home again. Of course you can, but the home will be different. Do we change, or does the world change while we're gone? Here is a little bit of the answer.

Time and the River

When you are a 2-year-old child, a single day represents a much larger portion of your total life than when you are 22, and so the child's perception is that time passes slowly. Your second day of life is half your life, the third day of life a third, and so on until, when you have racked up 80 years, a single day represents only an infinitesimal portion of all your days upon the Earth. After 80 years a single day, compared to all those you have lived, seems to pass quickly.

For a child, everything is new and memorable. For someone in mid-life, everything is old and, unless outstanding, forgettable. The secret to feeling young is to never stop exploring the new and to make every day count for something. It isn't that we have to do something outrageous to remember each day, but at least we ought to feel like we could.

When you are a 5-year-old child and catch your first fish, it is the biggest fish you have ever caught because it is the only fish you have ever caught. You will likely remember not only the fish, but the water from which you pulled it. But, when you are my age and have caught too many fish to count, it takes a very special fish to be remembered.

If I remember a fish perfectly in my mind's eye, I also remember the water perfectly. I remember not only the fish's home address and general neighborhood, but the zip code.

So perhaps this is the formula for how home waters come to be home waters: first fish plus first fish-water equals home waters. As the old fisherman said, "All fish are memorable, but some are more memorable than others."

If you adopted your home waters in childhood on the day you caught your first fish and then moved away from that place, you may yearn to return someday to find that old fishing hole, perhaps to revisit a less troublesome time and place. These waters are that misty place of long ago and far away. It is the place where we caught our first fish and where, as we've polished the legend, the fish were always huge and bright and hungry. Should you ever take this sentimental journey as my brother and I did, be prepared for a curious phenomenon.

A Little Therapy for the Inner Fishing Child

On your way home to home waters, remember these things.

First, you will find that despite decades of growth, the cottonwoods are shorter than when you left them. The river will be smaller or, if a lake, it will be rather more a pond than a lake. Both will be shallower.

The great boulder you once stood on to cast will have been chiseled down to a mere rock. Where the water was once deep and dark and a little frightening, you will find nothing to fear. The bite, by the way, will be pathetically slow and, should you catch a fish, it is more likely than not to be puny by comparison to the ones you remember.

"What the hell," you ask, "is going on here?"

What is going on is this. The brain records visual scenes exactly as the light stimuli pass into the eyes, strike the retina, and are fed onto the visual memory banks. Since children are short, the angle of the visual feed is less sharp than it is for adults. Visual memory does not adjust itself to correct for how the world "ought to look" when you are three or four feet taller. Thus, when you once again inspect the trout stream of your youth, the current visual image does not line up with the one you etched there as a kid. Result: Because you're taller and looking down, the stream appears both narrower and shallower.

If you want the revisited trout stream of your childhood home waters to fit comfortably over the old so that your heart is not broken, get down on your knees. From this angle, the old world will once again look "right."

If, per chance, you should choose to revisit your home waters in this manner, and someone should stop and ask what in the world you are doing crawling around your old fishing hole, just tell them a crazy psychologist told you that Thomas Wolfe was wrong; from the right perspective, you can go home again.

The Good Medicine of Home Waters

Some fairly reliable scientists have made a case that since moving water produces an atmosphere heavily laden with negative ions, it is these weak environmental energy fields around water that account for the bracing effects reported by surf fishermen, river fishermen and cascading stream fishermen.

Water-jostled, negative-ion, heavy-air molecules are necessarily breathed in while casting and fighting robust fish. According to negative-ion enthusiasts, such inhalation therapy works a genuine tonic on those of us who — trapped like rats in carbon dioxide-filled office buildings — are starved for fresh air.

The data here are quite controversial, and no one really knows much about the good or bad effects of positive or negative ions on human mood or behavior. It could be that, for example, it is not the negative ions around fishing water that enhances mood but rather the simple, therapeutic effect of beautiful natural settings.

Either way, though, the results are close enough for me to take appropriate action. When it comes to ion fields, why take chances? After all, man evolved in weak natural electromagnetic fields, not in the high-energy fields of modern electricity that powers the concrete-and-steel high-rises in which too many of us spend too much time. We evolved around water, not water coolers.

Compared to the less than 20 hertz or so of our ancient, natural magnetic past, we are now exposed to daily doses of 60 hertz, especially when indoors or trapped in a glass-encased, urban-hassle factory. For the record, animal researchers have shown that artificially created electrical fields like those we build into our work sites and homes are not only more powerful than those produced by the Earth herself, but can affect things like hormone production, sleep-wake cycles and mood.

Several researchers have found that solar magnetic storms which blast and bathe the Earth from time to time in magnetic plasma and expose everything to increased hertz loads — sort of like ringing a cosmic bell — cause everything from the destabilization of bee dances, to rodent hyperactivity, to increased admissions to psychiatric hospitals.

Reading between the lines of this research, it seems that the more unstable or unusual the electrical field you happen to be zapped by, the more unstable or unusual you may act and feel. Dr. Frankenstein's monster was, after all, just another surgical patient until he got a jolt through his bolt.

Since I made it a practice to hold all things electrical in high regard — I once nearly electrocuted myself installing an ice maker — the next time my wife drags me through a mall riddled with too many hertz for an entire morning of shopping, I am going to repair myself. For health reasons of course, I will escape that very afternoon to my favorite trout stream and attempt to balance my electromagnetic energy fields.

Having inhaled gallons and gallons of toxic mall ions all morning, I figure to recuperate by inhaling gallons and gallons of non-toxic, healthful fishing ions all afternoon. Falling water and thrashing trout produce tons of negative ions. What better way to keep one's electromagnetic gyro working within normal limits than to get out there and inhale those negative ions?

If this sounds like fishing through a Star Trek episode, then I apologize. But the fact is that the world is not as we came into it. We have changed it. We have upped the amperage. The science of subtle geophysical energy effects on human behavior is but twenty years old, and barely into its infancy. No one knows what effects magnetic fields, natural and unnatural, have on our mind, body, moods or behavior.

The fact that rats and bees and birds act weird during solar storms, that migrating birds and rainbow trout rely on the Earth's weak magnetic fields for direction, and that all life evolved under such gentle forces ought to alert us to the possibility that, at least until we know better, there are energy relationships between us and the Earth that we are only beginning to appreciate.

Until we better understand our relationship to these forces, the smart money spent on health care is on fishing home waters, fishing often around moving water, and to not be dumb by exploring the back of plugged-in refrigerators with a metal screwdriver.

I know. With the aid of but a 79-cent screwdriver and 120 volts of alternating current, I have gone where no man has gone before.

The Parapsychology of Fishing

Some say that psychic phenomena such as extrasensory perception are not aberrations of the human mind but rather a form of routine animal communication under certain electromagnetic conditions. The nervous system is entirely electrochemical in nature and subject to the subtle forces of physics, so why couldn't psychic phenomena and geomagnetic-field activity have some sort of relationship with one another? Not a few psychologists working in this area say such relationships exist, but the definitive studies are simply not in.

I don't know about other anglers, but sometimes when I am out fishing in great fields of negative ions caused by moving water, and especially if an ozone-laden storm front is closing in on my home waters, the heavy air causes me to feel a special oneness with nature. It is as if I am in a special state of hyperalterness during which, it seems, I can communicate more perfectly with the life around me.

More than once under such conditions I have "called" the

hit *before* the cast. The called strike comes and an ancient key opens a cosmic door. It is as if I can predict the future.

This is a very weird, powerful and yet wonderful feeling — although not the sort of thing you want to spread around to people who don't fish, lest they roll their eyes and move on.

The people who study so-called mystical experiences suggest that the explanation for such euphoria and heightened internal arousal are not due to the supernatural, but to the natural effect of nature's forces on nature's own machinery — in this case the neurochemistry of the human brain. Electrical stimulation, including that caused by seismic activity deep in the earth under your feet, appears to directly affect neurochemical brain activity, resulting in increased sensory powers and enhanced perception.

Imagine that while fishing your home bass waters during a powerful storm front you hook a 30-pound largemouth bass. With the hook set and the fish fighting, a subduction earthquake of, say, 7.5 on the Richter scale, strikes right under your boat. Earthquake lightning simultaneously fills the sky above as the earth below shakes and shifts. Your graphite rod pulses, not only from the huge bass, but from the physics of Mother Earth adjusting her girdle.

The bass, invigorated by all the natural goings on, starts to pull you out of the boat instead of the other way around. The waters are pitching and parting.

The sky darkens. Rain begins to pound down on you while bolts of lightning leap out of the earth to meet bolts of lightning streaking down from the clouds.

A sudden gale whips the black water into whitecaps. With the rod arched, the line about to part, and the great bass slowly pulling you into deep water you might, given this awesome coming together of natural forces, interpret your high state of internal arousal as a religious experience, complete with visions, disorientation, physical and perceptual irregularities, and out-of-body sensations. Unless you are stone dead, you ought to at least experience a huge "WOW!"

If you then landed what, in fact, turned out to be the next world record largemouth bass, you would no doubt be sainted.

However, if you broke off what, in fact, would have been the next world record largemouth bass, you would no doubt be suicidal.

Either way, one thing is certain: You would never again wonder where your home waters are.

Sacred Waters, Holy Waters, Healing Waters, Home Waters

Your home waters may be sacred to you, but they may not be sacred to others. Or, your home waters may be sacred to you as well as every other fishermen who ever comes to fish them. For your sake, I hope your home waters are off the beaten track.

Around the world there are holy waters and sacred places. The Black Hills of the Dakotas, Mount Fuji, Ayers Rock, Mount Sinai, the Ganges River; the list is long, not short. Sacred places and holy waters are anointed by human enchantment, not elected by vote.

Down through history people have been drawn to these natural places for their power to inspire and heal, and so anglers are drawn to their holy waters and home waters for angling's great cure. Let me now make a case that home waters, fishing waters and all bright waters have powerful healing qualities.

The Psychology of Sunlight and Bright Waters

Hippocrates, the father of medicine, long ago pointed out that, "Such diseases as increase in winter ought to cease in the summer, and such as increase in summer ought to decrease in the winter."

Hippocrates was a very wise man, and I interpret this particular observation to mean that fishermen tend to grow depressed and testy during the winter when fishing seasons are mostly closed, and tend to feel happier and more mellow during summer when fishing seasons are mostly open. A fisherman's season of discontent generally begins with the first snowfall.

Cabin fever amounts to that gradually worsening condition of winter discontent that occurs between ice-up and ice-out. A psychophysiological malaise common to northern climes, it is not just a figment of the angler's imagination and — except for those who learn to enjoy ice fishing — a bad case of cabin fever deserves both sympathy and understanding. Here is the understanding part.

According to the research, our biological clocks, our very lives and sense of well-being, are tied not only to the circadian rhythms of each passing, 24-hour day, but to the seasons of the year. All living things — from blue-green algae to stockbrokers — have two internal clocks, one that marks the timing of dusk, and another that marks the timing of dawn. Our daylight tracking systems govern not only daily rhythms, but seasonal rhythms as well. From the weasel changing coats from brown to white and back again, to antler growth to fish-migration schedules, all living things live according to the beat, beat, beat of light and dark, light and dark.

Thanks to oil lamps, Edison's electric light bulb and jet travel, we now have the capacity to foul up these natural rhythms. Some say we are paying a steep price, both in general discomfort and in psychiatric symptoms. Delay, retard or advance the natural circadian rhythms of the body and under which that body evolved; and you start to feel out of sorts, out of sync and even out of, as we professionals say, *it*.

The average fisherman gains 5 pounds over the winter months, sometimes more, and sometimes loses weight if he or she is clinically depressed. Weight gain, lying low, sleeping more and conserving energy are human adaptations to ice-up and the long dark nights of winter. Humans long ago evolved a very efficient fat storage system, without which the first ice age would have taken most of us out. As everyone intuitively knows, Thanksgiving is a very poor time to begin a diet because the unconscious wisdom of the Stone Age body is screaming: "Pile on the fat, fool! Winter is coming!"

Weight gain, lethargy, irritability at being disturbed, hunger for those bright home waters; these are the symptoms of the winter blues. Having just tied five salmon flies this evening, five bead head nymphs, and cleaned and oiled my fly reels twice this morning, you might guess that I'm writing this paragraph under slate gray skies in early January only 100 miles from the

Canadian border. My cabin fever temperature is spiking a bit this evening, so I can tell you honestly that there are only so many passive, winter fishing activities one can engage in before one wants to jump up, grab an ax, rush out to the nearest lake and chop a hole to open water.

Open water cheers us. Open water draws us to it. Open water reflects the light and reflected light can heal us, especially if we are suffering from cabin fever or, as it is known clinically, Seasonal Affective Disorder, a subject I will return to in just a moment.

In the second century, Aretaeus wrote, "Lethargics should be laid in the light and exposed to the rays of the sun, for the disease is gloom." Sunlight was a good cure then, and it is a good cure now. There is nothing like lying in a boat in the broad sunlight, or casting trout flies to water glittering like diamonds on a bright winter day to cure a case of the second-century glooms or 20th-century cabin fever.

Seasonal Affective Disorder, known as SAD, has only been researched for about twenty years. In that time its existence has been clearly documented and SAD is now listed as a medical condition, a condition in which the sufferer experiences a downturn in mood as a result of insufficient sunlight. Not enough sunlight and the brain's ability to produce the neurotransmitter serotonin is compromised. The symptoms include lethargy, sleep disturbance, loss of interest and eating problems. Seriously affected fishermen may not even want to have sex. Here's how SAD is believed to occur.

Sunlight strikes the retina. The retina sends electrochemical signals to the brain which, in turn, kick starts the pineal gland. The pineal gland then fires off messages to other parts of the brain to enhance serotonin production. Serotonin is the neurochemical key that helps turn on an improved mood. All the latest antidepressant medications basically are naturally occurring chemical compounds which, when circulated through the blood stream, affect how serotonin is metabolized in the brain. Bright lights seem to enhance general serotonin production.

Depression is the common cold of modern life or, as a psychiatrist friend of mine cracked the other day, "This man isn't depressed, he's Prozac deficient."

There are many kinds of depression and SAD is just one of them. Fishermen, loving sunlight as they do, might be especially prone to SAD. In northern latitudes, the symptoms of SAD must begin after November 15, and remit when the sun is again on the bass pond in April and May. For some sufferers, SAD is a very serious problem, and the rate of this depression increases as you move north or south from the equator.

About 10 percent to 12 percent of the people living as far north as the Canadian border experience a significant downturn in mood with the approach of winter, whereas only about 2 percent of fishermen living in Southern Florida experience such symptoms. In Alaska, everybody knows just about everybody is depressed and irritable during the winter. Whereas, a friend of mine who teaches in Guam — where the sun is always straight up for the same number of hours every day — reports the rate of SAD is zero.

The Fishing Cure

Cures for SAD are obvious: Fly to Mexico for marlin, Arizona for trout, the Bahamas for bonefish, and Christmas Island for more bonefish because fishing near the equator is the surest cure of all. Or you could go cheaper and simply buy one of the commercial sun lamps currently on the market, turn it on, and read fishing magazines. Personally, I keep a little year-round trout stream in my hip pocket so that, when the dark clouds blow away for a few hours and the sun pops out, I can dash out there for a few hours of therapy.

Winter sunlight strikes your retina, thus causing your little pineal gland (located directly in the center of your brain) to jump around like a Mexican jumping bean. Neurochemically, the pineal gland shouts to the rest of the body, "Hey! Summer's back!" Since reflected light is even more powerful than direct light, fishing gives you an even more powerful dose of rays, which may account for the euphoria you experience after a day on the bright waters.

Sunlight and summertime, as Hippocrates also suggested,

is the season for euphoria and its extremes of hyperactivity, mania, and fishing from dawn until dark — or until your arms drop off, whichever comes first.

Last, some theorists have argued that since the rate of depression has been rising steadily the world over since 1915, when they started keeping statistics, perhaps it is because since then we now spend more and more time indoors. Thus, we are reducing our exposure to the natural cycles of light and dark under which our species evolved. Could it be, these experts ask, that the true price of the indoor, indirect and artificial lighting that permits us to distort our more natural rhythms, is paid at the expense of our discontent?

Well, of course this must be the explanation. So, here's my prescription to cure cabin fever, Seasonal Affective Disorder, the glooms and mild cases of ordinary depression and grumpiness: Go fishing three times a week, preferably when the sun is shining; and don't go see a shrink until you've tried the fishing cure.

The trouble with shrinks like me is that we're expert at missing the obvious. Fortunately, we compound this error by giving you medicines you don't need and excuses you didn't ask for. Don't be like the millipede that went to see a psychologist with only a small problem and left the office barely able to walk because now, after only fifty minutes of help, he had to try to negotiate the world with a thousand tiny little crutches. Fishing therapy costs less, is drug free, and won't cripple your mind with a lot of excuse-making and psychological mumbo jumbo.

If fishing therapy fails to relieve the symptoms of your despair and discontent, then see a qualified provider — and by qualified I mean a shrink who fishes.

Home Waters to Call Your Own

If you have not yet found yours, I believe every fisherman can find his or her home waters. It is an important thing to do, not only because going there may work a psychological, physical and spiritual cure when you need one, but because all things are connected and some water, someplace, needs you.

If you love your home waters, and give back as much as

you get, then you will stand up and be counted when those waters are threatened. If every fisherman adopted some water as home water and stood up for it with the same grit and tenacity as for his terrestrial home and hearth, together we could save the most precious, most endangered thing on the planet: clean water.

Here is a last passage or two from the essay I wrote about my home waters, Rock Lake:

It's funny how the brain works, how it makes permanent certain visual memories. I can go to home waters, cast to the corner of a rocky cove, and remember, with perfect clarity, a trout I took from that exact same spot maybe fifteen or twenty years ago. I can't remember who was with me or how old I was or what was happening in my life or then, but I can remember the trout, the color of it, the heft of it, the sex of it, the fly it took. It's better than a camera because, with the remembering, there is a tightening in the throat you don't always get from film. And one hopes, if there's a dance after this one, you'll get to keep these best-held memories.

But the fish are only part of home waters. The other parts are people, the people you've taken there in a kind of this-is-mine pride, or the friends you've burned sunlight with on the broad waters, and the kids you've raised there. Yes, raised there. People think children are raised in homes; not so, children are raised in families. And where a family fishes together, so it comes together. Maybe you've fished a thousand waters, but if asked where of all those places you'd most want to be together again for one last fishing trip, the answer will be obvious. Why? Because that is where the bulk of the treasure is stored.

I've fished a lot of different waters and plan to fish a lot more, but there is always one place where, to paraphrase Robert Frost, when you have to catch a fish, they have to let you catch one.

Be careful what you invent, lest it invent you.
                                            — author

Rod Maker, Reel Maker

"Okay, so if it's against camp rules to give it to him, can I trade him for something?"

"What do you want?"

"A fishing bow and arrows. You said he was the camp fisherman?"

"He is. He supplies the pavon, morocoto, catfish, everything."

" '*Pincers bonita*,' he called them."

"Beautiful pliers," Dennis Bitton, my host and old pal, translated from Spanish. Dennis, thanks to a job he'd taken in South America, had invited me to fish for peacock bass in the Amazonas Territory of Venezuela's Orinoco River country. "A trade will work," Dennis continued. "A trade is better than a gift. Everyone keeps his pride in a trade."

"But what if Luis won't go for the deal? I still want a fishing bow and arrows."

"That's why they call it trading," Dennis smiled. "You may have to ante up. On the other hand, I'm pretty sure Luis has never seen a Leatherman."

A Leatherman is a kind of Swiss Army knife on steroids.

An all-purpose hand tool that folds up into a package smaller than your fist, about the only thing you can't do with a Leatherman is pound nails or launch rockets. At the heart of a Leatherman is a pair of stainless steel, full-sized regular and needle nose pliers. Loaded in the handles so that they fold out for use are an awl; Phillips screwdriver; small, medium and large screwdrivers; a knife blade; a metal/wood file; a can and bottle opener; and a ruler. The opposing deep jaws of the pliers are honed to chisel points which, when brought together under pressure with the grip of an ordinary human hand, will cut shark hooks, heavy line, or 50-pound steel leader. The Leatherman is a triumph of human tool making and represents, at the very least, 50,000 or so years of human thought and cultural evolution.

After a week of camping and fishing with a Leatherman, it becomes increasingly hard to imagine the great outdoors as all that difficult, which was no doubt why Luis repeatedly praised my Leatherman, *"Pincers bonita!"* A few thousand years ago, a man with a Leatherman could have ruled the world.

Mr. Luis Meets Mr. Leatherman

Luis was not exactly a Stone Age man, but his father probably had been, and his grandfather most certainly was. The outboard engine arrived in the Orinoco basin in the 1930s, changing everything. Within three generations, Luis and his children had become modern men and women. And it showed.

On our first day of fishing on the Orinoco, the boat motor failed some dozen miles upriver from camp. We began a slow, downriver drift. The nearest marina was hundreds of miles away. I felt a small pang, not so much of disappointment, but of fear. My first day in the tropics and here I was adrift in a river the size of the upper Mississippi, except that it was full of piranha. Fortunately, the guide couldn't speak enough English to describe our peril, if there was any.

What I didn't know then, but do now, is that all the native guides and fishermen who live along and on the waterways of the Orinoco and Amazon river basins are expert, outboard-engine mechanics. Since their survival depends upon such expert knowledge, they have to be.

Except in the instant case. It appeared Luis had no tools with him.

In Spanish, he asked if I had a knife. I open the Leatherman's blade and handed it to him. He smiled at the Leatherman and then quickly cut a sliver of wood from the boat decking. After I showed him how to turn the knife into a pair of pliers, he then pinched the metal rings that hold the gas line to its fittings and pulled the fuel line free. He blew through the line to unclog it, replaced the hose and clamps and, after handing my tool back to me and pulling on the Yamaha a couple of times, had us underway again. No big deal.

Two things became immediately clear. Had we been in a traditional, oar-powered dugout canoe for the last forty-five minutes, we would still be within walking distance of the camp and safety. Second, since there is no high technology to let you down in a dugout, you don't need a Leatherman or duct tape or bailing wire or more gas or a sparking plug or a plug wrench to save your life. All you need is a paddle, a sense of direction and a strong back.

Technology is a blessing wrapped in a curse; it can carry you far, but it can drop you hard, and in a New York minute.

Only the day before I'd had a similar thought about our sometimes dangerous dependence on high technology. The pilot who'd flown us from Caracas over the jungle to the fishing country had allowed one wing tank to run dry before switching to the second tank. A quiet man in dark glasses who chain-smoked filterless cigarettes, he never bothered to explain to the rest of us why the engine quit or why, for example, we were suddenly plummeting toward eternity.

Just as a vast wilderness of rain forest rushed up at us, fresh gas hit a sparking plug and — as with Luis' fix on the 40-horse Yamaha — we were once again the king of beasts, masters of the world, and back in charge of the known universe.

Whether you are temporarily stranded in an airplane in the middle of a cloud 15,000 feet up, or temporarily stranded in a boat in the middle of a wild, piranha-filled river, it is only at these moments that we realize how dependent we have become on our tools. More than any other fishing creature, we fishermen are helplessly dependent on our tools, as anyone who has lost his only rod overboard or broken the handle on his only reel can tell you.

Evolving from stardust, we are now able to make everything from star drags to starships. Man is nothing if not a toolmaker and, if man doesn't watch his values and how he spends his life, he may soon become little more than the sum total of his tools. In an exploding electronic world, I've wondered, what will happen when kids can go fishing in virtual reality instead of reality? How will they choose?

Luis had never seen a Leatherman. Before handing it back to me that first morning, he studied it. I then showed him how it worked and the myriad of functions contained in the handles. Each time a fish needed releasing that afternoon and each day we fished thereafter, he smiled and asked for the *"pincers bonita."* I knew he had a pair of pliers somewhere, but each morning we fished together, he had conveniently forgotten them.

And why wouldn't he admire them? An ordinary pair of pliers gives an ordinary man the thumbs of a gorilla, but a Leatherman gives him the cleverness of a thousand generations of toolmakers, each passing along a little better idea than his father before him. With a Leatherman, Luis — just two generations from the Stone Age — could have the biting strength of a jaguar, the razor teeth of the piranha, a stainless steel blade that defied rust, and enough mental leverage to pry open a small world. The more I realized this, the more I wanted him to have it.

Across the Cultural Chasm

I'd fished with other guides, but I especially liked Luis. The rules of the Manaka Jungle Fishing Camp were straightforward: No matter how much you liked them, the guides were not to be given modern fishing gear, apparently on the argument that introducing such high technology to these aboriginal peoples might enable them to destroy their own, life-sustaining fishery. The sports practiced catch-and-release, and we were expected to leave the jungle and its fishes pretty much the way we'd found them, although a "thank you" in the form of a pair sunglasses, gringo cash, insect repellent or fishing pliers was okay at trip's end.

Luis had shown me a couple of wonderful days of angling, and so I wanted him to have the Leatherman rather badly. Neither of us spoke fluent Spanish, although his was much better than mine, and yet I felt a strong bond with him about the fishes. You could tell Luis loved the fishes. He was respectful of them, gentle with them and talked to them. When the freshwater dolphins were nearby and I had exhausted a fish with a fly rod, he protected the captured fish he was about to release by moving into shore to be sure the tired fighter could make it to cover before the dolphins could catch it.

Explaining in sign language that a battle-weary pavon was no match for a dolphin, he would cradle the fish in his hands, moving it gently backward and forward in the water until it was fully revived. Then, moving the boat close to shore, he would release it with a kind word.

"We'll go up to the village tonight," said Dennis toward the end of the week. "Perhaps you can work a trade with Luis then. He would prefer a trade, I think. If he makes a good trade, his stock will go even higher in the village."

Having been a bow-fisher from boyhood, I very much wanted a bow and a pair of fishing arrows from the Amazon jungle. I could always get another Leatherman, but I might never meet another man like Luis. While we were different in many ways, we were both fishermen, both family men, both men who loved the wild and the fishes. A man from a different world and culture, Luis would teach me a thing or two before my fishing trip was over.

Fishing Tools and the Tackle High

A fishing rod is a highly specialized tool. So is a fishing reel, with or without a star drag. Fishing line is a tool. Hooks are tools. Lures are tools. Snap swivels, colored beads, spinner blades, hand carved or molded plastic minnows are tools. Put all these tools together and you have a fishing machine so divine most anglers cannot own enough of them.

I don't know about other fishermen, but when I pick up a perfectly designed, finely machined, smooth and beautifully crafted fishing reel, and then attach it to a matched, balanced, tapered graphite rod of heavenly proportions and flex — well, it's as if my brain releases a great, cascading flow of morphine-like endorphins that, when they hit the pleasure centers in the old noodle, compare favorably with the rush of a heroin high, or so I've been told by addicts.

And why shouldn't there be something called a tackle high? We anglers have been questing for the perfect fishing outfit since the very beginning of fishing. Each time we find some wonderful new fishing tool, why wouldn't we have a "Eureka! I have found it!" kind of experience? Compared to heroin, a tackle high is clean, safe and, if not cheaper, at least you don't have to stick yourself with a needle.

In my experience, tackle highs can last as long as the tackle. I have a few fly reels that, just by picking them up and slowly pulling the line out to that sweet, dragging music of click-click-click, can transport me to faraway rivers where the fish are as long as your leg.

We modern anglers may not realize it, but we now enjoy fishing tools so wondrous that a fisherman from 500 years ago could never even imagine them. Luis's grandfather, isolated in the jungles of Venezuela only a hundred years ago, could never have imagined them.

Thumbs, Precision Casting and High IQs

Many years ago I was hunting deer up near the Canadian border and had been sitting for a couple of hours when a ruffed grouse flew into the tree above me and settled on a limb not 15 yards away. A legal bird, I wanted that grouse for lunch. But, I didn't want to explode a .308 round to pay for it, so I picked up a rock, stood, aimed and let it fly. Grilled over an open fire, that grouse went very well with a Winesap apple and canteen of cold, spring water.

Killing game by throwing things — rocks, sticks, spears, harpoons — is as old as hunting and fishing. It is no doubt how we first began to hunt and fish. Interestingly, throwing things may be one of the pathways by which we humans grew such big brains.

In my wandering search for the origins of fishing, I recently found a new theory that ties stone throwing and hunting and fishing up with brain size, and further attempts to explain the explosion in human intelligence we hominids have experienced over last 100,000 or so years.

For this theory to work, though, humans had to first develop a thumb. Thumbs are very important to fishermen. You have to have a thumb to grab a rod properly. You need a thumb to get a grip on a reel handle. When a fish is running hard on a level-wind reel, you need a thumb to "thumb the drag." Fishermen who cannot tie their own flies say of themselves, "I'm all thumbs," meaning they have too many thumbs and not enough fingers.

Thumbs are much more important for *Homo sapiens* than any of us realizes. The other day one of my sons was at home visiting with his girlfriend, a modern girl with feminist inclinations. When I complained that my wife, Ann, was late getting home to fix dinner, this beautiful young girl remarked to my son, "Gee, that's too bad. Doesn't your father have opposing thumbs?"

Suddenly in deep, post-feminist water, I had nothing to say. I took the wise advise of the old fishermen, who said, "Sometimes it's best to just keep quiet and take your medicine."

Opposing thumbs made tool-making possible. Without thumbs, there would be no tools, let alone fishing rods. But before tools, there was a need to throw rocks.

In a nutshell, this new theory holds it was the requirement of *when to release* a rock when thrown that resulted in the human brain gradually gaining size, weight and efficiency, thus making us all smart as whips. Those rock-and-stick throwers with the best timing and release killed more game, became alpha males, married more often and had more kids. Over time, the best hunters and fishermen became Darwin's survival machines, or Darwin's bass.

Whether you pitch baseballs for a living, throw darts for fun, launch space flights, toss trout flies or cast bass plugs in competition, a well-timed release is at the top of the list of things you must do well if you hope to be successful. The release of the line to cast a lure is nothing more than pulling a remote trigger on a projectile whose energy has been loaded into the arc of a fishing rod on the backcast.

The timing and perfection of the release of the string is so important in Zen archery that the teaching masters insist a beginner practice only releasing the string for the first year. Then, they get to try an arrow. If the release is perfect, imagination will take care of the flight of the arrow. While not as critical in casting a lure, timing the release is still everything in launching a good cast.

To reach a rising fish with a fly, or to drop a bass plug perfectly amid some distant lily pads, the line must be released at the precise moment. Too soon, and the lure flies high and falls short; too late, and the lure flies low, and falls shorter. We're talking split-second timing, as a millisecond too soon or too late and your efforts fail miserably. Essentially, to be a good caster, you must have perfect timing.

So, what goes on in the human brain and body to achieve this kind of timing? Quite a lot, it turns out. Whether perfect timing is required to throw a rock, release an arrow, complete a down-field pass, cast a bass plug, or send a shooting head a hundred feet out over a steelhead river, what goes on inside us is nothing short of miraculous.

It takes eighty-eight muscles to coordinate the throwing of a projectile like a baseball or bass plug. To throw a fly or plug to a distant target with any accuracy requires the brain to sum up all the necessary instructions to all eighty-eight muscles; visually find, fix and estimate the range to a given fish or log or lily pad. Then, like some great orchestra conductor, the brain must get all those nerves and chemicals and muscles to do exactly what is required at *exactly* the same moment.

To hit the target the release must be perfectly timed. Only something as complicated as the human brain could possibly coordinate all that is required to get this enormously complicated job done. Yet with a little practice, even small children can master all this neuromuscular activity and deliver decent casts in a matter of minutes. Apparently we humans come equipped with a built-in, rock-release mechanism. I know that at my age — after a billion backcasts — I am now able to not only deliver lures to far targets, but can chew gum and tell lies all at the same time.

Chimpanzees throw rocks and sticks. They also require the same eighty-eight muscles to throw something. But chimps don't come with big, built-in, rock-thrower brains. Chimps throw long, but not straight. Any human being with a decent arm can win a rock fight with a chimp. Chimps throw to intimidate, not to kill, although there are scattered reports of chimpanzees disabling small game by throwing sticks. Man, on the other hand, learned long ago that if you could throw well, you could knock down a banana or a grouse for lunch, or drive off a predator. Perhaps he learned to fish in the same way.

The history of our hunting and fishing tools is the history of our success as a species, although early man as fisherman has gotten scant attention until recently. Scientists excavating an ancient village submerged for at least a hundred years along the Sea of Galilee recently found strands of fiber from the Stone Age. Since there were piles of fish bones found with these 19,300-year-old twisted plant fibers, one hypothesis is that the baskets were used to catch and keep fish. At an even earlier site in the ancient Africa of our human origins, archaeologists digging in the Kalahari Desert have found barbed bone projectile points mixed in layers of perch and catfish bones, again suggesting that fishing was important to survive another day, another year and another generation. The Kalahari fishing operation was 40,000 years old.

I have my own theory about how fishing first began. Since I am unencumbered by proper academic degrees in the fields of archeology and anthropology, I figure I can muck around in prehistory without taking any serious heat if my notions don't hold water. So here's my theory.

An Irresponsible Theory of How Fishing Got Started

As man was first learning to get up on two feet for all its built-in advantages — better heat dissipation, improved ambulation and speed, free hands with which to carry sandwiches and fishing rods, and improved opposing thumb strength to open those pesky twist top cold beers — he was also exposed to the greatest drought in the history of Africa, or so the experts tell us. According to my readings, the African continent was drying up at the time the human brain dramatically leapt forward in size and function. Something called "desertification" was taking place.

Desertification means just what it sounds like: Due to climatic changes, temperate zones were becoming deserts. Patterns of rainfall changed. Green forests were giving way to blowing sands. River flows dropped lower and lower. Lakes and ponds began to dry up.

Able to walk upright by this time, the bipedal fishing mammal had gained a great advantage: He and she and baby could follow the retreating green of the forest, keeping up with the herds that had to follow the water courses where the fishes lived.

An omnivore, man would have eaten fish if he could find them. But how to catch them? If man first became a fisher in these hard times, how did he gain an advantage over the other fishers: birds, mammals and reptiles?

I have a fanciful answer, and it goes very well with about four fingers of scotch and a crackling campfire. Here it is.

Having been out and about during a drought where I live in eastern Washington, I know something about desertification, if only on a small scale. As of this writing, our current drought is into its eighth year. On a summer hike through the backcountry few years back, I came upon a shallow lake that was — as near I could tell studying the old shoreline — less than one-third its former size. There were birds of prey working the lake for the trapped fish — much as there must have been birds of prey working the shallowing waters discovered by my ancient

African grandfathers — and so I spent a couple of hours investigating this quite natural phenomenon.

As I was to learn in a few minutes, the lake was filled with dying tench. Tench are a European import to America, and while a favorite of anglers there, here they are considered a nuisance. Tench feed only in summers and hibernate during winter in mud cocoons where, because of their specialized systems for oxygen utilization and resistance to carbon dioxide build-up, they can live out of water even longer than the carp. Tench can also survive short droughts because of this ability to survive in low liquid environments until the rains return and fill the pond or lake again. Because of these camel-like characteristics, tench are sometimes the only fish found in isolated, marginalized bodies of water of the kind I had discovered on that summer afternoon.

They're not much to look at compared to a golden trout. But had I been an ancient fisherman in search of a meal for my family, the sight of feeding herons in shallow water would have signaled food and been a cause for great celebration. Here were fish for the taking, swimming in plain sight with their backs out of shallow water.

But how to take them? Since I wasn't fishing the day I discovered the dying lake, I didn't have a rod and reel with me. Or a net. Or a spear. Or anyone to help drive them up on the shore and strand them. I was tool-less but, being a clever human, not quite clue-less.

Why not wade out and catch one with my hands? Slipping off my hiking boots, I waded in the mud after them.

Bad idea. Tench are heavily coated with an extremely slick shield of heavy mucus. You can grab them, but you can't hold them. They're a strong fish, and you need talons or a heron's beak, not fingernails.

I returned to shore and sat down and studied on the problem. All around me lay bits of broken lava. A 40-watt bulb popped inside my skull: Why not stone them? They didn't call it the Stone Age for nothing. Man started out throwing sticks and stones at enemies, fruit hanging in trees, and small animals and birds. So, why not fish?

On my fifth or sixth stone toss into the schooling fish, I stunned one sufficiently to have a chance to rush out, get my hands under its belly, and flip it onto shore. The fish weighed about a pound. Germans may regard a baked tench as a particular delicacy, but I was not so much interested in fixing shore lunch as I was in examining my prize and then imagining if this is how fishing got started.

With the lakes and ponds and rivers drying up just as man was expanding this range and becoming a better bipedal walker — even without sophisticated harpoons, or nets, or weirs, or bows and arrows — he could have been a very successful fisherman, especially if he fished with his family and friends. He'd have had trouble in deeper waters, but not in shallow water. Fish trapped in shallow water, or passing through shallow water on a spawning run are easy to take, as any Alaskan brown bear can tell you.

But is there any evidence for such a theory? Well, or course there is.

Researchers studying ancient, now-dry, African water holes have found the bottoms of these littered with thousands and thousands of fist-sized stones that appear to have been thrown there. Since only humans are likely to have thrown that many stones, what would have been the point? To make splashes? Probably not.

Some researchers suggest that the stones were thrown at watering game animals. But since this is a book about fishing, why couldn't they have been thrown at fish? Every angler knows that the bottom structure of all the good fishing water the world over is currently littered with millions of lead sinkers, snagged plugs, downrigger balls and goodness knows what all else, so why not fishing rocks?

The First Fishing Rock

According to neurophysiologist William H. Calvin in *The Ascent of Mind*, the common Acheulian hand ax of our Stone Age ancestors is not an ax at all, but a throwing stone — most likely used to kill or disable, in Calvin's thesis, big game. In my thesis, the Acheulian hand ax was also used to kill big fish.

These hand axes show up all over the globe, sometimes in great numbers, and especially in the beds of dried up lakes.

Why, Calvin asks, did our ancestors bother to chip a sharp edge all around these discus-sized tools and then lose so many of them? If they were used for skinning or fleshing, how come you'd have a sharp edge right where you would most likely hold the tool? And why, when you throw one of these bilaterally symmetric, pointed, flattened hand axes, does it sail like a discus, turn itself over in mid flight, and tend to land point down, sticking deeply into the ground?

Hummmm. ...

To test the aerodynamic properties of the hand ax, Calvin recruited university discus throwers to toss fiberglass replicas of hand axes. They sailed like a discus. Even though they tried, they could not get these hand axes to fly other than in an on-edge trajectory, thus suggesting that the hand ax wasn't designed for chopping or skinning or fleshing, but for throwing.

Throwing at what? Well, what have you got? Herd animals come to mind. Fish trapped in shallow water might be worth a toss, especially since the Nile perch is endemic to Africa and can weigh up to 300 pounds. If you caught several fat, Nile perch in shallow water, why not bean one with a hand ax?

Individual big game animals like lions and bears are hard to hunt and kill. But herd animals, like zebras and buffalo, tend to bunch up when under attack. So do fish. The "safety in numbers" defense works well if you keep to the middle. As herd or school size increases, the percentage of animals on the periphery decreases, thus giving the average creature inside the pack or school a better chance of surviving the average predator attack.

But a bunch of Stone Age hunters and fishermen are not your average predator, especially if these hunting parties are slinging razor sharp stones that, because of their form and aerodynamic properties, always come slicing down out of the sky edge first. Pound for pound, a sharp stone is more deadly than a dull one, and any game animal or fish hit in the spine, head or neck with a heavy, sharp stone will be stunned sufficiently — if not killed — that ancient hunters might have been able to scramble in for the kill, as I did with the tench that summer day.

As Calvin's theory predicts, you ought to find a lot of hand axes around old water holes. And you do. In some areas, hand axes are so thick on the beds of ancient water holes as to appear as if they grew there. You can imagine that as herd animals were encircled by groups of hunters, their tendency to pack them-selves into tighter and tighter groups for defense simply made the lobbing of sharpened rocks more effective. The same would hold true for herded fish.

Sort of like shooting at the side of the barn, all you have to do to kill a herded fish is to get close enough to lob in a shot. Imagine ten fishermen lobbing hand axes all at once into a pan-icked herd of zebra or tightly packed school of fish. In a kind of grand flock shot, someone was sure to hit something.

Even more interesting, when hand axes are thrown by experienced discus throwers, they spin through the air, thus becoming a spinning, sharp-edged, cutting tool zooming through space. Once it strikes a fish or animal, it doesn't just bounce off, but digs in, thus causing much more injury and rais-ing the likelihood of a kill. Hit hard on the head, neck or spine, all vertebrates tend to stagger and even go down. A head shot on a big perch would likely kill it, which is why Calvin has sug-gested the ancient hand ax ought to be renamed the "Killer Frisbee."

From Throwing Rocks to Throwing Flies

All this may be more than you ever wanted to know about how throwing rocks might have led to throwing flies. However, consider that it was our graduation from making a flock shot to throwing a spear that ensured our survival and led to ever greater brain size. The better the release, the greater is the accu-racy and the more success in spearing fish. And with each gen-eration of a better fishing tool, only those with enhanced brain capacity could use such tools efficiently, thus gaining advantage over the Joneses.

With bigger brains, more focused concentration becomes possible. With bigger brains, ever better timing of the neuro-muscular systems becomes possible. And with bigger brains, the old toolmaker discovered the rock-throwing sling, the bow and arrow, catapults, Chinese cannons, flintlocks, the forward cast and flippin' rods — each one with its own perfect moment of release.

Dr. Calvin's theory that man's sudden growth in brain size over the last couple hundred thousand years is due to his evolving a better and better timed release certainly makes some sense to me, whether it has any merit or not. The journey from throwing rocks to rocketry, and from flock shots to moon shots, has been a wonderful ride. But somehow I'm not surprised. After all, we humans have always wanted the same old thing: a little better fishing rod than we had awhile ago.

Luis and the Leatherman

While it has taken thousands of years to evolve and perfect the rod and reel, it takes man-the-tool-user only minutes to master them. After showing him the fundamentals of casting a fly line and how to set the drag on a fly reel, I left Luis near our boat to experiment on his own. His first few casts were awkward and fell short. Line speed was slow and his loops were too big. Then, suddenly, they improved. I checked my watch. In less than ten minutes Luis was laying out very decent 40-foot casts. He stripped the fly at the right speed. I watched him for a moment or two longer, and then started fishing myself.

The next time I glanced over at Luis, he was fighting a very nice peacock under the big arc of a 9-weight fly rod. He controlled the fish well, taking line in by hand, rather than on the reel. Once he had the fish against the shore, he looked up to see if I had witnessed his first peacock on a fly rod. The native men in those parts don't show their emotions much, but there was no mistaking Luis-the-fisherman's grin.

Like any man or woman anywhere on the planet surface, tool-using is in the genes that blueprint the brain. With a little education and training, Luis could learn to fly an F-14. No modern human of average intelligence is long confused by any tool whose purpose and operation can be shown or explained.

Likewise, if we reverse the arrow of time and could find an instructor, any modern human should be able to master any ancient skill, practice or tool. Had I only had the sense to ask,

I'm sure Luis would have taken me night fishing using his ancient methods under a tropical moon when the great fishes of the Orinoco rise up to the surface.

When a fish is shot with an arrow in the light of the moon, the long manaka palm shaft tipped with a steel barbed point is grabbed to haul the catch into the dugout. But, if the fish is too big, you must follow the shaft until the fish dies. And you never shoot a fish too big to land. There are catfish up to 400 pounds in the Orinoco. Had I not been locked in my 20th century rut of rod and reel, I might have enjoyed a night of fishing the way it has been done since Luis's people first came to live in the jungles.

On the last day of fishing, I went with Dennis to meet Luis in his village downriver from camp. The Leatherman was offered in trade for a fishing bow and a couple of arrows.

Translating for Luis, Dennis smiled, "Luis says he just happens to have just such a bow and arrow." In a few minutes, the deal was struck. No haggling. We shook hands and smiled at each other.

Through Dennis I told Luis that I, too, was an "*arco*," a bow fisherman up in the United States and perhaps he could answer some questions for me. Luis smiled; he'd be happy to.

He quickly explained the design and details of the arrows, why the shafts needed to be over 5 feet long, why cormorant wings fletch the best, and why a special hardwood was needed to make a strong tip. Then, as he showed me how to draw an arrow to shoot a fish, I asked him what sort of wood was used in the construction of the bow, a bow design that has not changed for perhaps 10,000 years.

Luis studied my face for a moment, as if I had suddenly gone stupid. He then turned to Dennis and said something in Spanish.

Dennis grinned. "Luis said to tell you that the wood one uses to build a fishing bow is the 'appropriate' wood. He seems a little mystified that you wouldn't already know that."

Be not afraid of sudden fear ...
— Proverbs 3:25

The Phobic Fisherman

Several years ago I received a desperate phone call from a woman whose fear was so great she could not even name the thing that terrified her.

"Someone gave me your name," she began, somewhat hesitantly. "They said you were good. Do you do work with phobias?"

"Yes," I said. "What kind of phobia do you have?"

"I can't say," she replied, her breath suddenly coming short. "I can't even say the word. Their name makes my skin crawl. For that matter, I'm not very fond of the word crawl."

"It must be a ... "

"Don't say it!" she interrupted. "Or I won't even come in."

Remembering that the patient is always right, I asked, "How would next Tuesday at one o'clock be?"

"That would be fine. But remember, don't say the word. I call them my 'friends,' and I want you to call them that, too. Understood?"

"Yes," I said. "Understood."

Little could I guess from that first call that I would be challenged by the most difficult phobia I had ever encountered; that I would learn more than I ever knew about the nature of primal fear; and that, before we were finished, I would need several of those long rubber bass fishing worms to work a cure.

The "Why now?" question we psychologists always ask ourselves when someone makes a first appointment was answered as follows. Recently moved to the Northwest from a major Eastern city, this 32-year-old mother had nearly killed herself and her daughter when, upon seeing the object of her fear lying in the middle of a curving road while driving home one afternoon, she screamed, threw her hands into the air, and very nearly crashed the car.

For fear of seeing another, she was afraid to drive except after dark. Because one might be lurking under the tomato vines, she could not go into her garden. She could not go for long walks down quiet lanes near her home in the country. And she could certainly not go stream fishing with her husband.

If you have guessed that my patient was "snake phobic," you are exactly the kind of highly intelligent, educated reader for whom this book was intended. Most likely a fisherman yourself, it is more than probable that you have had one or more snake encounters. If you have not encountered a snake while afoot in the field or stream, you have very likely seen one sunning itself on the countryside tarmac. Confronted with an identical situation, you may have swerved to avoid the snake, stopped to let it move along, or you may have aimed your tires over its midsection and said, "Good riddance!"

Humans are seldom neutral in their feelings toward snakes. Some don't mind them, and a few like to see them, but most fishermen I know would just as soon pass the day without a snake encounter, herpetologists not included. In poisonous snake country, a good day of fishing is a "no snake day." To protect one of my favorite trout waters, I often say to anglers who are pressing me for directions, "Yes, the rainbows are huge, just like the rattlers."

"RATTLERS!!!"

"Don't worry," I assure them. "Most of them are so big you can't miss 'em."

"Ah ... er ... and where else do you recommend I go fishing?"

Fear is a wonderful motivator: You just have to know how to use it. I admit that the snake-infested-fishing-hole ploy was invented back in the Pleistocene, and while I hate myself for using it, I am — like other crafty anglers — not above such shameless behavior to protect a secret spot. Besides, there could be rattlesnakes where I fish.

Snakes can ruin a lot of fishing, so perhaps an examination of our aversion to them might be a profitable way to spend a few minutes — that is if you can't, for some reason, be out fishing just now. If you can be out fishing, put this book down immediately and go.

Before this chapter is out and after I have explained primal fears and such, I shall loop around to the case of the "Snake-Phobic Lady," cure her, and thereby demonstrate how a crack clinical psychologist can leap tall buildings in a single bound. Well, maybe short buildings. Would you believe a pup tent?

The Natural Selection of Emotions

Fishing was not always the calm, relaxing sport it is today. During the Stone Age, fishing was probably not even a sport, in part because fishing could be hazardous to your health. On an extended fishing expedition 20,000 years ago, perhaps five anglers went out, but only four returned. On arrival back at camp and to account for the missing man, Zag might shake his head and report, "Good fishing, too many bears."

Among the things that made fishing dangerous were several large carnivores, alligators, crocodiles and snakes. Fail to avoid these, and your fishing days could be shortened up considerably. Moreover, as with most fishing trips, someone usually falls and sometimes breaks a bone. No fishing trip is complete without cutting a finger. While these are mere annoyances now, in the Stone Age such events were life-threatening. There was nothing to minimize pain and suffering like antibiotics, anesthetics, tetanus shots, first aid kits, plaster casts, sterile surgery, search and rescue teams and Tennessee sipping whiskey. (Tennessee sipping whiskey is strong medicine for just about anything bad or painful that can happen to you on a fishing trip; it works equally well in case anything good happens.)

As a result of all these dangerous forces selecting the fit from the not-so-fit, modern fishing man now comes complete with a number of interesting survival tools, including the emotions of anxiety and fear, among others. In Darwinian terms, our emotional reactions were selected to help us survive, not to make us happy. You may not like feeling anxious or fearful, but once you understand that these two emotions are the early-warning systems that allowed mankind to avoid predation by bigger and faster killers, perhaps you can understand and accept them not as weaknesses, but as blessings.

Here's how it happened. Two possible ancestors are fishing for perch one day when a hungry saber-toothed tiger approaches them through the tall grass. They both spot the cat. One fisherman experiences the symptoms of fear — rapid heartbeat, deep breathing, sweating, increased glucose and epinephrine output, itchy feet, and a powerful urge to spring into the only tree along that section of the river. The other fisherman does not experience this "fight-or-flight" response, but goes on chatting about the benefits of spitting on your bait.

The cat charges.

One guy leaps. The other continues to watch his bobber.

Only one of them becomes your grandpappy.

When you feel anxious, and many millions of people do, it is important to remember that nature doesn't care if you're uncomfortable: All nature cares about is that you survive. Too much anxiety costs energy, and spending energy needlessly is not biologically smart. Knowing when to worry is the key. Since anxious people are all tensed up to avoid getting hurt or killed, it may be instructive to look at a simple study on the merits of being timid.

The Smallmouth Bass and the Timid Guppy

Can anxiety, fear, worry and timidity save your life? Yes, especially if you happen to be a guppy trapped in a fish tank with a smallmouth bass. In this study, guppies were observed over time and then separated into three groups: timid guppies that dashed to cover at the slightest threat, ordinary guppies and bold guppies.

On seeing a smallmouth bass, timid guppies darted away and hid in the corners, ordinary guppies carried on what they were doing, and bold guppies stood eyeball-to-eyeball with the smallmouth. After sixty hours, 40 percent of the timid guppies remained, while only 15 percent of the ordinary guppies were still alive. How many bold guppies survived?

None.

Lesson: It is better to respond to a thousand false alarms than to get killed just once.

Have you ever heard a twig or limb crack in the woods behind you when you were out fishing? If it was a tiny, little crack, you may have turned to check out what sort of small animal might have made it. But if it was a big crack, you probably held your breath, stiffened a bit, and either froze or began a slow scan of the woods behind you. It is those individuals whose resting anxiety level is tuned to respond quickly to a possible threat, and who also enjoy accurate signal detection, that have a clear survival advantage.

Among the standard issue signal recognition equipment we all inherit is our predator-detection machinery. We can spot shadows in the timber. We "listen up" at the cry of a cat or a branch breaking in the bush. Thanks to eons and eons of natural selection, we all come equipped with a quite reliable snake detector.

A slithering movement out of the corner of our eye, a rustle in the grass, the sound of snake scales ratcheting over granite, the buzz of a reptile's rattles — these are just a few of the stimuli which can bring an otherwise serene angler to full alert.

In some anglers, a snake alert converts instantly into something my old friend Patrick F. McManus calls the "full linear panic." Once ignited, a full linear panic involves running at high speed through fishing country, during which the angler only changes direction when he ricochets off something solid, like a tree or large rock. If he panics in open country, the results may include only minor injuries and exhaustion. In thick woods or cliff country, however, the resulting medical expenses can easily run to four figures.

Some argue a fear of snakes is taught to us by our parents.

Another camp claims the fear of snakes is part of our built-in neural system of automatic detection-alert-arousal equipment and that no teaching is required. As is often the case with this old nature-versus-nurture argument, the latest research suggests both are right.

Fishing in Snake Country

First, we are not alone in our fear of snakes. Chimps and baboons don't much like snakes and will avoid them if they can. Confronted with a real or rubber snake, rhesus monkeys jump out of their skins. Stepping back to pull in a nice trout one day, I looked down to find myself astraddle a small, diamond-back rattler coiled between my wading boots. While I didn't exactly jump out of my skin, I did elevate with sufficient force to leave stretch marks.

But like most primate programs, experience with snakes determines how we respond. Without adult supervision and absent any experience, baby chimps will reach over a snake to get a banana. But not if their mother is around. If mother sees the snake, she will let out a scream, and then so, too, will junior. And a good scream it will be. One exposure to a snake and a screaming mother activates the primate snake-detector. It is a one-trial learning experience and is basically never forgotten.

At least as clever as chimps, humans can have later experience with snakes that modify any built-in or conditioned aversion to them. Were this not so, humans would probably have killed off all the snakes, good and bad, a long time ago. By pairing a banana with a rubber snake, chimpanzees come to accept and tolerate "snakey" things. Despite the inherent risks that snakes present, primates and humans can learn to get along with snakes quite well, even taking them as pets. If this weren't so, I was going to have a very hard time charging a fee to treat my snake phobic lady with bass worms.

I did, however, have prior experience in working with snakes and the fear of snakes. I tried a snake deconditioning experiment with my oldest son when he was just a boy. An undergraduate psychology major at the time, I had taken Jeff with me on a catfish fishing trip one warm, spring afternoon.

Given the opportunity for a natural experiment, I attempted to rid him of any fear of non-dangerous snakes.

Only 4 years old at the time, the boy wandered away while I watched the bobbers and — as luck would have it — the lad chanced upon a fresh hatch of baby garter snakes. He ran back to me to announce the find and was both alarmed and curious. We found the little, green slivers cutting through the grass, and I assured him they were perfectly harmless.

"Don't worry," I said. "These are baby garter snakes, and garter snakes don't bite."

This would have been a grand suggestion except for one little problem. Not five minutes later Jeff came up behind me with a foot-long garter snake dangling from that web of skin between the thumb and forefinger. The snake had a firm jaw lock on the boy's skin and a little blood was weeping from around the bite. Jeff, whose eyes were rather enlarged with more disbelief than pain, looked at me and said, "Dad, garter snakes *do* bite."

Arriving home sometime later to face the boy's mother, I had a lot of explaining to do about the snakebite: Why I would let a child play with snakes in the first place, and when, in God's name, was I going to stop conducting all these crazy, irresponsible psychology experiments on the children. I would have launched a perfectly rational counterargument, but as I hastily explained, I had a lot of catfish to clean. As I recall, for the next couple of days my otherwise warm and healthy family life caught a small cold.

But back to the experiment. Even with the little snake locked on, Jeff did not panic. Better still, I did not panic. Had I panicked, the boy would have panicked, perhaps developed a full-blown snake phobia and, in the bargain, never gone fishing with me again. Had his fear of snakes spread, he might have begun to avoid not only snakes, but places where snakes live, i.e., the great outdoors.

In Darwinian terms, I suppose we humans should thank all the snakes for helping make us what we are today. Natural selection says that people who spot dangerous snakes and avoid them tend to live longer, whereas those who don't spot dangerous snakes tend to leave the gene pool under the general medical category of "snake bit." Thanks to the cobras, cottonmouths, rattlesnakes, venomous pit vipers and those large, bone-crushing boas, we have fewer and fewer snake-stupid people with which to contend these days. Through their biting, poisoning, crushing and eating those of our ancient ancestors who were a tad slow around things that slither, the scaly ones have helped select for our highly adaptive, hard-wired, built-in, shock-proof, rust-resistant reptile detector.

Not counting the few that can kill us, we very much need snakes. Without them, the balance of nature would tilt dangerously out of control. Without snakes, the rodents would soon rule the world, or try to. The key is to: Respect all snakes; avoid the ones that can kill you; love the ones that keeps the mice out of your grain; and never kill one you absolutely don't have to.

A Fear of Flying

As to other fears and phobias and difficult-to-explain human behaviors, it is interesting to speculate that perhaps some of the more common ones were selected for before and during the Stone Age. Among our pre-packaged fears are the following.

"Agoraphobia," the fear of open places, makes sense if you are out on the African savannah during a fishing trip with your pals and you get separated. Suddenly alone in lion country, a twinge or two of fear makes good survival sense. More than one angler has got "turned around" in the woods, and the panic you feel at being lost feels very primal, very ancient indeed.

"Hydrophobia," fear of water, made more sense before big, safe boats and floatation devices, but even now it is a useful fear. We lose far too many fishermen each year who do not properly respect the water they love.

"Acrophobia," the fear of heights, always makes sense — then and now. The human body was not designed to bounce.

Obsessive hoarding makes sense if you live in a world of chronic food shortages.

Worry and anxiety about cleanliness was adaptive in a world filled with disease and close quarters, and still is in some fishing camps I've visited.

Fear of strangers makes sense when strangers have a nasty habit of killing you first and asking questions later.

Generalized anxiety tends to occur in unfamiliar surroundings, and it should.

The roots of our fears and current phobias run to ancient, ancestral roots — roots pruned by the forces of natural selection in our original, evolutionary environments. Bring these vestigial but very real, heart-thumping fears into modern settings, combine them in unnatural environments, and you have a formula for an interesting array of new fears and phobias.

For example, the fear of flying combines acrophobia with claustrophobia, a fear of being trapped in a tight, closed-in places, and adds xenophobia, a fear of strangers, into the mix. Throw in loud noises, high speeds and "agentaphobia," a fear of life insurance salesmen, and you have a recipe for genuine terror. I know. I was once trapped for an hour in a small, commuter jet between two life insurance salesmen during a thunderstorm.

The Case of the Snake-Phobic Fisherman

Since most primate programs are open, it is theoretically possible to cure any phobia with the exception, perhaps, of the one just described. In the case of curing a snake phobia, it is the emotional side of the equation that needs fixing. Intellectually, we all know we should not be afraid of a non-poisonous snake. The trouble is, our ancient survival machinery needs to be taught the difference between friend and foe.

If a chimp can be taught to tolerate snakes, then I should be able to help a 32-year-old executive overcome her fear of non-poisonous snakes. So let's loop back to the beginning.

After shaking hands, I seated a woman we shall call "Beth" on the couch in my consulting room and asked how she came to call me. She explained that she had gotten my name from someone at work and, having just moved to the Northwest from a large metropolitan area, she realized just how dangerous and incapacitating her phobia now was. "I have to do something about my 'friends,' " she finished.

"Your 'friends'?"

"I call them my friends because I can't stand to hear or say the word. They move like this," and with that, she made a wavy, S-shaped movement with her hand.

"Oh, you mean snakes. You suffer from a ... "

"Please!" Beth gasped. "Don't use the that word! I can't bear it! If you say that word again, I will leave this office and never come back."

She was quite visibly experiencing a sub-linear panic attack. A full linear, McManus panic attack would have her ricocheting around the room, knocking over bookshelves and table lamps.

Her breathing was quick and shallow. She clasped her hands and wrung them. She fidgeted on the couch. She glanced at the door, as if she was about to make a hasty retreat. "That door's not locked, is it?" she asked.

"No," I assured her, "and I will never say the name of your friends again until it is okay with you. You are going to be in charge of what happens here. Okay?"

"Okay," she said, relaxing only a bit. "Have you a glass of wine to calm me down?"

"I'm sorry," I said. "But, I can teach you how to relax." And with that I quickly taught her a simple breathing exercise to help her gain some control over hyperventilating and fear of losing complete control of her autonomic nervous system. When she felt a little better, I proceeded.

"I'm curious," I said. "If you knew you were moving here, and especially to a place in the country, why didn't you go to the phobia clinic in your hometown? There is a very famous one there."

Beth studied my face. "Maybe you don't know as much about phobias as you think," she said. "Anyone with a real phobia wouldn't go near a phobia clinic."

"Why?" I asked.

"Because you psychologists will just make us confront the thing we fear. That's the last thing we want. It's why they call it a phobia."

Right away, given my special training, I knew I was in deep trouble, perhaps even over my head. Here was an intelli-

gent, educated executive who knew more about how a true phobic would respond to the promise — and threat — of a cure. If
it involved contact with the thing most feared, the cure could
always wait. And in Beth's case it had. She had been terrified of
snakes since early childhood.

For the next several visits, Beth told me her story. As happens in the development of some phobias, hers had a traumatic
beginning. As a 7- or 8-year-old girl, she had been traveling
through the Southwest with a cousin, an aunt and her mother.
The group was on their way to a summer family reunion. They
had stopped in a small town off the interstate to spend the night
and — as if Stephen King had written the scene — here's what
happened.

It was a hot and muggy evening, with crickets singing and
night moths fluttering in the heavy air. As the girls were preparing to go to bed, Beth's mother threw open the motel door to let
in a little cool air. And there, crawling up the lattice of the
screen door, was a huge, black snake on its way to the light fix-
ture and all the bugs attracted thereto.

As a good primate mother, Beth's mother shrieked. Then
her aunt shrieked. Then the girls shrieked. The only creature in
the immediate vicinity not shrieking was the black snake, who
was only climbing the screen door for dinner.

Shrieking has almost no effect on snakes and so, after
awhile, Beth's mother got on the phone and called the motel
office. "Be right down," said the man at the desk. "Happens all
the time."

A thoughtful gentleman, the motel manager came running
with a rake and a hoe. He quickly raked the snake from the
screen door and, mindful of his terrorized customers, advised the
mothers to send the girls outside so they could see firsthand
what happens to nasty old snakes that go around frightening
innocent children. For reasons we will never know, the adults
agreed.

The man then raked the big snake into middle of the dirt
parking lot and, without further ado, chopped off its head with
the hoe. Animated by its now headless condition and spewing
blood in all directions — including onto the girls' faces, hands,

arms and nightgowns — writhing parcels of black snake were hacked up by the manager into finer and finer pieces until, in the end, there was no snake left longer than a hot dog.

Except, of course, the one in the Beth's head. The snake in Beth's head remained full length, very much alive and quite well, thank you very much.

"That should cure 'em of any fear of snakes," said the manager. "Now I'll just cut a line in the dirt around this sucker and leave him here till morning. That way, the little ones will know this snake can never hurt them again."

And he was right. That particular, harmless, black snake never did frighten the girls again. But, being a quick study, Beth with the snake in her mind started on a journey which was to bring no end of grief, change her life, and eventually inspire her to call me. This is the answer to the "Why now?" question I began with.

A phobia is nothing more than a fear with a face on it. The fear can be great or small. When the fear is great, one of the things we learn to do is to avoid that fear. In Beth's case, she began avoiding snakes immediately, and then forever.

At school she did not take biology classes because snakes show up in textbooks. She did not take long walks in the country, because you might encounter a snake on a walk in the country. As she grew older, she found herself avoiding the women's apparel departments because there might be a snakeskin handbag on display. She moved to the city to avoid possible snake encounters, and when she and her husband were having dinner one evening and a man wearing a cowboy hat with a snakeskin band sat down behind them, she asked the waiter to move them to another table.

By the time she moved to the Northwest, into the country and became my patient, her family had become professional "snake handlers." They screened all magazines coming into the house before Beth picked them up because, if Beth happened upon a photo of a snake in a magazine, she would scream and throw the magazine. Since they do not have a snake button to control snakes suddenly appearing on television, even this form of entertainment produced anxiety. As Beth put it, "You have no idea how many little 'friends' there are out there until you live in terror of them."

Beth could not garden. After the incident which triggered her calling me, she was afraid to drive her children to school and back. She could not go fishing except in a boat. To hike along a trout stream and fly fish was unthinkable. The only place she felt safe was at her office, in the heart of a city or in her home — and even then she feared she might open a door and find a snake crawling up the screen door or posing as a footstool on her porch.

Working a Cure

The approach to treating any phobia is fairly straightforward; you simply help the patient remain internally calm while they are repeatedly exposed to the very thing they fear. The procedure is called desensitization, or counterconditioning, or — as my grandpa put it to me after a horse threw me when I was 7 years old — "You got to get back on the horse right now, or you won't ever learn to ride." I didn't and — with one unpleasant exception as a teenager showing off for a bunch of girl scouts — I have never again tried to ride horses.

The psychologist's job is to construct a fear hierarchy, what frightens you first, second, third and so on. Then arrange a series of what are called successive approximations. This, when coupled with a relaxed patient practicing perfect control over his or her autonomic nervous system, permits the patient to face down any irrational fear one step at a time.

But because our fears of snakes, heights, deep water and such are built into our nervous systems, they are not so easy to rationalize away. The fear we experience with things that slither, growl and go bump in the night is more a biological, survival imperative than a rational decision. Therefore, it helps any phobic patient to be reassured their fearful response is not only natural, but suggests superior intelligence and learning capacity.

Psychologist's interpretation to the snake-phobic patient: "You must be exceptionally smart and have a high IQ. Just imagine, you learned to avoid snakes on your very first exposure and did not even need to be bitten."

The trouble with Beth was that she had been avoiding anything snakey for so long that just finding a place to begin was a major obstacle to her therapy.

With Beth's help and agreement, we decided the first step was to get her past her avoidance of the S-word so that we could at least talk like two sane people. Since she could not read the word snake without getting the willies, I took a pencil and pad and asked her to watch while I made an S on the paper.

A full, curvy S reminded her of a crawling snake and made her skin crawl, so I backed up to a straight line. Then, with her watching, I made another line with a very slight S-curve in it.

As we had rehearsed, she was to raise her finger or speak up if she felt any rise in anxiety. We defined her anxiety as a feeling of discomfort that could range from zero to ten.

Beth could control the rate of exposure by simply signaling me that she was approaching, say, four on her "snake-Richter scale." We could then ease off, back up, and let her relax again until she was comfortable with the earlier stimulus. Then, once she was back around zero or one or two, we would proceed to the next step, but only with her permission.

This may be difficult to believe, but it took Beth and I several hours to decondition her to the written letter S. Beth could routinely say the letter S in normal speech, as speaking the letter has no visual similarity to the original fear stimulus, that old, Oklahoma black snake slithering up the screen door. By the way, this is the same black snake that lies buried in Beth's ancient memory, in mine after her therapy and, fortunately or unfortunately, in yours. All of us, you see, have an archetypal snake imbedded in our ancient brain; the same one, in fact, that shows up in your vision of the Garden of Eden.

Once we got past the S in snake, the rest of the letters went quickly. For the first time in years, and although it almost made her vomit, Beth was finally able to actually say the word "snake." But she needed practice. So with the best interest of my patient at heart, I gave her a homework assignment: She was to say the word snake 500 times on the way home from our appointment. Then on the way to our next appointment, she was to say it 500 more times. Out loud, of course. This meant other drivers would likely see her talking to herself. I told Beth, with her wonderful sense of humor, that if anyone looked funny at her in traffic on the way home, she could hold up a sign that read, "Don't worry, I'm seeing a psychologist."

By the next week, the word "snake" was rolling off Beth's tongue and she reported a growing sense of confidence. She was ready for the next step. "Mind you," she said, "I don't want to come to love these slimy bastards. I just want to be able to tolerate them."

Fears that work themselves into full-blown phobias eventually spread throughout the nervous and sensory systems. In Beth's case, this meant that not only did she fear the sight of snakes, but also the sound and feel of snakes. Of these, her fear of actually touching a snake was the most pronounced.

We worked though the hissing sounds snakes make by my simply making increasingly loud hissing sounds through my teeth. Then, I had Beth practice snake sounds. This took less than hour. She could now say snake and make a fake hissing snake sound. She turned a psychological corner on her fear and began to find the whole procedure rather laughable. While she could not yet look at drawings or photographs of snakes, and she was miles from touching one, she was making enormous progress.

To help Beth overcome an actual visual encounter with a snake, I stumbled across the perfect tool: a series of Gary Larson's "Far Side" cartoons in which snakes play ordinary members of human-type families. In one of these, a family of snakes is sitting down to supper and in each bowl is a small rodent. One of the kids says to the mom and dad, "Oh, not gerbils again!"

Together with my crude snake drawings and the healing humor of "Far Side" cartoons pasted on her bathroom mirror, Beth was able to get closer and closer to looking at an actual photo of a real snake. On the day she won the battle, I gradually exposed more and more of a full-sized, coiled cobra by sliding a piece of plain paper down the face of a photograph. Beth controlled the rate and amount of exposure, practiced her breathing and relaxation response, and made me stand on the far side of my office while she kept her hand on the doorknob.

But she made it. No panic. No overwhelming fear. That day, she bounced out of the office with the brisk step of a winner.

The last step in Beth's treatment was to overcome her fear of actually touching a snake or, in case she wanted to bait her own hook someday, at least a worm. "I'll never touch a snake," she said, "except perhaps with the tire of my car. But if it humors you to see if I can, I'll give it a go."

This is where those big, Texas-style, bass-catching rubber worms came in so handy. By cutting one up into small segments, I was able to coax Beth into touching and holding a piece no bigger than a pencil eraser. To the slimy plastic, I believe her first response was, "Ick!" But she persisted. Over the next several minutes, I passed her increasingly longer segments of rubber worms. She controlled her anxiety while I controlled the size of "snake." By the end of a single hour she was able to hold a 7-inch-long plastic worm without rolling her eyes in terror.

"Keep it," I said, folding her hand around the bass bait. "Now you can go fishing with your husband. You're cured."

And she was.

If we choose to let conjecture run wild, then animals, our fellow brethren in pain, disease, suffering and famine — our slaves in the most laborious works, our companions in our amusements — they may partake of our origin in one common ancestor — we may all be netted together.
— **Charles Darwin, 1837**

Dinner in Seattle

'A nd what will you gentlemen have?"

"Is the salmon fresh?" asks my cousin, Steve.

"Of course," says the waiter. "This is Seattle."

"Then I'll have the salmon," says Steve. "Oh, and by the way, is the salmon you serve from an endangered run?"

The waiter pauses. "I don't know, sir. Would you like me to try to find out?"

"No, thank you," says Steve. "I was just curious."

"And you, sir?" the waiter asks me.

"I'll have the grilled tuna steak," I say "and a glass of your house Chablis."

"Should we be eating salmon these days?" asks Steve when the waiter has gone.

I think for a moment and answer, "I don't even know if we should be eating tuna."

With the order in and the food on the way, Steve and I fall into a familiar discussion about fishing in Alaska one day. It's an old conversation, the kind of comfortable fishing talk old pals slip into without much fear that they might actually go and do it. However, with the Pacific Northwest fisheries in steep decline lately, Alaska is becoming less of a dream and more of a necessity. An old Alaskan fisherman recently told me, "Go now, before it's too late."

Too late?

Naaaaa. ... Alaska will always be there.

Won't it?

Deep in Denial, the Head Predator Dines Out

Denial of reality is a wonderful thing, and it's a specialty with us humans. Denial is a psychological defense mechanism that permits us to ignore what our senses tell us, overlook the facts, and pretend to ourselves and others that things are not all that bad, when in fact, things are quite bad indeed. Denial enables us to not only tolerate terrible tragedies, but it allows us do what we want to do, rather than what we need to do.

If you're good at denial you can remain fat, sassy and comfortable, at least in the short run. If you're not so good at denial, you tend to accept reality early on, plan accordingly, and have a better chance of surviving in the long run.

Worriers and fretters tend to be poor at denial, but they always remember to bring a spare rod and a first aid kit. The rash and happy-go-lucky who rely on luck, not planning, tend to be good at denying the possibility of negative outcomes. While they are fun to have around in good weather, you don't want to count on them to remember the lunches or foul-weather gear.

We all need denial. It is an important psychological defense against not only the ordinary setbacks of ordinary life, but against great tragedy or terrible loss. Without a little denial, most of us couldn't sit through the evening news.

Fishermen are quite capable of denying unpleasant reality. In my case, I try to be fishing most evenings when the news is on. Fishing while Rome burns is denial in its finest form. But it can be costly.

Anglers who deny that bad things might be happening to the fisheries they love choose, however unconsciously, to stand by and dither rather than accept reality and act. If, as a fisherman, you are not experiencing a little hand wringing about what's happening out there to the fishes, then either you don't read enough, or you have mastered denial completely.

There is one other form of denial worth mentioning. We psychologists call it "magical thinking." It works like this. Even though the river I fish is suffering from serious threats to its water quality, somehow, from somewhere, a hero will emerge just in the nick of time and save us all from disaster. Children use magical thinking all the time. On them it looks okay, but on an adult it looks like Alfred E. Newman — pretty goofy.

Up in my Northwest country in the early 1970s, those of us whose denial of reality was insufficient to the threat started to raise hell with the Corps of Engineers and our elected representatives about the negative impact two more hydroelectric dams would have on the middle Snake River and the anadromous fish runs of the Columbia River system. We were called alarmists. Now we're called visionaries.

With most of the wild runs on their last legs and with only a handful of sockeye and kings left these twenty-five years later — trust me on this — there is no joy in "I told you so." The last part of this chapter is an elegy I wrote about the middle Snake River for *Field & Stream* a few years ago. It's a downer, so if you'd rather stay in denial, skip it.

Running Against the Clock

Won't Alaska always be there?

I have been to Alaska and plan to go back. It's a big place and there are zillions of fish. Surely, there will always be Alaska and zillions of fish.

I remember meeting an old Nez Perce woman years ago who said that when she was a girl — back before the dams were built on the Columbia and Snake rivers — there were so many steelhead and salmon in the Lower Clearwater run above Lewiston, Idaho, you could "walk across the river on their backs." These fish knitted together the soul of the people.

Reading some early history from my hometown newspaper the other day, I learned that as late as 1909 there were salmon and steelhead runs up Marshall Creek, a small, spring stream not two miles from my house. These were big runs of big fish.

Then, the dams went in on the Spokane River.

Everywhere you look, fish are not running against the current, but running against the clock. That ticking sound you hear is not the counting device of a fish counter, but the timing device on the human population bomb. The head animal is crowding out, eating up and moving in on every other living thing, including itself. As overcrowding forces more and more of us to retreat into ethnic, religious and national groups for safety and security, we are not even safe from each other.

Want to know how much denial you're in? The next time you read a newspaper article, just about any article, slip on your Darwinian survival glasses for focus, imagine mankind competing with itself and every other life form for the same finite resources, and then ask yourself this denial buster: Is this problem due to too few resources and too many humans?

I know the answer because I have spoiled many a dinner party with what my wife, Ann, calls my "gloom and doom questions." I still run this experiment every so often to remind myself of why I got one of the first vasectomies in history — it was so long ago the doctor used a stone knife — and why I belong to and support several organizations that are trying to do something to break through our massive and collective denial about the true source of most of our problems.

Denial Works Best Without Numbers

We've got a pretty good count on how many people there are. We've got a pretty good count on how many white rhinos are left. But we don't have a good count on the fishes.

Fish are not so easy to count: until they are all gone. Even I can count the king salmon in Marshall Creek. Counting fish costs money, not a lot of money. The fish biologists I talk to who are trying to save some of the wild fishes tell me that one way to solve the political problem of dwindling stocks is to simply stop funding the counting projects. For those who choose denial over reality, no number means no crisis means no political problems.

If ordinary people occasionally employ denial to avoid unpleasant realities, governments and politicians specialize in it.

Stop the funding and you bend reality to your own ends. No money, no reality, no problem. Wildlife are especially easy to sacrifice on denial's altar.

"Fish in trouble?" asks the politician. "How do you know?"

"We know. We fish these waters."

"Gee, no numbers? Too bad. Call us when you have some figures."

"You're supposed to get the numbers."

"Getting numbers isn't in the budget. Sorry. Next problem?"

Fishing a river in North Idaho's panhandle a few years back I met a government fish counter. His summer job was to snorkel through some of the world's finest wild trout habitat and count and measure fish. Swimming with a length of perforated PVC pipe marked off in 1-inch gradations, his mission was to measure the number and size of the remaining bull trout in the St. Joe River watershed. We had a nice chat. He assured me the big fish were there, but the stocks were dwindling. I told him I had a foot-long cutthroat get ripped off my fly by a huge bull trout. The young man nodded and smiled. Nice kid.

These several years later, that college boy's summer trout-counting job helped place the Rocky Mountain bull trout on the threatened list. And just in the nick of time. Most of us fishermen don't recognize a real hero when one rides in to save us.

The plight of the fishes is especially vulnerable to human denial because fish are elusive. Since fish don't look like baby harp seals — they are cute and look like baby humans — no one much cares except fishermen when the fish are in trouble. Some species of fish are nearly impossible to count. When you can't count the fish, or when the numbers can be disputed, those interests with the most at stake often have their way.

Does the average citizen really care that the American Fisheries Society recently reported that haddock, cod, redfish, hake and pollack are down 80 percent to 90 percent from their 1970 populations, that the National Marine Fisheries Service is considering ordering a stop to all groundfishing on New England's Georges Bank, and that if this happens thousands of fishermen will be out of work, their souls unknitted by the loss of the fishes that help their people stay together? Not, I'll wager, if that citizen can still buy a two-dollar fishwich in a fast food joint.

Does the average fish-eating public realize that the great majority of marine fishes are what scientists call "nearshore dependent" and that the vast open seas are neither vast nor open when it comes to critical habitat for spawning and food supplies for these fishes?

The National Marine Fisheries Service states that virtually all gamefish, except billfish and tunas, are in some way dependent on the same shorelines, bays and estuaries we are now polluting and changing to suit our current fashions and to meet human needs. Among only the estuarine-dependent fishes, here's a short list: amberjack, bluefish, cobia, snook, pompano, Spanish mackerel, king mackerel, most snappers, most groupers, some halibut, California corbina, Atlantic salmon, striped bass, winter flounder, weakfish, black drum and all my long list of Northwest salmons and steelhead.

With over one-half of the U.S. population living within 50 miles of our coastal waters, it is not a food chain we are threatening with our wetland fill-ups, channelization projects, freshwater diversions, and conversions of fish nurseries to governmental and commercial docks and piers and industrial sites, but an entire food web — the very web of life itself.

The massive loss of coastal habitat for marine fishes only means one thing: less fish, and less sport and commercial fishing. You cannot reduce inshore-dependent fish and shellfish by 75 percent to 95 percent of historic levels and not experience a glut on the garage-sale market of old saltwater fishing tackle. Someone, some group, some organized group of human predators has to pass beyond our current level of denial and make habitat protection the priority it needs to be, that is if there is to be any fishing left to manage in our future.

The public needs denial so that it can continue to believe that there are always plenty of fish just under the surface, around the bend in the river, or drifting in great schools in the ocean deep. As that famous citizen of the world Alfred E. Newman would have replied when told that of the seventeen major fisheries in the world, nine are in severe decline, "What? Me worry?"

Indeed, why worry? Even though some 30,000 employees of the cod fishery are out of work along the Grand Banks, and the Georges Bank is right behind them, there will always be plenty of fish up in Alaska. If not there, then out in Montana. If not in Montana, then down off the Oregon coast. If not on the Oregon coast, then in Chesapeake Bay. Or over in Idaho. And if not in Idaho, then up in Alaska. If not in Alaska, then surely out along the Grand Banks. Surely the fish will never run out.

That's what they said about the cod and flounder and haddock before the Grand Banks stocks crashed. That's what they said about the huge New England halibut of the Georges Bank back in the mid-1800s when fishermen brought in 20,000 pounds of halibut a day and just before the grand fish was fished to near extinction, leaving so few halibut today regulators don't even bother to count them.

That's what they said about the North Sea groundfishery, until the seven European nations that compete for those fishes fished them out, and are now headed to the coasts of Africa and the Indian Ocean to fish them out.

That's what they said about the great Pyramid Lake cutthroat runs. That's what they said about the Red Lake sockeye run and, for all I know, that's what someone said about the Marshall Creek kings.

Denial of reality is fishing's most dangerous threat. Denial linked with politics is positively deadly. Scientists count the fish as best they can. Scientists are not permitted to engage in denial because of an old scientific truth: Numbers don't lie. Fish scientists plot population declines with numbers and computer models and tell fish regulators what is going to happen if stocks, age classes and spawners are not protected by reducing the take.

The regulators write regulations to protect the fishery, but the fishermen and commercial lobbyists pressure the politicians to deny reality and tell the regulators to go to hell. The regulators then deny the scientists' numbers and soften up the regulations.

Result: The scientists eat a lot of Maalox; the regulators

pee down both legs; the politicians get re-elected; the fishermen keep fishing; and the fish go on the endangered list or become extinct, whichever comes first.

If you stand back and watch humans do this denial trick a couple of times — whether it is fishes, trees or watersheds — you have to ask yourself an obvious question: How come they call this species intelligent?

Only a handful of scientists and conservation and population-control groups are facing the problems squarely; the rest of us don't even want to discuss it, at least not as long as our home waters are safe and we can get a fishwich for a couple of bucks.

Just before this book went to print, however, a ray of hope shot through the darkening sky. Something called the Alliance to Save Fisheries was formed. The alliance unites boat builders, marine manufacturers, marine trade organizations and the sport-fishing industry in a common cause to save the nation's fisheries. Headed by the National Marine Manufacturers, American Sportfishing Association and the National Marine Trades Council, the goals of this group are to: lobby for change in fishery management practices; identify fish species vital to angling's interests; work to achieve gamefish status for certain stocks; promote improvements in fish habitat; and curtail the depletion of large pelagics like sharks, billfish and tuna.

If you can find a way to support these and other conservation efforts, the future of angling can be about as bright as you choose it to be. If you can't, then perhaps it's time to look a little deeper into the mirror.

The Supreme Predator

It's right about here in the history of our species that we need to take a long, deep look into the reflecting glass, into the true nature of our being. We need to see ourselves for what we are; the best damned predator in the history of the world. Well, at least in the modern world.

A few centuries ago the best damned predator in the world was the cave bear, or the lion, or depending on where you lived, the last big carnivore that killed and ate uncle Fred. Before those big, carnivorous mammals, the best damned predator in the world was tyrannosaurus rex, and now his big brother recently discovered in South America. And before rex, more than a half a billion years ago when all life was still underwater, the seas were ruled by giant killer shrimps. Called *Anomalocaridids*, one of these beasts grew to more than 2 meters in length — longer than 6-and-one-half feet — swam like a manta ray, and could crush the toughest, shelled seafood in a circular mouth filled with a ghastly ring of teeth.

The point is this: Since the very beginning of life on the planet one creature, a predator, has sat at the top of the food chain. If that predator could have somehow eaten all of its prey, it would have died out and another predator would have taken its place. Stupid predator, you say? Maybe, maybe not.

No top predator in the history of life has had the brains to add two and two and get four, or make a phone call. No predator but man can build a gill net, throw a harpoon, build a dam, or cut down a forest and destroy an entire ecosystem — and with it our own food chain. The last time I looked through the slits in my denial blinders, we humans were up to all of this and more, much more.

Back at our dinner in Seattle, my cousin Steve and I had ordered seafood. Salmon and tuna. Had I ordered crab instead of tuna, the crab legs would have come pre-cracked. Unlike the crustacean eaters of the deep sea, we did not have to lay in wait and grab supper for ourselves. Other humans would do that for us. We didn't even have to clean it or cook it. That is the beauty of being human, you don't have to crush your own seafood, clean, catch or cook it. You just enjoy. If the world is running out of fish, you simply switch your denial lever to "on," and ask for seconds.

The Incredible Shrinking Salmon

Because our fellow humans are such wonderful predators, and because we cannot find a brake to apply to our population juggernaut, my cousin Steve's filet would come from a small salmon, not a big one. People don't catch big salmon in the Pacific Northwest much any more. Trophies are few. Strong recent evidence suggests that Pacific salmon are shrinking and that, in just a dozen years, the average size of a returning mature salmon is down 25 percent.

Result: fewer big fish.

Probable cause: the supreme predator.

I would have grilled tuna steak. Tuna are not endangered. Yet. Or at least I don't think they are. I'm very fond of grilled tuna steaks and therefore want to stay in denial as long as I can about the condition of the tuna fishery — which means I should probably stop reading the newspapers.

Knowing a little about one aspect of the tuna fishery, I gambled the restaurant was not going to serve me a filet of great bluefin tuna. Pound for pound the most valuable living thing in, on, or above the earth, I doubt if I could afford a filet of great bluefin even if they had it.

According the International Commission for the Conservation of Atlantic Tunas (ICCAT), the stocks of this most sought after fish have been depleted by 90 percent since the 1970s. Cause: overfishing. A highly migratory fish, a truly good count of their numbers is difficult, if not impossible.

Solution to the pressure from the supreme predator for more bluefin? The ICCAT recently announced an increase of 200 metric tons to be taken in the Western Atlantic.

When the supreme predator is hungry, he generally gets what he wants. If money is no problem, he always gets what he wants. Currently, it is very wealthy Japanese who want these giant bluefins. They want them especially for the fatty rind they call "toro." Two bites of prime toro goes for $75 in U.S. currency. That's right, two bites.

The very finest toro never reaches the public market in Tokyo because it ends up in the private dining rooms of the rich and famous. Please understand that a prize bluefin tuna is worth up to $60,000 U.S. dollars on this market, and even an average fish is worth $20,000. If you catch one while sportfishing, land it and return to harbor, you must decide between your taste for tuna fish sandwiches and, say, a new boat and motor. On every dock there is a Japanese tuna buyer who will write you a very nice check for your catch.

With one fish worth more than a new Mercedes, what

kind of fishing methods will the supreme predator employ? Having only read about it, I think it seems that hunting down and killing a giant bluefin tuna could be favorably compared to hunting down and capturing an enemy submarine.

With the potential to make such high profits, the commercial boys use both a fast boat rigged with a 28-foot spotting tower and spotting planes. The spotting planes stalk the sea lanes as if on patrol for enemy subs, while the fishermen in boats use Lorans and satellite signals to station themselves in places where the fish have been killed before. Once fish are spotted by the pilot in the aircraft, their position is radioed to the boat. The crews then race to the bluefin so that a master harpooner can drive a whaling-type harpoon into the fish.

To make sure the great fish does not pull out hundreds of feet of line in its fight for life, it is then administered enough electric shock to stun it into submission for the haul up to the surface. Before dragging it into the boat, it is given the coup de grâce with a pistol shot to the brain. Too much fighting by the fish bruises the flesh and builds up lactic acid, thus impairing the taste of the *toro*, and lowering its price. We *toro* aficionados certainly wouldn't want that.

Will there always be great bluefin tuna from which to dice away the *toro*? Perhaps.

Will there always be a great bluefin to take with the rod and reel? Perhaps.

But perhaps not.

When you couple our human capacity for denial together with our unwillingness to place the welfare of a lowly fish above today's fashions for table fare, you have a very hazardous blend of psychological, economic and political forces with which to contend. These forces work together for short term gains, not long term investment. A fishery is like a healthy bank account; if you don't get greedy or stupid, you can live nicely off the interest. But hungry humans are notorious for eating up what's close, easy to catch and cheap.

The Worldwatch Institute reports that while the Pacific, Atlantic, Mediterranean and Black Sea all suffer from serious overfishing, the number of humans is growing by 1.6 percent per year. That equates to adding the population of Mexico to the dinner list every twelve months. Third world countries rely on fish for protein more so than the first world countries, but the first world countries have already fished themselves out of business and are now headed to third world fishing holes to fish them out of business.

If the great fisheries are lost, the great fishing cultures from Nova Scotia to Malaysia will follow. If the fish go, so will the people. If we were smart enough, and could act quickly enough, we might turn it around. But this would mean getting rid of the people to save the fish.

The Finnish fisherman and philosopher Pentti Linkola, who spends most of his time fishing and thinking about the world's problems, says that what the world needs most right now is a famine and a good war. By wiping out most of the human race, the rest of nature might have a chance. Linkola compares humanity to a sinking ship with 100 passengers and a lifeboat that can hold ten. "Those who hate life try to pull more people on board and drown everybody. Those who love and respect life use axes to chop off the extra hands hanging on the gunwale." You may think Mr. Linkola a crank or crazy, but in fishing- and nature-loving Finland, he is a national symbol and one of the country's most celebrated authors.

As the historian George Santayana said, "Those who cannot remember the past are condemned to repeat it." He did not say ancient history, or recent history, just the past. My take on modern man is that, thanks to his tremendous capacity for denial, he doesn't like history very much, doesn't read it, and doesn't want to read it. This is not good news for the fishes.

Most of us are proud to be human. We think this is better than being, say, a coyote or a robin or a brook trout. As Darwin machines, we are the master predator. The head animal seated at the head table and served by the head waiter, we predatory hominids are mighty damn proud to have won all the fights for survival and finally made it to the top of the food chain.

But what if winning is really losing? What if we change the world to suit us and the suit doesn't fit, or falls out of fashion? According to geomorphologists — people who study the shapes of landforms — that skinny, no-account hominid called man now moves more earth in a year than any other single, natural geologic process, including wind, water or ice. By brute force, mechanical power and less direct influences, we move 40 billion tons of soil and rock annually, or about 7 tons for every man, woman and child on the planet surface.

"We do clearly see ways in which human beings are changing the surface of the planet," Jeffrey Hoffman, a shuttle astronaut, said not long ago. From space, the visual impact of highways, housing tracks, and dam building is far greater than the natural action of even the Mississippi River and rivers like it. To sculpt the very face of our home planet to suit us, we pave the valleys in concrete, shave away our timbered mountains to resemble punk hair styles, and straighten and dam our rivers so they look like T-squares.

For such uniformity of geometric pattern — and to save a few nickels on our electric bills — we replace the irregularity of nature with what we think is a better fit for human needs today. Outguessing nature, we think we can make her work harder, be more efficient and dress her up to look like nature "ought" to look. But human fads and fashions are notoriously transient. Does anybody really know what we're doing?

The Snake that Spoke

At that dinner in Seattle, the waiter didn't have a clue about from where the salmon we ordered came. It could have come from a Taiwanese gill netter. It could have come from the Fraser River where, in recent years, the stocks have been overfished. While doubtful, it could have been one of the few remaining inshore-dependent salmon trying to make it back up the Columbia into the Snake, over nine hydroelectric dams, and on to what remains of a spawning gravel somewhere in Idaho — that is, if timber companies haven't clear-cut the headwaters and cattle haven't eaten away and stomped flat the riparian area, causing the creek to silt up, warm up, color up and fill up with cow shit.

When I first moved to the Northwest thirty years ago, there were salmon in the Snake River. Lots of them. I never caught a salmon from the Snake River. I never even fished for one. But the river spoke to me and told me they were there. More than once, I saw a salmon roll, and found post-spawn Chinooks rotting along the shore while I fished for bass or steelhead. One day, I told myself, I'd learn how to catch them.

Now it's too late.

Thirty years is not a long time in the history of a fishery, but it is a long time in one man's life. It is enough time to personally observe in only three decades a progressive, relentless loss of privacy and places to fish. It is enough time to know that Santayana was right about our failure to know history and learn from it. And it is enough time to experience loss. Consider this little essay singing Kaddish for the middle Snake River.

"The Snake That Spoke"

I have a picture of a boy, about 6 years old at the time, holding a spinning rod in one hand while he poses with what looks to be a 3-pound smallmouth bass. He is smiling broadly. Behind him rushes the great Snake River. The boy is a man now; the photograph is beginning to fade a little, and the rushing river behind him is gone. Probably forever.

In the years we fished the middle Snake, an old Indian man lived in a shack near a place called Almota, not far from where the boy caught the bass. I don't know who he was, or to what tribe he belonged. Respecting his place and privacy, we never disturbed him. Someone told me the old man lived off the river, fishing mostly. We saw him only a few times. Then, the dam builders came. And then he, too, like the rushing water, was gone.

I don't go down to the Snake to fish much anymore — partly, I suppose, because the boys are grown up and gone, but also because I can't seem to get up the enthusiasm. Like an angry old man once said, "They keep changin' things around on me!" In my case, I liked the Snake better when it could speak to me — whispering in winter, roaring in spring.

One of those places where it spoke was around a little jut of rocks near an old railroad siding called "Indian." I'm not sure that the one Indian had anything to do with the other, but I imagine that somewhere in that distant, unwritten history of the Snake, they did. Behind the jut of rocks at Indian lay a big eddy and pool and, behind that, a long, shallow bar. When the runs were in, the steelhead rested there by rank and file and in water so clear you see them plain enough to make your heart jump.

I fished Indian often; summers for smallmouth, fall and winter for the big sea trout. One August day I took my family there for a picnic on its sandy beach and, eating fresh apricots bought from an orchardist who ranched the high bench land across the dusty river road, we sat in the shade of old trees and showed the boys how to let a carp run with a dough bait before setting the hook with one long sweep of the rod.

The jut of rocks and eddy I knew as Indian is gone now, gone under the pool behind Lower Granite dam. Mind you, this is a damn fine dam, and together with all the other dams built along the middle Snake, it seemed like a good idea at the time. Like everyone else, when I throw a switch, I expect a light to come on. But trading-fishing-holes-for-wattage changes more than just the rush of water; it changes everything.

There's a marina now at Almota not far from where the old Indian lived. And a bar with cold beer and liquor. Picnic tables. Manicured lawns. Taps where you can draw clean water. Even showers. Squared up in straight lines, the river is cased in concrete and riprap, almost as if dressed in a Corps of Engineer's uniform. On the Fourth of July a cast of thousands appears: big silver boats trolling skiers, thin-clad coeds from the university, and kids fishing jigs for crappies under bobbers floating in the bluish oil slicks around the docks. RVs, tents and two-cycle thunder. Boom boxes booming while barbecues billow with smoke from the fat of the land. An American dream, some say, come true.

But somewhere upstream away from the crowd and under the slack water is that little jut of rocks, that place where the boy's bass took and the great trout rested, and you could cast straight to the fishes because the river had nooks and crannies and lairs and lies and character so vivid it deserved a name like Indian. And the river could speak: whispering in winter, roaring in spring round the little, stone altars where we fishermen knelt to worship.

Worship is not too strong a word. A fisherman's world is his water. When he isn't near it, he yearns to see it, to wade into it, or to drift over it in his canoe. And it wrenches his soul to see it fenced, blocked, choked, channeled, shunted, stopped or stalled. Like the old Indian who lived in the shack near Almota, a fisherman's water is nothing if not sacred. I know I am not alone in this practice: When returning to an old and hallowed fishing hole below a jut of rocks, I will often ask, "Hello. Have you been well?"

The middle Snake of Idaho and Oregon and Washington can no longer reply. Like the old Indian I, too, have gone away. But on those rare, summer days when I return to the river to try for a bass like the boy once caught, and when the evening air is still above the water that barely moves, I sometimes lean into that coming night and listen, once again, for the Snake that spoke.

Just enough of me, way too much of you.
— P.J. O'Rourke

Should There Be a
Creel Limit on Fishermen?

I can see her coming for some minutes. She is wearing a dark green parka and a bright yellow hat, and she carries her head high. The rain doesn't seem to bother her. Her stride is brisk, and she seems to be an experienced hiker. As she closes the distance between us, I think I can see a hint of gray at the edges of her yellow hat and judge her, with the best of gentlemanly intentions, to be about my age. Standing ankle-deep in the stream near the trail, I continue to cast to a wonderfully stubborn trout I had found finning in a shallow pool behind a large boulder. An encounter with a stranger seems unavoidable.

She is alone.

I am alone.

We are alone together high in the Eagle Cap Wilderness Area of Eastern Oregon. Even during the peak of the fishing season there are not all that many people cluttering up this little groove in the planet's surface, so this juxtaposition of strangers is a rare one.

It is a Sunday morning. On Sunday mornings I believe you

are supposed to be a bit more social, a bit more tolerant and understanding of other members of your species. If a fellow human is in need, I think you are obliged to be a better samaritan on Sunday morning than, say, on Friday night. But as nothing I had read in Miss Manners covered this particular situation, I wondered, do I speak? First, or only if spoken to? Or, will a tip of the hat and smile get me by? If I really don't feel up to it, do I even have to smile?

Questions to Judith Martin, alias Miss Manners: If a man has gone far into the wilderness to be by himself and is quietly fishing alone and a single, woman hiker passes within 10 feet of him, is he required to acknowledge her presence? Or could he, for example, stay about his business and imagine that the lady is passing him on a sidewalk in, say, Manhattan?

One of the reasons I am alone in the Eagle Cap this Sunday morning is not to be social. If I'd wanted to be social I'd have stayed in the city. Besides, I find that when I've got several miles of trail and a couple of ridges between me and my fellow man, I'm a lot more tolerant and understanding of him. (I have imagined that if I could ever get away into the heart of the Montana's Bob Marshall Wilderness and stand knee deep in a wild cutthroat stream all by myself for, say, a month, my feelings toward mankind would positively glow.)

But I am in the Eagle Cap for only a weekend, and frankly, the woman moving inexorably up the trail toward me seems an intruder. When I escape to a wild place, that place seems to become mine — as in the infantile possessive, "Mine! Mine! Mine!" As I follow her progress toward me, that old angry question pops into my head: "What is *she* doing here?"

The woman can see me now, but we are still too far apart to exchange eye contact or words. And now I can see the dog at her side: a wolf-sized German shepherd large enough to yank down a bull elk. Instantly I am reminded of Winston Churchill's remark about the German character: "They are either at your feet or at your throat." I do not fear dogs, but I maintain a grudging respect for those with meritorious reputations.

Questions to Miss Manners: Should one speak to the lady's dog? Or should one speak to the lady first, and then to her dog?

If the dog is rude and plunges into the pool one is fishing and frightens one's trout, is one permitted to speak sharply to the animal? Can one swat it with a fly rod or, perhaps, crack its skull open with an oak wading-staff?

As the trail and the woman and the shepherd disappear behind a thick stand of evergreens I have, unfortunately, more time to cogitate.

What if, Miss Manners, the lady is a windbag? What if she is desperate for conversation and will not leave when one has, as politely as one knows how, turned one's back and got on with the task of trying to catch a trout? Is one permitted, for example, to simply charge off upstream and leave one's visitor dangling amid, say, idle observations about mountain weather patterns? And I remind you, Dear Guide, that we are not in a downtown restaurant or in the drawing room at Uncle Fillmore's estate but, rather, deep in a mountain wilderness.

My guess is that Miss Manners has never found herself in quite this spot, although that is only an assumption. From my misdirected reading in Emily Post and such over nearly half a century, I have yet to come upon a single line devoted to what might be proper etiquette under the present and looming circumstances. Presumably the relationship between the civilized male and civilized female of our species remains the same regardless of location — or so I gathered some years back on the occasion of insulting a woman fly fisher by asking if she was lost. Her reply: a pained grimace and eyes slitted down to a knife's edge — accompanied, I might add, by a soft drumming of her fingers against her rod handle.

Trotting ahead of the woman, the shepherd can see me now. He pauses and his ears come up. I can imagine him thinking, "Ah ha! What manner of game is this?"

The German, now sure of his mark, leaps forward.

As I do not relish having to explain my presence to a dog with a considerable fang-and-bite advantage, I make ready for introductions by getting a firm grip on my wading staff. Just beyond, I see the lady in the yellow hat step clear of the woods.

I am making a great deal out of this chance wilderness encounter, but I have my purpose. It was not until this precise moment that I realize that man has finally lived out his Malthusian nightmare and reproduced himself into that gasping, wretched, overcrowded mass of humankind — the one population experts have been yapping about since their mathematical conclusion first woke them with a start in the middle of the night.

Here she is, in the flesh, numero 5 billion — the very person everyone's been looking for since July 1987 when the human infestation was to have surpassed this impossible-to-grasp number, thence plunging it forward into an even murkier future. And I am about to meet her.

Here.

Now.

High in the Eagle Cap.

Five billion people. And counting. So many people. Worry, worry, worry. The old population problem has been a spook in man's closet of fears so long, I imagine most people have a hard time getting up any real anxiety over the subject. Until, of course, you meet your lady in a yellow hat. It is not 93 million new people a year that frightens you; what frightens you is a woman coming at you in a yellow hat.

And here she is.

The shepherd, now closing in quickly, gives me only moments to inspect my 5-billionth human being as she clears the timber below me and moves directly forward into my private, personal wilderness space.

Allow me to digress a moment to comment that, in my opinion, personal wilderness fishing space is much larger than personal urban fishing space. In the wilderness you need an area ranging from several thousand square acres down to the equivalent of a baseball diamond, with you casting from the pitcher's mound. In urban fishing, you are grateful for the roominess of a standard dugout and will settle for not having your hat snagged off your head by the guy casting next to you.

Here she comes, my single lady in a yellow hat trailing nine zeros behind her, the vanguard of 5,000 million others just like her stretching endlessly down the trail and out of sight. If there is such a feeling, I feel existentially crowded; and if there isn't such a feeling, my guess is there soon will be.

Apparently familiar with the implication of an officer's swagger stick, the lunging German takes his eyes off my throat as I lift my wading staff ever so slightly to remind him of his rank in the animal kingdom. A stern glower and he skids to a stop, lays back his ears and comes to parade rest. He seems to be content to be at my feet, so I loosen my grip, nod, and acknowledge his canine rank.

I look at the woman as she closes to ten meters. I was right about the gray hair and her apparent age. Our eyes meet. She has a deep tan and light blue eyes. She smiles. But I think I see something in her eyes. Is it perturbation? Is she, like me, dismayed at finding another biped fouling the scenery so far from our usual and customary roosts?

Question: Am I *her* 5-billionth person?

Is she suddenly feeling existentially crowded?

She will pass but a few feet away. I smile, but do not speak.

Her smile broadens. Apparently, she feels no need to speak.

Our communication is perfect. We do not need to pester Judith for advice. We need no words between us or to ask after one damned thing or another. All we have to do is get by the next few seconds without trashing this quiet, wild setting with some sort of human blathering.

We make it.

The lady in the bright yellow hat disappears into the green willows where the trail curves toward a meadow turned blue with lupine. Dismissed with a wave of my fly rod, the shepherd lopes after her.

For a moment I watch where she has vanished. Then, she is gone, and suddenly I am back in my Eagle Cap, and she in hers. The rain dimples the pool where my trout is still finning slowly, right where I left him. Then, from high in the timber above me, I hear a solitary vireo warble down a drainpipe.

Creel Limits and Carrying Capacity

Since I didn't quite vent all my spleen about too many humans in the last chapter, allow me to set up my soapbox and take off again.

Whether it be 5 billion people or 5 billion dollars, I have never been able to bend my mind around big numbers. A billion doesn't register. A woman in a yellow hat does.

Although it actually makes denial easier, even a little number like a million gives me trouble. Solving for X, in my experience, is basically impossible. Math-challenged since childhood, my handicap severely impairs my ability to understand things like slot limits, weight limits, or what sort of population limits, if any, ought to be placed on human beings.

I don't know about other lovers of fishing in wild places, but I've been trying very hard lately to get a grip on what to do with all the hominids crowding into the places I love to fish. There are days along one my favorite trout streams where, because there are so many anglers traipsing around behind me, I need to yell, "BACK!" on my backcast just so that I don't snag some poor devil.

Some years ago I tried to fish North Carolina's Nantahala River on a warm, spring day with my brother John. To get a fly on the water, I had to learn the Nantahala In Between Cast (IBC). You need the Nantahala IBC to get a fly or lure *in between* all the other fishermen, kayaks, canoes, drift boats, inner tubes, rafters, paddle wheelers, bystanders, moonshiners, children-at-play, lost sinners, and God knows what all else the flatlanders drag up into the Smoky Mountains to make up that colorful chain of bow-to-stern traffic that parades through whatever riffle it is you're trying to present, however patiently, a damned trout fly. In the aggravation department, New York City gridlock is nothing compared Smoky Mountain "rifflelock."

And it isn't just the East Coast either. I just came back from a trip to New Mexico's world famous San Juan River where 19-inch rainbow trout are practically routine. Consider my guide's comment when I attempted to dead drift a nymph off the toe of my boot and into the mouth of a 22-inch trophy finning quietly at my feet.

"It isn't considered sporting to catch the wader feeders," he admonished.

"Wader feeders?"

"The ones sucking in nymphs at your feet."

He meant that because there are more fishermen per linear mile on the quality water of the San Juan than there are pickets in a busy fence, the trout have completely adapted to the presence of booted, angler legs. Time and again huge, beautiful wild trout swam up to claim a feeding station a foot or so downstream from my ankles and calves.

"It's weird," I said, looking down at the back of a trout I would cast a country mile to hook. "Trout are supposed to be spooky."

The guide nodded, shrugged his shoulders and waved at the fifty or so fishermen standing in our bend of the river, "The fish gotta eat, so where they gonna go?"

Personally, I didn't hear the population bomb go off. I heard a slight pop, but that was about it. Five years ago up in the Eagle Cap, I did run into that 5-billionth person everyone predicted was going to show up sooner or later, but she wasn't wearing a sign. Since then, our species has been adding about 95 million humans to the planet every year. Maybe more.

It took from the dawn of humanity until 1830 to get to our first billion people. Before 1830, folks pretty much knew each other, knew who they were going to marry, and what they were going to do when they grew up. We were all, to quote Crocodile Dundee, "tribals."

Then things got confusing. We started multiplying like rabbits. To add the second billion humans took only 100 years, from 1830 to 1930. The next 3 billion of us arrived over the next six decades. Expert projections are uniformly gloomy for rifflelock around your favorite trout stream. Whether or not the farmers can stay ahead of the horde in food production, things are going to get more and more congested around your home waters.

Teeming will overtake tranquillity. It won't matter much

where you live. You can teem in Calcutta or you can teem in Mexico City or Philadelphia or Los Angeles, or you can teem out on your favorite lake, pond or stream. But you *will* teem. I've been to the cities of Tokyo, New York and Phoenix and the Madison River in July: Teeming sucks.

In a recent survey, the Izaak Walton League of America asked its members, "How have your outdoor recreational areas changed in the last 20 years?" Of the respondents, 93 percent reported more people; 84 percent reported their recreational area had been developed; 69 percent reported fewer fish were available; 68 percent said their area no longer existed; and 64 percent said there was less game. To what do we own these losses and degradation of recreational areas? Too many hominids.

Too many people, and what those people need and want to sustain themselves, is at the bottom of most of our sorry crimes against nature. Name any problem — ozone depletion, atmospheric pollution, global warming, wetlands destruction, clearcutting, soil erosion, impure water, the collapse of fresh and ocean fisheries, etcetera, etcetera, etcetera — and then remember my denial-buster question.

Fishing Math Made Easy

The trouble with big numbers like millions and billions to describe a problem is that they don't cause little beads of sweat to pop out on your forehead. So let me show you how you worry more effectively with numbers you can feel in your hip pocket. Worry with me, then act with or like me, and maybe you won't have to learn the Nantahala IBC to fish your home waters.

Since the human population crisis threatens those who love nature more than most, here's my formula for effective worrying.

Divide the total number of new humans added to the planet each day by the total seconds in a 24-hour day and you come with a palpable number: *three new humans per second.* Three humans per second is a number you can bend your mind around.

If it took you one second to read that last phrase, and you

were reading it while sitting on your sofa, put those three new people right there on your sofa with you.

Sofa crowded? Feel it?

Now, having read the intervening sentences, it is six seconds later.

There are now an additional eighteen people in your living room with you — a sum total of twenty-one.

And now twenty-four.

And now twenty-seven.

And now thirty.

And now thirty-three.

Take a deep, relaxing breath; the mad psychologist is right behind you.

And now forty-two. That deep, relaxing breath, added nine new souls.

And now forty-five.

Time to move the party out on the deck?

And now forty-eight.

If you don't get a twinge of claustrophobia right about now, my experiment isn't working very well.

And now there are fifty-four.

If this isn't working by now, stop reading and look at the sweep second hand on your wristwatch. Watch it go once around the face of the clock.

Good.

In those sixty seconds, 180 more people have joined your house party, thus totaling about 232 since you started this experiment.

If you invited all these folks into your house or lake cabin or apartment, you must be a truly pro-social person. Tempers are, however, getting a little hot around the bathroom.

As a fisherman, I now want you to move this experiment outside where it belongs. Indoors are pretty much the same anywhere you go; its outdoors where we find things like fishing and quality of life. Take this experiment to your most-cherished home waters.

Did I feel a little resistance in the line?

I thought so.

Now we're getting somewhere.

Drifting along on Williams Lake the other day, I tried this mental experiment with the population bomb in my 12-foot fishing boat. It sank in three seconds. Before we could even find something to bail with, we were on the bottom.

Later I tried it in my son's 21-foot Lund. We flipped over in five seconds.

Out on a stretch of the Grand Ronde River just upstream from its confluence with the Snake River, I stood alone at the head of a perfect steelhead pool below a long set of rapids. In the time it took me to tie on a Green Butt Skunk — about twelve seconds — I looked up to find thirty-six anglers crowded into the shallows with me. Blinking my eyes made them go away, but this trick won't work forever.

The way I see it, those of us who love fishing the mountains and rivers and streams and beaches and bass ponds hidden in quiet woods have more to lose from the population bomb than those who don't really give a damn about things like fishing. Movie-goers can just build another theater; golfers another golf course. They aren't building anymore Madison Rivers.

Barring some sudden, spontaneous, simultaneous, contagious and universal bloom of rational thought among all the humans of the Earth, it seems to me it might be an awfully good idea to acknowledge our denial, examine the population bomb, defuse it, get a vasectomy and stop the madness.

It is only a matter of time until each of us meets our lady in a bright, yellow hat.

You see the way the Fisherman doth take
To catch the fish; what Engins doth he make?
Behold how he ingageth all his wits,
Also his Snares, Lines, Angles, Hooks and
     Nets …
  — John Bunyan, **The Pilgrim's Progress**

How Shall I Catch Thee? Let Me Count the Ways

Last Sunday I took a young psychologist fishing on Clear Lake, not far from my home. Hoping for browns, we were lured by trout on a blustery day in early March. A young man born and raised in Philadelphia, Mark has the right stuff: He took the advice of Vermonter Horace Greeley and American trout fishermen everywhere, "Go West, young man. Go West!"

Mark is not yet a fly fisherman, but I am working on him. Like the freedoms guaranteed by the Constitution of these United States, Mark holds the effectiveness of a spinning rod to be self-evident. Despite several thrashings, he persists in the belief that a spin rodder can outfish a fly rodder. On this windy day in early March, my intention was to make him eat spinners and die.

Mark would fish Rooster Tails, while I would use my killer, hand-tied, black-and-orange woolly buggers on a sinking line. By late afternoon we had both done quite well. While Mark had caught the most, I had caught the biggest; a deep, wonderfully colored 19-inch male. Our expensive equipment and fishing finery had served us well. Little did we know that just down the lake a 16-year-old was making national news fishing with a golf club.

"Kid hooks long one with 5-iron, tees off pros," read next morning's headline in our local paper. Paul Harvey picked up the story and broadcast it all over the country.

The kid in question was Tanner Grant. The "long one" was a 5-pound brown from the very same lake Mark and I had been fishing the very same afternoon. While Mark and I had been battling for the most obscure, least meritorious prize in fishing, the Equipment Oscar, young Mr. Grant had fashioned a broken golf club into a fishing rod and caught a great prize. Modestly, the boy said, "I made my reel out of an old coat hanger and ran a 25-foot line through some old loops and hooks that I found in a junk drawer. It took me about two hours to rig it all together."

Local rumor has it that several fishermen sharing the same dock as young Tanner the day he caught the big brown were so undone by the experience, they exchanged face-slaps to revive their faith in angling's high technology.

The History of Fishing Tackle, from Rock Throwing to Golf Clubs

Historians of fishing tackle agree that while some fishing methods have remained unchanged for thousands of years, there have been short periods of rapid change and development, just as in the evolution of species. New ideas lead to new technologies. As a provocative thesis to keep you from slipping the hook here, consider this question: Does the development of increasingly sophisticated fishing tackle serve as a rough index to the continuing evolution of human intelligence? An admittedly wild and irresponsible notion, it still seems to fit pretty well into a book entitled *Darwin's Bass*.

Before I give you more details about how fish have been and are caught — more details than anyone but a fisherman would stand still for — let's begin at the very beginning and clear up a couple of terms.

Fishing is about catching. Catching is about survival. Hunting and fishing are both about catching to survive. Man may be able to live on bread alone, but occasionally he likes a little smoked salmon on his bagel. You cannot have smoked salmon on your bagel unless you first hunt and then catch, or grab, a salmon.

Hunting and fishing are one and the same thing. Both started in the same place and at the same time, or approximately so. Hunting and fishing differ from gathering, but only a little. In gathering, or handpicking, your arm and hand are all you use. In hunting and fishing you extend or expand the length, grasp, grip and effectiveness of your reachers and grabbers through the use of projectiles or tools. A modern deer rifle is a better-thrown rock; a landing net, a better hand. Half-close your eyes and let your mind defocus a bit, and you will see that a fly rod, line and hook, are really just a long skinny arm with a bent finger and a sharp fingernail.

Both hunting and fishing are about capture and catching. Deer hunters returning from the woods are asked by people unfamiliar with hunting, "Did you catch anything?" Tuna are harpooned, but so are swimming deer. A crab caught underwater is fishing, but a crab out of water is hunting. Catching gear in both enterprises is often identical, as with harpoons, spears, arrows, hooks, traps and even modern firearms. From the drawings on ancient Egyptian tombs, some believe nets may have been used in hunting even before they were used in fishing.

Attitudes, Attitudes

Something interesting happened to our attitudes about hunting and fishing along the road to this season's fashionable prejudices. As the land fell into the hands of the rich and the powerful, hunting birds and mammals became the sport of the royals. Fishermen gradually slid down the social register where, in many countries today, they remain still. The adjectives "humble," "poor" and "ordinary" stick to fishermen like stink to catfish bait.

Historically, except for the salmons of the British Isles and a handful of other upperclass fisheries sprinkled around the globe, fishermen have not been the kind of people you'd want your daughter to date — that would lead to marrying down, not up. But that seems to be changing. Especially here in America. If fishing, and I mean sportfishing, enjoyed the same status as hunting, perhaps the fishes would stand a little taller in our hearts, minds and courts and move a little higher on the list of things to be mindful about.

We fishermen must be careful, however. Hunters are taking a terrible beating down at the public prejudice polls just now, and if we anglers don't support them against such gross ignorance and bigotry, we'll be next. Having dinner with an editor in New York a few years ago, I was asked if I hunted. I said I did. "I suppose you fish, too?" He sneered. I replied that I did, but — in a thoughtless effort to redeem myself — added that I mostly practiced catch-and-release, to which he erupted, "Oh, I suppose if I hooked you in the lips, dragged you all around this restaurant and then let you go, that would be okay, huh!?"

If you love fishing, support hunting.

First Beginnings

Long before the fishhook or spear or first net was invented, people fished with their hands. Handpicking is the simplest form of fishing. It is still practiced today, even here in the United States by those who wade and feel for catfish hiding along the muddy banks of rivers.

Handpicking fish is considered such a great skill that to honor the ancient tradition during the famous Nigerian fishing festival in the River Argungu, the first prize goes to the angler who takes the first fish with his bare hands. Prizes for the fastest boat and biggest fish caught on traditional tackle come later.

From Greenland to the Kuril Isles, handpicking salmon is as old as human memory in those parts. Called "tickling" by the British, the trick is to sneak up on a stationary salmon or trout, dip your arm in the water, move your hand carefully along the fish's belly until you reach the gills, then slip your thumb and fingers inside and lift and toss the catch up onto the beach. To mitigate against slippage, the Lengua Indians of Gran Chaco use a ribbon strung through small vertebrae to improve their grip. I gather tickling a fish should not lead to a laugh, lest you miss your grab *and* the fish.

Some reports exist that sharks can be taken by grabbing their dorsal fin and pulling them into the boat. This kind of angling no doubt inspires considerable excitement, especially if the shark proves bigger than one first estimates, and I imagine poor practitioners are not much good at the piano.

As a boy my parents took my brothers and me to the ocean beaches of Southern California to handpick grunion, the only legal way to take these small, silvery fish. This odd little customer rushes into the beaches to spawn, completely stranding itself as it deposits its eggs. The runs occur only at night and shortly after high tide following a full or new moon. Grunion runs last only a few hours, but thousands of these slim, beautiful fish roll in on the tide and can be seen wriggling and flashing on the sand in the moonlight as you scurry about to handpick them.

I might note that the romantic possibilities of a warm California night with a full moon to wriggle under has not been lost on human California beach lovers. With a successful moonlit spawning run, you can expect baby grunion to hatch and ride out the next high tide in about ten days; it takes about nine months for the rest.

Fish have been caught by hand the world over. Fishermen have used lights to lure fish into the shallows for handpicking. Stranding fish by driving them with everything from trained otters to horses to squads of young children beating the water have all proved successful. The Maoris of New Zealand strand fish by damming up a stream, creating an artificial creek, chasing fish into the false creek blocked on one end, and then re-diverting the main flow. The trapped and stranded fish are then gathered by hand.

Fishing with Your Feet and Other Appendages

The African lungfish likes to burrow into the mud during dry spells. Hidden underground in their cocoon-like sheath of slime, fishermen tromp around the mud flats stomping their feet. When you stomp your foot right above the fish it growls, making a distinct grumbling sound, as in, "Who the hell is up there?!" Once the fish gives itself away, the fisherman can dig it out with bare hands or a simple trowel.

Fishing with your feet is not limited to lungfish. North Sea fishermen, Indians of the Pacific Coast and many Asian fishing cultures take flat fish like turbot and flounder by treading in shallow, ebb tide waters until a fish is felt under a bare foot. Then, holding it with one foot, they reach down and grasp it with the hands. This kind of fishing must be exhilarating when you step on an eel or the spike of ray.

Flyfishing for coho salmon one fall in Alaska, so many fish were trying to swim past me through the mouth of an estuary they were bumping into my wadered legs. Since most were ignoring my fly, I thought perhaps I could spread my legs and catch one between my thighs, thus inventing a whole new style of fishing.

I was wrong. There is an old story from Easter Island that when the first Polynesians arrived, the fishing was so good that fish could be caught between your legs. Even today there is a fishing hole in the Islands called, "Fish-Catching-With-Thighs."

The First Fishing Tools

One way to enhance your luck at handpicking fish is to find very dumb fish, slow fish, sick fish, fish buried in mud, or fish that have been stupefied by some means or other. Stunning fish before handpicking them goes all the way back to rock throwing and the probable development of human intelligence. From the Olduvai Gorge in northern Tanzania where our pre-human ancestors have been excavated, both fish bones and pebbles have been found together. If the stones were used to stun fish, then Lucy, our African grandmother, would be the very first fishing hominid, thus adding a bit of weight to my theory and personal experience with how to capture a tench sans a $400 fly rod.

Native Australians use boomerangs — not the kind that return — to stun fish. Projectile throwing is well-known in hunting and in every primitive society, so why not for fishing?

In cold weather where ice forms, all sorts of hammering and stunning methods have been used to prevent fish from escaping to shallow water under ice. The Chinese long ago invented rock hammering as a way to discombobulate fish hiding under river stones so they could be scooped or netted.

In modern times, the most prevalent form of mechanical stupefying is the Dupont Spinner. A Dupont Spinner is a small charge of dynamite which, when properly fused and dropped into fish-filled waters, is many times more effective than a black-and-orange woolly bugger or even a Rooster Tail spinner.

In the Turkish Black Sea fishermen make dynamite eggs of paper and twine and hunt for fish by slowly rowing over coastal waters. One guy rows while the other guy, chain smoking, rides up in the bow and keeps a sharp eye for schools of fish. The chain-smoking is necessary so that when a school is spotted, the short-fused fishing egg can be immediately lighted and tossed into schools of fish. Since the explosion must be instantaneous with the bomb striking the water, thus requiring a very short fuse, I gather fishermen without impeccable timing are not much good at the guitar.

The controversial sport of spring pike shooting with modern rifles in North America is hardly new or even novel. For many years in parts of Europe, it was considered quite sporting to build small dams on spawning rivers so that returning salmon had to come out of the water briefly to continue upstream, at which time they could be shot-gunned or picked off with rifles.

The trick for the marksman was to place the shot at the point of the salmon's nose and just before the leap. Stunned fish could then retrieved by net or dog. Apparently, some of these salmon-retriever genes persist in present day bird dogs, as I have personally owned a brace of Brittany spaniels who, while occasionally indifferent to a winged pheasant, seemed quite obsessed with helping land struggling rainbows.

Boomerangs, explosives, thrown stones, hammering ice and rocks, and other mechanical approaches to injure, kill or hamper the escape of fish seems to be a worldwide phenomena. On a trip east a few years ago, I saw a photograph of a huge northern pike in a barber shop in Bryson City, North Carolina, under which was written the following legend, "Largest pike ever taken from the Tuckaseegee River with a .30-.30."

Such a photograph would now be considered in poor taste. But it is important to remember that hungry people cannot afford fishing ethics, and only in recent historical times have people been able to restrain themselves in the killing of fish.

Hookless Fishing with Ichthyotoxins

Fish poisons, or ichthyotoxins, are as old as the oldest native legends. As with any creation myth, we will never know exactly who, what, where or how any of the hundreds and perhaps thousands of naturally occurring fish toxins were first discovered and used. Fish stupefied by poison rush or rise to the surface where they can be caught by hand, scooped up in nets, or easily speared.

Perhaps the first tackle shops in human history were run by medicine men and women who, for proprietary reasons, must have kept the secrets to which plants and which preparations were the most powerful fish-getters. When such fish toxins could also kill fishermen, those anglers who mistook their bottle of fish bait for their bottle of beer were, thereafter, not much good at anything.

Fishing with poisons is particularly prevalent in the tropics, but is known throughout South America, Asia, Europe and North America. The list of ichthyotoxic plants that produce a narcotic effect on fish is long, not short. The European kokkelseed is called the "fish seed." Crushed into powder and made into doughballs, these seeds of picrotoxin are then sprinkled in still water or ponds where, after the fish eat them, they rise to the surface for the easy grab.

The best known and most widely used fish toxin is rotenone, made originally from cubé plants. Now made synthetically, rotenone has been used by fishermen in Southeast Asia since before time. For the Festival of the Fish Drive in Malaysia, great heaps of cubé root are crushed and pounded into rotenone juice and spread into the water, thus allowing everyone to reap a great harvest.

My own Washington Fish and Wildlife Department occasionally throws festivals of a similar nature to rid our lowland lakes of undesirable species. Announcements in the local newspaper bring hordes of fish scoopers to the lakes when it's time to kill off low-class fish like bass, and replant with high-class fish like rainbow trout.

Note, I am only joking about matters of class between fish. But to listen to trout fishermen call bass "trash fish," and to listen to bass fishermen call trout "trash fish," says more about how we humans love to talk trash than it does about the merits of a fish. There is nothing so pathetic than for an otherwise intelligent human being to fall prey to things like "fishism" and racism, since neither condition does us proud.

Fishing with the Animal Act

Somewhere along our evolutionary trail we made a deal with other animals and birds, and even other fish, to gang up on those fishes we want to catch. We've formed teams. We've teamed up horses, dogs, otters, remoras, the ever-friendly porpoise and especially birds.

Dogs may have been our first, volunteer fishing buddies. Like wolves, dogs naturally hunt together and like to follow a leader. Just as a beagle naturally drives the rabbit past the shotgunner, all over the world dogs have been used to drive fish into fishing gear, especially nets. But dogs have also been trained to hunt down fish, catch them in their jaws and retrieve them to fishermen standing on shore. The first "me-and-Joe" fishing book may have been a me-and-Spot book entitled, *Spot! See Fish! See Spot Catch Fish!*

Dogs have been trained to retrieve mechanically stunned fish, poisoned fish and fish herded into shallow water. Dogs of the Kamchatkans in eastern Russia are fed mostly a fish diet year round and learn to fish successfully on their own without, I might add, a fishing rod or license. There are reports of dogs trained by Hungarian shepherds to catch a single fish, as in, "Fetch that one, Spot. No, no, *that* one!"

Horses can't cast worth a damn, but they can drag fishing nets through shallow estuaries, which is mostly how horses help us catch fish. The Maoris of New Zealand, however, hunt snapper from horseback. After spotting a fish, they ride slowly after it until it is exhausted and then, dismounting, pitchfork the pooped-out fish onto the shore.

In a more vigorous approach, Shoshone warriors once caught a mess of trout by piling brush across a stream to make a temporary weir. Leaving a few men at the brush pile, a half dozen riders then circled downstream and charged upstream, slapping the water with lances and coup sticks. Pressed against the brush dam, the trout were handpicked and tossed up onto the bank for a quick lunch.

The greatest sturgeons ever taken from the Snake River down the road from my house were hooked with large, baited hooks tied to ropes which were tied to wagons. Teams of horses pulled the wagon, rope and sturgeon out of the river. Some of these fish weighed as much as 1,800 pounds. It is not reported if any wagons or horses were ever pulled *into* the river by a sturgeon, but one can always hope. I personally have hooked, but never landed, several of these magnificent fish while fishing for catfish and carp. Such big fish should live forever.

Izaak Walton described trained fishing-otters in *The Compleat Angler* in 1653, but fishing with otters predates his observations by many centuries. Marco Polo witnessed Chinese fishing with trained otters. In Sumatra, India, Burma, northern Africa, Europe and just about anywhere otters are found — except in the Americas — they have been trained, like sheepdogs, to frighten fish into nets or waiting spears. Scandinavians have trained otters to specifically catch trout.

Imagine the following conversation between a couple of frustrated Scandinavian fly fishermen.

"Well, Sven, they're sure playing zipper-mouth with us today, eh?"

"Yep, Ole, they sure as hell are. I can't buy a rise. I say to hell with them, let's break out the otters!"

Fishing with the Birds and Fishes

Fishing with cormorants goes back to time immemorial, mostly in the Orient. Europeans did not fish with cormorants until the 16th century, at which time cormorants were, like hawks, used in royal sport. In these pre-fly rod days, a Master of Cormorants was a member of the English Royal Courts of James I and Charles I. A good fishing cormorant was as valuable as a quail-hunting hawk.

Cormorants are caught in the wild and trained to fetch; the finding comes naturally through natural selection. Some species are raised from eggs and taught to work for fishy wages. With a ring around the neck that permits only the shakers to pass through, all the big fish go to the boss. In productive waters, cormorants can catch up to 150 fish per hour without a backcast or backlash, giving them the undisputed title to "Best Fisherman."

Fishermen have also used other fish to catch fish. The remora, a member of the perch family, has a strong sucker, or adhesive disk, on its back where the dorsal fin ought to be. This the remora attaches to larger fish for a free ride. By putting a ring through the tail of the remora, attaching a line to the ring, fishermen in various parts of the world let the remora swim out, attach to a bigger fish, and then haul them in together. Although you get double the fight, rod and reel are optional. I might add that the remora's free-ride technique has been used by tax-hungry governments since the time of the Pharaohs.

The Evolution of Hardware

A fishing spear is a long arm with better finger nails. Fishing spears are found in every fishery in the world and new evidence from Africa suggests man has been carving barbed fishing spears for at least 90,000 years. These artifacts suggest fishing may be our oldest means of gathering protein. Moreover, they suggest that organized fishing with friends and relatives, fish camps, fish-camp campfires and tall fishing stories may have been the basis for our earliest bonding into social groups — the very same groups that became capable of strategic planning, culture, oral tradition and, finally, written history.

Spears come with single points, two points, Neptune's favorite, the trident, and with multiple points, barbed and unbarbed. Harpoons, eel combs, and bows and arrows fall into this general category of things you throw or shoot to grab fish.

The short list of other hand-assisted fish-getters includes: clamps, tongs, rakes, dredges, traps, polehooks, ripping hooks, fish harrows, mid-air fishing traps for jumping salmon, scoop baskets, cover pots, gill nets, seines of all kinds and manner and so many different kinds of nets that describing even a part of them would take another book.

Hook, Line, Fly and Lure

Compared to all the other ways to catch fish, a rod, line and hook are dwarfed in their use and comparative effectiveness, which is no doubt why the fishing rod is the symbol of the sport.

"I love to use a rod," said an Alaskan native who was fishing the same silver run in the same estuary the day I thought I might invent thigh-fishing, "but I can't support my family one hookup at a time." The silver salmon we were both after swam past me and into his gill net where, struggling for a time before dying, they helped make his car payment. To be able to catch with my fly rod so many salmon as he, I'd have made his damned car payment.

Britain is considered the home of sportfishing with a rod and line, thanks mostly to a Western view of history and our monumental failure to read or know our collective human history. In fact, the Japanese record fishing for sport by Empress Zingu (170-269) when she bent a pin, baited up with rice, made a line from her silk garment, stood in a river and caught trout. Chinese reports of fishing are even older, but Sister Zingu may be the first recorded sport fisherman of either sex.

Gorges and hooks preceded flies and lures, but not by much. The gorge, a short length of bone or wood sharpened on both ends and grooved in the middle to hold bait, came first. Tied to a line and aligned with the bait, the gorge is swallowed. It then turns sideways and catches in the throat or stomach. Spider web, yarn of silk, twines and other fibrous materials have been baited and used to entangle fish or eel teeth.

Experts agree that the first fishhooks were probably made of wood, and most likely occurred naturally in the environment. Natural thorn hooks were still in use in parts of Europe into the

20th century. Hooks were also made of bone and carved from stone long before the first metal hooks made it to the scene. Compound and complex hooks for big fish can be seen in the halibut hooks made of steam-bent cedar by early Northwest Indians.

A recent discovery in Zaire has produced the first fishing spears and the first-known carved bone fishhooks. These were found in Africa, not in Europe. European fishermen came up with barbed hooks only 14,000 years ago, while African fishermen invented complex fishing tools some 76,000 years earlier. This carefully dated finding upsets some rather favorite racist notions about who were the first technologically advanced toolmakers and the first modern, intelligent humans.

The idea that humans only got smarter after they moved north to Europe is incorrect, according these findings. Since these artifacts predate any found in Europe by tens of thousands of years, it would appear that Africans were catching-and-keeping with barbed hooks and spears while Europeans were still catching-and-releasing — although not intentionally and probably with considerable cursing and fist-shaking.

These fishhooks and barbed spears were found, by the way, near an old catfish spawning area on the Semliki River between Zaire and Uganda where local people still fish today, thus making this spot the oldest-known fishing hole in the world and giving Africa the uncontested title to the original Home Waters. It seems Africa was where the river first ran through it.

First Lures

A written record of the first fishing lure does not exist. But I would not be surprised if the archaeologists someday find bird feathers and bits of twine near ancient fishhooks. In ancient times in the South Pacific, bonito rigs were fixed with mother-of-pearl, tortoise shell, whale bones and feathers and even human bones. These were clearly lures, the barbs of which were made of turtle shell and the shank of whale bone.

In the greatest voyages of all times, the Polynesians carried this fishing gear with them, and it wasn't until the Europeans brought them metal hooks that these traditional lures were given up. Hooks connected to shiny bits of metal, the original jigging rigs, are found in archeological sites all over Europe.

The Bronze Age brought bronze hooks. From prehistoric digs, fishhooks have been found made of gold, iron, copper and brass, thus reflecting man's steady march toward laser-sharpened stainless steel dry fly hooks. Now, we all fish with tempered hooks, protected from the elements by bluing, plating, galvanizing, tinning, nickel, gold- or silver-plating and even, in Japan, enameling.

The first mention of fishing with something like a fly comes from ancient Greece. (An old teacher of mine once said that nothing moves in this world that was not Greek in origin.) Claudius Aelianus of Macedonia wrote in the third century that some fishes in the river Astaeus preferred an insect which flew above the river and for which the fish would gladly jump. When captured, these *hippuri* were too fragile to be impaled on a hook, and so imitations of them were made with wool dyed in red wine and with small feathers from the head of a cock.

By the time the first book about fishing was written in 1496 by the mysterious Dame Juliana Berners, European flyfishing was well-established. Dame Berners mentions not only rods, lines, floats and such, but the twelve essential fly patterns for her home waters. No drawings of the flies were included, and the first drawing of an artificial fly appeared only in 1620. Some authors suggest that, based on their written descriptions, the Japanese were into flyfishing even earlier.

Thy Rod and Thy Reel

Line-fishing gear was used long before it became sporting and long before something like a fishing rod came into common use. Handlines of all kinds exist, usually operated by pulling baited hooks with the hand, but also by holding fishing line in your mouth. Some anglers loop the line over one ear to feel the bite, or attach the fishing line to the toes of the feet, thus freeing up the hands to row or play cards.

Fishing with line attached to your peripheral parts may increase sensitivity to the bite and free your hands for other duties, but you want to be careful. More than one fisherman has lost a finger to a hot fish and a cutting line, thus making him not much good at the banjo.

Pole and line fishing without a reel is common the world over. In some places the angler uses one pole and one line. In other places, like Tanganyika Lake, fishermen use bi- or even trifurcated branches with a hook and line attached to each, thus allowing single, double or even triple hookups. An ancient drawing from Egypt shows a man pole-and-line fishing with one pole but with many lines attached to the single tip.

The development of the fishing rod, as opposed to a fishing pole — a fishing Pole is a person fishing from a bridge in Warsaw, Poland — is considered the beginning of sportfishing. A first-class fishing pole is to a fishing rod what a toy wagon is to a Mercedes.

Early fly rods were made of Tonkin bamboo, then split, then reinforced with bone and other materials. The first two-piece rods came from England where, some have speculated, such a "sneak rod" could be smuggled into the best illegal water just as poachers smuggled in the first folding guns.

The Chinese invented the first reel many hundreds of years ago and mounted it on the rod. This was a major advance in thought and technology in sportfishing as it allowed the angler to store more line than he could cast by hand or stone, or from the tip of a rod. It also permitted the first fish to be taken on the reel, thus allowing some early Chinese fisherman to shout to his buddy, "Big fish! He spooled me!"

The fishing reel didn't make it to Europe and to our old Father Izaak Walton until the 1600s, at which time the design had changed from wood to metal to, now in its latest incarnation, handsome fly reels like the Hardy.

The decision to purchase a new rod and reel follows the evolutionary steps we have taken in the development of fishing tackle. These are as follows.

Step one. We wake up one morning hankering for a new rod. We hanker for awhile, save up some cash, and then say to hell with hankering and buy the rod.

Step two. As soon as we have the new rod in hand, we say, "Gee, without a reel, this new rod is just a stick." Then we go out and buy the new reel.

Step three. Since we've now spent too much money, a money fight erupts with our spouse.

Solution to the new rod-and-reel problem: Since marriage is not much good without love, never shop for a new fishing rod without enough cash to buy the reel at the same time.

A Letter to Sir Izaak Walton

Dear Mr. Walton,

In case we don't happen to meet streamside some day in the Great Beyond, I thought perhaps you might like a quick update on how things have progressed in the sport you helped start a few centuries back.

You'll recall, I'm sure, that fishing is the recreation you gave such a boost with that book of yours. And by the way, your book is still in print, which ranks its lasting power right up there with the Holy Bible.

What prompted me to write this letter is that I was out fishing the other day, and just down the lake a young boy caught a very nice brown trout with a golf club. No, he didn't club it. Absent a proper rod, he fashioned one out of a 5-iron. You know, one of those sticks the Scots use to bat around those little white balls they curse so much. In turn, it permits them to justify drinking great quantities of those wonderful single malt Scotch whiskeys that, as someone once said, God permitted them to invent so they wouldn't conquer the world. A bit Scottish and a bit Irish and a bit fond of single malts myself, I can understand His reasoning perfectly.

At any rate, I thought you'd like to know that we sport fishermen approaching the 21st century don't use things like golf clubs (except in a pinch), shotguns, poisons, nets, clubs, otters, dogs, horses and such. Rather, we use rods and reels exclusively. But we're entering a new age just now, and fishing is about to change. Perhaps forever.

Sportfishing is one of the most popular sports in the world just now. If the complexity, design, beauty, form and function of our fishing gear is any reflection on the quality of human thought, then we are truly in a classical age not unlike that which the Greeks gave us some centuries past. If we could only address all our other problems with the same intelligence and passion we bring to building better fishing gear, mankind's future would be a lot brighter.

Consider that we now have spinning rods, casting rods, trolling rods, fly rods, rods for something bass fishermen call flippin', back bouncing rods, worming rods and specialized rods for every kind of fish God ever made. We've got salmon rods, trout rods, tarpon rods, tuna rods, bass rods, crappie rods, muskie rods, walleye rods and rods for fish I have yet to meet. They make these rods out of bamboo, fiberglass, graphite, boron and mixes of these. One rod has no eyes because the line feeds through the center of the rod blank. Izaak, it takes a fisherman about two lifetimes to finally round up all the trout rods he needs, let alone the ones he needs for bass and walleye and saltwater fishes.

And lures? We have whole industries devoted to lure design, development and mass manufacturing. We call these lures plugs, spinnerbaits, poppers, jigs, crankbaits, spoons, divers and such. They go by names like Hot Lips, Pig 'n' Jig, Hawaiian Wiggler, Fat Rap, Hawg Boss, Rapala, Dardevl, Shadling, Bomber, Mr. Twister, Fuzz-E-Grub and hundreds more. Some are covered with diamond dust, others are loaded with batteries to light them up, and most are so realistic they look good enough to cook and eat.

And flies? There are more "standard patterns" of trout and salmon flies than there were citizens in London the last time you visited. I've even invented a couple myself. The whole world of flyfishing is so broad, deep, wide, colorful, artistic, lovely, enchanting and wonderful that more books have been devoted to it than to any other aspect of fishing. Flyfishing has become a culture unto its own. Literature, art, drama — these are a but a small part of angling with the fly. The fundamental pleasures don't change, Izaak, they are still there, still raw, still exciting and still holy.

If I had a bit more time I'd tell you about developments in fishing lines, fishhooks, reels, downriggers, smart trolling motors and something they call sonar. Would you believe you can now see the fish underwater? We have even created the use of artificial moons shot up into the sky to spy on schools of fishes in the ocean so that, when a school is spotted, you can steer a boat directly to their location via a telecommunication to your on-board FAX machine.

The big risk we sport fisherman face right now is that we will soon invent the perfect gear, the perfect lure, the perfect fly and, in so doing, remove the last vestige of chance from angling. This would be a terrible turn of events, Izaak. As chance disappears so does fair chase, and fair chase is the very heart of sport.

Still, you can't keep a good idea down. A good idea has to be a little frightening to be much of an idea. I just hope that fishermen everywhere will realize that as we gain more and more advantage over the fishes, we will also see the need to handicap ourselves to keep the spirit of fair chase fair.

Hope all goes well with you.

Sincerely,

Paul Quinnett

Paul Quinnett

P.S. Izaak, I happened to go back to Clear Lake last night to see if the browns might be on the prowl so I might catch just one for my supper. They weren't. But I did row by that dock from which the lad caught the big trout with the golf club. Like fishermen in your time, Izaak, we still like to ape one another's success, which no doubt accounts for why I saw perfectly grown men fishing with not only 5-irons, but 7-irons, 3-irons and sand wedges.

*Question: How can you tell when a
   fisherman is lying?
Answer: His lips move.*

   — **anonymous**

Flies, Plugs and Rubber Bugs:
The *Compleat* Psychology
of Deception

When James Callaghan wrote, "A lie can be halfway round the world before the truth has its boots on," he was probably thinking of fishermen. Fisherman are notorious liars, not just *about* the fish they catch, but *to* the fish they catch.

No fish is caught by the truth. A fish is always caught by a lie. In the case of angling, the lie is the hook hidden in the worm, grub, fly, shiner, plug or rubber bug. A good lure is nothing if not a clever deception, a sneaky way to exploit the dining habits of the fish we seek.

All fishermen well understand that to lie successfully to another fisherman requires a little practice, a steady eye, and just enough self-deception to be convincing. A fishing lie that can't dress well enough to pass for the plain truth isn't much of a lie. As the old fisherman said, "Tell the same lie often enough, and it becomes the truth."

If we fishermen occasionally lie to ourselves and to each other in a modest effort to adjust the world to our own harmless ends, we lie to the fishes with a vengeance. We have always lied to the fishes. My very own father taught me to lie to the fishes when I was still quite young and completely innocent, and since he was a religious man, I consider myself to have had exceptionally fine training.

There is nothing paradoxical about this statement. Once you are raised with the Gospel and have a firm grasp of how strong truth is, it takes only the slightest effort to noodle it around a bit to make it even more powerful. It is people who have never known the truth who have so much trouble bending the facts without breaking them.

As a trained clinical psychologist with thirty years in the trenches between truth and fiction, I have gained a keen insight into how and when the truth — if it ever does — wins out. Not only have I been lied to by the painfully slow and obviously pathological, but by the best and brightest of sociopaths. I have seen truth twisted to low purpose, high purpose, political ends good and bad, and soundly ignored in the interest of prejudice. I am not so pessimistic about the merits of truth as I am in awe of the power of the lie.

As every politician, world leader and fishing lure manufacturer knows, it is the appearance of truth that convinces, not the actual truth. Something close to the truth is often more believable than the exact truth, or so I can only judge from the fact that some of the least effective trout flies I've ever used are exact replicas of the insect they are intended to mimic. I have, by the way, discovered the perfect trout-fly lie, which I will get to in due course.

When it comes to deception, we anglers stand in the first rank. We are simply the best. Hands down. Not only do we lie well and convincingly to our own kind, but we are nothing less than sensational when it comes to lying to other species. It is our success as liars to the fishes that makes us fishermen, and not simply people who go fishing. If you ever hope to feel like a full member in good standing of that magnificent tradition called angling, you must learn to lie well to the fishes and practice often. If lying is our trademark and deception is our craft, then to honor both we need to come to understand the complete psychology of deception.

The Complete Psychology of Deception

Homo sapiens come by lying naturally or, rather, by natural selection. There is little doubt that our success as a species is due to our ability to lie, and to lie well. Children are effective liars by the time they utter their first words. If curiosity and intelligence are the keys to our success as a species, so too is the provision of false information to self-protecting ends.

"I didn't do it, mommy," declares a 3-year-old the instant he has dumped an entire box of crackers onto the kitchen floor.

"Who did it, then?" asks mother.

"Ahhh ... Barney did it!" declares the child, spying a purple dinosaur on the television set.

"Barney? Barney who?"

"Ahhh ... Barney, you know, there!" The child points an accusing finger at the TV and maintains a wide-eyed innocent face. "He did it. Barney!"

"Where did Barney go?" asks mother, tapping her foot.

"Ahh ... back into the TV."

This is not a child with a gift for politics, this is just your ordinary child. Had this child been a political prospect, he'd have gotten a couple bucks from Barney for his campaign and asked for his mother's vote.

Mothers try to combat this sort of prevarication by making up various specialized sensory equipment and truth-detecting powers. My mother had eyes in the back of her head and could see through walls 10 miles in every direction. I must have been 6 or 7 years old before I realized I'd been conned by a better liar.

If I ask you to smile for the camera, you can do it, even though you do not feel like smiling. And you can do it convincingly. But you have to think for a moment to carry it off. If you laugh at something spontaneously, your face lights up without thinking. The first smile is faked, the second reflexive.

Neurophysiologists have shown that our brains come complete with two neural systems to control the facial expressions so necessary for effective lying. The system that controls voluntary expression is managed from the left side of the brain, whereas the neural system that controls reflexive or involuntary expression is controlled by both the right *and* left side of the brain. The neural system used in spontaneous smiles does not pass through the cortex where the editor sits. The editor is that part of your thinking brain that makes up lies. When you speak a lie, the lie is carefully evaluated in this higher brain center before being sent out on the wire, thus giving you time to adjust your facial expression to aid and abet the delivery.

Why, we should ask ourselves, do humans have such an elaborate set of neural pathways to control facial muscles? Why should every healthy human be able to override spontaneous facial expressions?

So that they don't give away the rush they feel when dealt four aces?

So they can become actors and actresses?

So they can tell tall fish tales and get away with them?

Consider, again, natural selection.

Down through the thousands of generations of humans meeting, greeting, trading, dealing and double-dealing with each other, it follows that those humans able to detect lying in other humans would gain, in the great stretch of time, some survival advantage over those who can't hold a poker face. Give yourself away through blushing, twitching, diverting your eyes, or by any number of other signs that the truth is not being spoken, and you won't win many hands of poker.

Likewise, those humans best able to pass off a lie for the truth, and best able to detect lying in others, will keep a greater share of the resources by sharp trading. They will keep the best fishing holes to themselves and, thereby, enjoy greater reproductive success for their immediate gene pool.

I fully confess that I have long practiced this wonderful gift from my ancestors by gently bending the truth to the following angler's ends: what kind of fish I caught, where I caught them, how many I caught, and on what. To keep things friendly, the omission of critical details is my specialty. Asked one day where I caught a wonderful brace of steelhead, I happily replied,

"In the Snake River." The Snake River is 1,500 miles long.

Eventually I came to learn that my mother had lied about eyes in the back of her head and having x-ray vision. Stepping boldly into the world of deception, I began to adjust the truth ever so slightly to achieve certain, occasionally noble ends. Who put the dent in the family car, for example. How to convince a largemouth bass that a ball of deer hair with a hook in it was a swimming mouse for another. I have lied to thousands and thousands of trout, and I am not yet finished. While not a born liar, I have become a reasonable facsimile thereof.

As a young man I received professional training in the art of the lie. Trained by the U.S. Army in espionage during the Cold War, I served my tour of duty in a foreign land where part of my job was to eavesdrop on our enemies. Their job was to fool us with false information, and our job was to fool them right back with false information. On both sides of this disinformation effort, cryptanalysts spent long days and nights trying to sift the truth out of mountains of lies. Now trading partners and allies, I'll leave the names of players in that great game as I found them in the 1960s: top secret.

What I came to realize about human nature and about the nature of truth in that time was that we, the enemy and us, all engaged in a great and dangerous game of ruse, fraud, deception, double-dealing, dissimulation, duplicity, misrepresentation, mimicry and, if we could get away with it, a little treachery. With the free world hanging in the balance, nothing was as it seemed. For a time during the Cuban Missile Crisis, I wondered if the best liar might not win after all.

Interspecies Lying

To survive, we humans have become the masters of deceit. A duck decoy is a lie. So is a spread of geese silhouettes. So is a turkey call, an elk whistle and a tuft of rabbit fur dangling on a breeze from a pine branch over a bobcat trap. To fool the fishes, fly tyers, lure designers, rubber bug and plug makers, all strive for the same result: a lure that looks like, floats like, moves like, smells like and even tastes like the real thing, but isn't the real thing. As with the evolution of living organisms, fishing lures are field tested and only the best designs survive.

My father's lessons to me on the importance of honesty in all matters might have been more convincing had he not taught them to me over a fly tying vice. Dad was a good tyer and, taking a No. 16 Mosquito from the vice to hold up for inspection, he might say, "If that doesn't fool them, nothing will."

An effective emerging-caddis fly floats down a river over pods of feeding rainbows and shouts, "Help! Help! I'm stuck in the surface film and can't get my wings dry! Oh my! Oh my! I hope some hungry trout doesn't see me!" An effective Muddler Minnow darts cross current, "escaping" pursuit. A broken-back Rapala plug swims as if it is wounded. Fishing without fakery is not fishing, and perhaps this is why a whopper is both a big lie and a big fish.

The Eyes Have It

Because predatory fish are headhunters and target the eyes of prey, we fly tyers and lure makers include eyes as a prominent feature of our deceptions. We repeat to the fishes that oldest of lies, "The eyes don't lie."

The first thing any creature looks for in another creature is the eye. No wildlife photograph or work of art is complete unless there is a prominent eye, preferably with a glint of life, that draws the viewer's attention to this universal point of inter-species reference.

It is often the eye of the prey that not only triggers, but directs the attack of the predator. Standing in high contrast to the rest of the body, the eye is the releasing stimulus that fires up the fishes' pursuit engines. As a result, some prey have evolved dark, contrasting eye-like markings at the expendable ends of their bodies. If you're going to be bitten, better the predator bite off a fake eye than a real one.

Many bait fishes and butterflies sport fake orbs on their fins and tails to lure the attack in the wrong direction. A few insects have evolved completely phony heads and eyes for the same reason. Judging from some of the laws being made in our nation's capital just now, it appears not a few of these empty-headed insects have been elected to Congress.

Distraction, Dead Drifts and Playing Dead

Distraction is another primary tool for deflecting the predator's attack. The nesting mallard drags a wing and staggers away from her nest, drawing the fox after it, only to recover and fly back to its eggs or ducklings. Some lizards lose their tails while under attack, and the tail — disconnected from the body — thrashes wildly to keep the predator's attention focused in the wrong direction. Fishing in bear country, more than one fisherman has used a shout or a scream or pistol shot to distract a bear from his string of fish.

Distracting large, carnivorous predators is a risky business, and I don't much enjoy it. "What tune works best to keep the bears away?" I asked my pal Rick Ries one afternoon as we hiked through dense cover on the way to an Alaskan river loaded with silver salmon. "Try 'Amazing Grace,' " he said. "That way if the bears get us, we'll have all the bases covered."

There's an old distraction story about two fishermen who happened upon a grizzly bear, disturbing its lunch. The bear immediately gave chase. As the anglers raced through the woods side by side, one said to the other, "I've got my camera. Have you got yours?"

"Yes," panted the other. "Why?"

"Because one of us is going to get one hell of a picture!"

Predators, including bears and fish, feed on living things. Their attack mode is typically triggered by visual cues, including size, color and movement. Playing dead can deactivate these releasing clues and cause the killer to pass on by.

Playing dead when that grizzly catches up to you is the best way to save your life. The reason given by naturalists for a bear's sudden loss of interest in something apparently now dead is that bears — like other large carnivores and unlike catfish — don't like stinky, old carrion. Putrefying meat and excreta can make a bear sick and so, if under bear attack, don't move, and try to smell bad, which, in the latter case, shouldn't be all that difficult.

Humans know how to play dead, and so do spiders, snakes, insects, and all kinds of birds and mammals. The North

American opossum is the uncontested master of the craft. Sometimes, and for some species, a fisherman must present his lure as dead, or just about dead.

Several years ago I took a long hike to a far river in search of smallmouth bass. What I found in those clear waters were not bass, but large pods of beautiful carp. The pods of carp circled and circled the clear pools, looking for food. An experiment occurred to me. Why not see if these carp can be caught on a fly?

I had caught a few carp on dry flies before, but always attributed these happy events to serendipity and the fact that I live a pure life. The carp in those cases were sucking in large numbers of dead, floating insects and, with my imitation among them, I thought the take inadvertent. I was wrong, but at the time I didn't know it. Now presented with a perfect laboratory of carp in gin-clear water, I opened my fly box and began a few tests.

First finding: I could not get a carp to rise to any of several, small dry flies.

Second finding: While I could catch their attention, I could not get a carp to chase or take a moving Muddler Minnow or, for that matter, any number of minnow-like flies, including several variations of the woolly bugger.

Third finding: The careful presentation of a small, light-colored nymph drew one carp out of a passing pod and to the fly. But when I moved the fly, the fish moved on.

Fourth finding: If I presented a little green scud so that the passing carp could see it falling to the bottom, *and then let it lie perfectly still*, a fish would swim to the resting fly, poise itself over it nose down and then suck it in.

Fifth finding: If you have not caught, fought, and wrestled 5- and 6- and 7-pound carp on a light rod, you need to get out more.

Here's a short list of lures and baits and flies for those fishes who like their food dead: dough balls, flesh flies, chicken guts for channel cats, salmon egg flies, dead suckers for pike, spinners from a baetis spinner fall and now, little green scuds for carp.

Is This Meal Dead or Alive?

I should add one other observation regarding this business of presentation. Compared to fishes that dine on dead things, predatory fish do not like their prey dead or, for that matter, to engage in un-prey-like behavior. Predatory fish like their prey to act frightened, sneaky and, if detected, to swim like hell to get away.

According to the laws of natural selection, a small shiner does not attack a big bass. Shiners this dumb left the gene pool a million years ago. Thus, when a big bass sees a little shiner gaining on him from behind, he says to himself, "Holy cow! I'm being chased by the Shiner from Hell!" No matter his size, a chased bass rushes for cover. Meals that don't behave like meals can be very unnerving.

Lefty Kreh has made this same observation about flies thrown and retrieved behind bonefish. When attacked by a crab, either head on or from behind, a bonefish flees. When the damsels are hatching in the Western lakes I fish, the catching is often much better from shore than from a float tube or boat because hatching damsels swim *toward* shore to mate and *away* from the trout, not the other way around. As Forrest Gump might say of lure presentation, "Unnatural is what unnatural does."

As a sometimes-predator myself, I prefer my food dead. Pasta with vegetables is dead food. Moving pasta is never a good sign. Having ordered pasta in a fine New York City restaurant a few years ago, I began to fork through my plate after detecting a little movement. Even a little movement is too much movement for pasta. Finding a live cockroach in my noodles, I bolted from that restaurant like a bonefish chased by a shark. A smart, one-trial learner, I have never again ordered pasta in New York.

Why You Never Own Enough Flies, Plugs and Rubber Bugs

Henry Walter Bates (1825-92) was a contemporary of Charles Darwin and one of his greatest admirers. He was one of the grand pioneers in tropical biology and, by himself, contributed some 8,000 new species of insects to the archives of sciences over the thirteen years he collected creatures in the Amazon basin. Among his many contributions to evolutionary theory was not only the idea that a good imitation may save your life, but that natural selection favors those creatures who lie with the greatest creativity.

I will, in a moment, work my way around to why you can never own enough fishing lures and to my personal favorite trout fly, but first you have to give the old college professor in me a little time to sharpen his hooks.

Henry Bates noticed that harmless insects were usually drably colored, whereas bad-tasting, poisonous insects were often decked out in bright, gaudy colors. The gaudy colors, he figured, most likely served as a warning sign to predators who might eat them. Bates then made a curious discovery; some good-tasting insects looked just like the bad-tasting ones, thus mimicking them in appearance, if not in content. This observation is now known as "Batesian Mimicry," and it is interspecies lying in its finest form.

If you are predator, you need to know what's fit to eat, and what will make you sick, or even kill you. A few humans, in their predatory mode, once ate the ripe roe, or spawn, of the Northern puffer fish and left the gene pool along with those bass-attacking shiners. In the case of birds who dine on butterflies, the trick is to avoid eating black-and-orange monarchs which, if you eat just one, will cause you to puke your guts out. Young birds only eat one monarch, then avoid them forever.

Enter the look-alike, black-and-orange viceroy butterfly. Most birds and most people cannot quickly tell a viceroy from a monarch. Birds who have sickened on a monarch do not give the viceroy a second look. Through mimicry, the viceroy enjoys the same survival advantage as the monarch and — like moving pasta — is forever deselected from the menu.

To catch most of the fish most of the time, all the angler has to do is mimic fish food; dead fish food for fish who like their food dead, and live fish food for those who like their food moving. The evolution of successful fishing methods follows exactly the evolution not only what fishes like to eat, but when they eat it and how.

If shad have been introduced to an impoundment filled with largemouth bass, you'd better have some shad plugs in your tackle box. If you're trout fishing in August, you'd better have some grasshopper patterns in your hat band. Matching the size, shape, color and movement of the fish's food chain in both time and space, and with reasonable imitations of that food, is the easy part.

The hard part is outwitting smart fish.

Fooling High IQ Fish

A smart fish, like a smart, butterfly-eating bird, has had negative and adverse consequences to certain dietary practices. Too many painful learning experiences lead to, for example, the educated trout. It could be an educated bass, or walleye or Northern pike, but for the moment let me pick on a large, old trout that has, due to a long life in a heavily fished catch-and-release stretch of river, been fooled so many times it has earned an honorary Ph.D. in stream entomology.

I know a trout like this. In fact, I know several of them. I have their names and addresses. These browns and rainbows have seen more trout flies than Lee Wulff. Fooled repeatedly in their youth, they have been hooked, hauled to the surface, squeezed, kissed and released so many times that when an amateurish Royal Coachman smacks the drink above them, something like this must goes through the old timer's mind, "Oh, good grief. Will the beginner who plopped that monstrosity on my front porch please get off the water and allow an old man some peace and quiet?"

If it be true that experience teaches all things to all creatures, then an old trout can wise up, too.

The Perfect Fly

Now let's suppose you are that wise, old trout and you have had to make a living sorting out the truth from the large assortment of lies handed you by every Tom, Dick and Mary who tries to match the hatch over your stretch of home water. You see the young fish fall for obvious fakes all around you, but your discriminating eye quickly spots the imitations. You wait, patiently, and sometimes into the dark of night for the real thing to come along. Ah, life is good when you are clever, discerning and wise.

Then, suddenly, there it is. The genuine article. A hookless meal. Floating as lightly as a mosquito wing on a summer zephyr, it settles ever so gently on the surface film and starts down the chute to the dining table. It is light-bodied and wears its skeleton on the outside where it belongs, not on the inside like some damnable fake with a hook in it. Dressed in a dull frock, yet with that subtle sparkle of life glowing on the inside, it seems barely tethered to the earth and floats high on the water, as if standing on invisible legs. You dash to the surface and suck it in.

What was it, old trout?

Too late, I have you.

And by what trick did I deceive the old fellow?

A No. 20 Griffith Gnat. I have fooled more big, educated trout under more difficult conditions in river, stream or lake, with a size 18 or 20 Griffith Gnat than any other fly. And here's my reason why.

Little more than a few wraps of peacock herl overwrapped, palmer style, with a grizzled gray hackle, a Griffith Gnat doesn't look like a gnat, a mosquito, a caddis pupa, a mayfly, or much of anything else in the insect world. Best of all, it doesn't look like any of the flies in my fly boxes.

It doesn't look like a Royal Wulff, an Adams, a Humpy, a Goddard caddis, an Irresistible, a Green Drake, or any of a dozen other of the standard dry fly patterns that appear with such regularity in fly tying books and heavily fished trout water. So far as I can tell, the only thing a Griffith Gnat imitates is another Griffith's Gnat.

It is my theory that the Griffith Gnat succeeds where other flies fail precisely because it does not look like any of the usual and customary fare presented to heavily fished trout, yet is small enough to be confused with just about anything edible, including small ants.

Applying fish psychology and what we know about how

living creatures learn, we know that the generalization gradient from pain-based learning is wide, not narrow. If you are badly burned by a match as a child, you are likely to avoid not only matches, but candles, cigarette lighters, stove tops, campfires and anything hot. If you are an old trout and been badly burned by a Muddler Minnow, you are more likely to leave all those shiners, sculpins and small fry alone and stick to ants and grass hoppers. If you have been burned by a Joe's Hopper, you may switch to caddis nymphs; if burned by a elk wing caddis, you may switch to ... and so on in your never-ending search for something that doesn't pull your lips off when you try to eat it.

Without naming names or places, I have watched experienced trout fishermen using so-called standard trout patterns thoroughly cover a stretch of excellent trout water and take only one or two small fish. Wading in behind them after a decent interval, I have covered the same water with a Griffith Gnat and sold many a fine trout on the tiny hook in the little lie. And should my gnat fail me, I take out my clippers, snip down the hackle until I cannot see the fly on the water, or even fish it subsurface, and then set the hook according to the flashes and tugs.

Just a couple of weeks ago, an evening midge hatch brought thousands of rainbows and cutthroats to the surface of a little lake not far from home. I caught trout on several small patterns, but none worked so well as a No. 18 Griffith Gnat.

At the other extreme, a California man named Alan Cole just built an absolutely huge plug for largemouth bass. The small size is 7.5 inches long, while the large model is 1 foot long, more than three times the size of more standard bass lures. Called the "A.C. Plug," early results show bass fisherman are catching some of biggest bass of their lives on this oversized hunk of wood. One Texas fishing guide has caught fifty bass on the mid-sized model, and the smallest of those was 6 pounds, 7 ounces. Is this not another case of fooling educated, old bass with something that cannot be confused with a standard-sized lure?

In the trout fly department, the 1995 Jackson Hole One-Fly Contest, a prestigious international flyfishing contest in which each member of a four-person team must fish only one fly, was won by my friend, Joe Roope Jr. of Castaway Fly Fishing Shop, and three other members of Team Coeur d'Alene. The entire team fished a Turck's Tarantula, an attractor fly pattern invented by Guy Turck of Jackson Hole, Wyoming.

A Turck's Tarantula doesn't look like a tarantula. A Turck's Tarantula doesn't look like a spider. A Turck's Tarantula doesn't even look like a trout fly. If anything, a Turck's Tarantula might pass for a grasshopper on steroids who somehow grew four long, white rubber legs. One of the nicest brown trout I've ever caught was taken from heavily fished water on Yellowstone's Gibbon River in the middle of the day on a Turck's Tarantula.

My theory? A Turck's Tarantula works on educated trout precisely because anything that weird and buggy couldn't have come from some traditional angler's fly tying vise. Experienced guides have told me: "These fish have seen everything. Throw something they've never seen before, and sometimes they'll go for it." Thanks, Guy Turck.

A Lure for All Seasons

You may deceive some of the fish all of the time, and you may deceive all of the fish some of the time; but you will never deceive all of the fish all of the time, unless you learn to lie like an expert.

Expert fishermen are experts partly because they offer the fishes not only what they want, when they want it, and how they want it, but if all these fail, something new and different and for which the fish has no genetic, personal or cosmic memory.

Presented with something resembling hookless food, fish hit the damnedest things. As a result, anglers collect, carve, build and tie the damnedest lures. What separates the expert angler from the amateur is not only skill, experience and knowledge, but the sheer weight and volume of his collected flies, spoons, lures, plugs and rubber bugs.

Fortunately for anglers and tackle manufacturers, there can be no final solution to the perfect lure. And there will never be. These many pages into the evolutionary psychology of fishing, the reasons should by now be clear.

So long as we catch-and-keep we will, over time, select out those fish that cannot discriminate between their real food and the fake food we toss at them. We have been doing this for several hundreds of years and, as a result, those fish who did not fall for the lure have stayed in the gene pool and passed along smarter and smarter fake food detection genes.

However, we have also made some lures so effective that some species of fish seem incapable of telling truth from fiction. The eastern brook trout of the early 19th century comes to mind, as does the wild westslope cutthroat trout — both highly susceptible to overfishing with dry flies. If caught and killed without regulation, such naive fishes will disappear before they have time to evolve and get smarter.

The interim solution is to catch and then release the fish we fool so that, over time, selection pressures will help produce a smarter, more challenging fish. The old trout with the Ph.D. saves his strength for spawning instead of chasing poor food imitations and, thereby, should live longer than his slower counterpart who exhausts himself in futile struggles against strong tippets. Even with catch and release, mortality is not zero.

According to natural selection, our old boy will then win the spawning race and pass along those genes responsible for making finer and finer discriminations about what is and what isn't real trout food. His fry will rise a little slower to the fakes, refuse a little sooner, and increasingly ignore sloppy presentations. Such fishes may even learn to tell a No. 18 Griffith's Gnat from a genuine No. 18 food item.

This, then, is fishing's future. Separated by minds more different in degree than quality, we are the moral species. Thus endowed, we help the fishes evolve into smarter and smarter fish, while they help us evolve into smarter and smarter anglers. To keep up the good race, one against the other, we humans must invent ever more clever imitations to fool ever more clever fish. Together fish and fisherman, we will go forward, arm-in-fin, co-evolving toward a wonderful, never-ending, reciprocal relationship of mutual respect and admiration.

I think, therefore I fish.
— Borrowed from René Descartes and a
popular T-shirt

Fishing in the Stream
of Consciousness

One moonlit evening not long ago I was deep in the pads once again casting a surface popper for lunker bass. Lunkers like moonlit evenings. I like moonlit evenings. "Lunkers in the Moonlight" is my favorite song. But tonight I was having trouble. My casts were good and perfect, but nothing moved. Then, just as I was about to reel in and head home, a huge, dark fish rushed up from the deep, opened its gigantic white maw and engulfed my deer-hair popper. The bass was so big I feared he might take bug, line, rod, boat and me all in one bite. I set the hook so hard I woke up.

Hook sets that wake you up in bed are proof positive that you can go fishing in the Stream of Consciousness, in this case the "Dreaming Fork" of the stream.

Fishing in your daydreams make up the riffles and pocket waters scattered throughout the Middle Fork of the great Stream of Consciousness, while fully conscious fishing takes place right where the Stream of Consciousness flows into the River of Reality. Other altered states of consciousness, like meditation and hypnosis, make up the South Fork.

In this chapter we will explore fishing in the various creeks of consciousness that flow together upstream from the River of Reality. We will hike high into the wild and remote headwaters and explore the mysterious country. We will pack a lunch and climb up to the meadows from which the first droplets of consciousness seep into pools and then trickle into tiny creeks that, braiding together, feed into the various Streams of Consciousness.

Any native trout caught on this journey must be released instantly. As everyone knows, all fishing in the headwaters of consciousness is catch-and-release.

Fishing in Your Mind

As fishermen everywhere know, you can go fishing in your mind, with or without a rod and with or without your eyes open. I can look at this computer screen as I write this line and simultaneously see the little rainbow that hit my fly last evening and shot up out of the lake like a silver dagger, shaking itself loose from the hook and knifing back into the green water. This ability to fish in the Stream of Consciousness, the Lake of Dreams and the Oceans of Imagination, presents us with the most perplexing problem in all of science: the human mind.

Mind is consciousness. And unconsciousness. And semi-consciousness. And all sorts of altered states of consciousness, some of which have not even been defined. All that man has been, and hopes to be, is tied to this yet immeasurable phenomena we call the human mind. Without consciousness and all its many manifestations and utilities, we ain't all that much.

When your body lives and your brain goes in a straight line, most experts consider you dead and that you've joined a new class of living things without minds: vegetables. When the doctors pronounce you brain dead, where does your mind go? Can it come back from wherever it goes? Does it stick around in your gray matter waiting for that gray matter to quicken again? If you unstick a valve somewhere in the brain's still-living machinery, can you return from Coma Creek?

Or, as the brain dies, does your mind begin some last great

voyage? Does it return to the one great consciousness that lies high in the mountains where the eternal snowpack feeds all living things, eternally freshening the headwaters of all our Streams of Consciousness? Or, at the moment of death, does the mind wink out to utter darkness and disappear forever?

Absent answers to these questions of consciousness, death remains the Riddle Fish of the Great Lake *Terra incognita*.

The Unique Organ

Because the human mind is unique, so too is the organ from which people agree the mind emerges. If you laid out the cerebral cortex that sheaths the human brain like a thin bonnet, the quarter-inch thick web would spread out to about the size of an average trout-landing net. Like a landing net, the cortex is all laced together.

The difference is that while the landing net has several dozen connecting strands in a geometric latticework, the cortex is made up of 10 billion neurons with some million billion connections in the most complex latticework in the known universe. If you counted all these connections at one per second, it would take you 32 million years to finish the job, and that's if you didn't break off the counting once in awhile to go fishing.

If you consider the number of possible connections between these neurons, one with another, one with a dozen others, one with a network of hundreds or thousands or millions of others, the number of connections shoots into the trillions, thus making the total possible number of intersections between the neurons in your brain greater than we can even imagine.

What we call mind or soul or consciousness somehow emerges from the almost unbelievably complex biological activity that takes place in this little organ between our ears. If we humans enjoy the freedom to choose, it is because somehow evolution has given us the capacity to transcend the limitations of our environment and to push back against the tyranny of external forces. With this thing called mind, we can even override those gene-driven traits and tendencies that seem to shape our personalities. It seems, if we believe in willpower at all, that we humans have now evolved sufficiently to take an ever more direct hand in our we shall live our lives.

Here are some sample questions asked by the people who study consciousness and the nature of the mind.

When you close your eyes and catch the same nice trout you caught yesterday from the pocket water of your visual memory, is it like catching the same trout again in an exact video replay, or is it more like a virtual reality experience in which the trout you catch again is whipped up by your mind out of old bits of this trout and that trout?

Or does your mind make up the trout you want to remember out of all its "troutness experience," and chip in just a tad of length and brightness? If so, does the mind have a "mind of its own"?

Or is the brain like a computer, able to store and retrieve visual negatives from coded files?

Or does the mind work on principles we will never understand? Perhaps the mind, following the known laws of the universe, but running beyond our power to know, operates on quarks and God particles.

As of this writing, no one has particularly good answers to even these simple questions, let alone the tough ones. Like the search for the headwaters of the Nile River in the last century, neuroscientists are some of the last great explorers. As curious fishermen, perhaps we can look over their shoulders and get a glimpse of that far country.

Two Theories of Mind

When you listen to people talk, it is pretty clear that they see their bodies as somehow separate from their minds. People with clear minds on their deathbeds say, "How can this be happening to *me*?"

The mind is "me." This me is somehow separate from the body that is letting the mind down by dying. As a young person, you may have broken a nice rod by stepping on it, and blamed your foot, as if your foot was an awkward appendage of a clumsy machine. With age and maturity, this separation of mind and body improves, and you learn to blame the rod for being in the wrong place at the wrong time. Only with great wisdom do you learn to blame your *self*.

That our minds are somehow more than a bunch of interconnecting neurons, however complex, is important to us for all sorts of personal, religious and spiritual reasons. It would be nice to catch a mind and study it. But no scientist to date has been able to test for, capture, measure and release a mind, let alone a fisherman's spirit. And yet, such a thing must exist if we are to think of ourselves more than mere meat.

The view that mind is somehow separate from body is called Cartesian Dualism, which is only fair since René Descartes wrote the original thesis. Descartes believed the mind dwelled, somehow, in the pineal gland, a small blob of endocrine tissue resting almost dead center in the middle of your brain. A curious little organ with no obvious purpose, yet mysteriously well-tucked away in a safe place, the pineal gland seemed like a good place for a mind to hang out. So that's where Descartes gave it a zip code. But just how the mind might arise from this little organ defied description, both in Descartes' day and ours.

One speculation from this early theory of mind is that there must be a little fisherman (homunculus) inside our heads, perhaps residing in the pineal gland. This little chap tells us what to move, think, imagine, dream, when to sleep, eat, fish, and advises us on such important things as when to set the hook. The little fisherman in our head is always conscious. It was the little fisherman inside my dreaming head, for example, that told me when to set the hook on the big bass that loomed up from under my bed floating in the lily pads.

According to this theory, the little fisherman inside our heads is a kind of ghost that neatly explains how we are able to catch fish not only in the Stream of Consciousness, but in all its forks and branches and lagoons and pools.

The trouble with this theory of mind is that, if you head up the Middle Fork in search of the source of the stream and the little fisherman, you can never find him. Or if you do find him, he will tell you there is a little fisherman inside *his* head that tells *him* what to do. No searcher for the little fisherman has ever come back with the littlest fisherman, let alone an answer as to who he is or how he got into our heads in the first place.

Nasty scientific problem: If you postulate a first, little conscious fisherman inside your head, then who is inside his head to tell him what to do? Another little fisherman? To explain a second, you need to explain a third, and so on and on and on all the way back to a fisherman so tiny he fits inside a quark with casting room to spare. If you postulate still another little fisherman inside the yet-to-be-found God Particle, you remain quite stuck in the mud and haven't yet got an answer worth a damn.

So the search goes on.

Can Computers Learn to Love Fishing?

A second theory of mind has been put forth by computer nerds. This theory is very popular right now and is based on the reasoning that a digital machine can emulate any computational system found in nature, including the human brain. Known as "connectionists," these folks build and study electronic "neural networks" which, they reason, parallel the functions of the human mind.

Their theory: If they just had enough money to build a big enough computer with enough interconnections, they could build the equivalent of a human brain, and a human mind would emerge. This particular science-fiction story line has been heavily overworked and was trite long before Captain Kirk graduated from flight school.

The trouble with the computer theory is that no machine can do what a human brain can do — then, now, or in the foreseeable future. If you built a computer by the same design specs as required to wire and duplicate all the connections in an average human brain, and relied on existing technology, the thing would be much larger than planet Earth — or at least that is what my brain guesses. I can guess about such things because, unlike a computer, I don't have to answer any foolish rules for internal consistency.

No matter its size or sophistication, no computer can ever answer these four, simple, ancient Native American philosophical questions: Who am I? Where did I come from? Where am I going? What is the meaning of my journey?

I don't know about your computer, but when I asked these questions of my computer, it let out a small plume of smoke and responded with considerably less animation than a fence post.

Which is not to say I don't like computers. I do. I love computers. Like a lawn service or fishing guide, I think everybody should have two on contract.

Nonetheless, to think that something as complex as the human brain can be duplicated with chips and circuitry is, at least to my mind, silly. You may teach a computer to tie a trout fly, and you may even teach a computer to design a trout fly, but you will never teach a computer to write a single interesting answer to the question, "Why fish?"

The great flaw in the computer theory of mind is that a computer has no sense of humor. Anyone who thinks a computer can ever be as funny as a human being is probably right, at least if the comparison is a personal one.

High up in the Headwaters of the Stream of Consciousness

Historically, we know there was a beginning of the human mind, and that before this beginning we have less and less evidence for things like art or law or ethics or language or fishing stories. To think of ourselves as human beings, we must associate our *being* with a life of the mind.

Beginning only a few thousand generations ago, we find the first, clear evidence for a life of the mind: culture, carved ivory, fishhooks, cave paintings, jewelry, tools, ritual burial, a belief in a life beyond this one and, while we have no recordings, tall fish tales.

Somewhere along this march to consciousness, something happened. Exactly what happened is not well-known or understood, but one thing is clear from the fossil record: We evolved a bigger brain. As true man emerged from his primate ancestors, his brain began to grow, adding about a tablespoon of gray matter per 100,000 years until about 250,000 years ago, at which time the brain stopped adding weight and size, especially in those who ran for public office.

Some experts think that to have thoughts, and to be able

to think about those thoughts, a creature must first have a big brain. Thus, a big brain is a prerequisite to whatever consciousness is. Generally, the more an animal weighs, the larger its brain. This is true between species, but not between individuals within those species. Comparatively speaking, I have a brain the size of a large cantaloupe while my wife, Ann, has a brain the size of a Texas grapefruit; she is smarter than me by half.

A big creature with a big brain, though, has a better chance of having a mind than a mite. For comparable body sizes, humans have bigger brains than all other primates, including chimps, monkeys and the apes. Moreover, our brain cells are packed more tightly — by 50 percent — than chimp brain cells, especially in the visual areas.

American Mensa, the high IQ club reserved for those humans in the upper top 2 percent of the intelligence bell curve, is no doubt composed of people with well-packed skulls. Fishermen have a similar elite club called "DENSA." At the lower end of the IQ bell curve, only steelheaders, trophy bass hunters and ice fishermen need apply. Anglers who have taken a very bad fall and knocked off half their IQ points on the bow of a fishing boat are also welcome to join, or at least that's what my invitation said.

For comparable body sizes, all primates have bigger brains than horses and cows and elephants, and all mammals have bigger brains than all birds. Birds, comparing body weight to brain size, have bigger brains than fish. Fish have bigger brains than reptiles, and so on down the brain-size rungs to the common angle worm which, while an interesting creature with a proto-brain and an ability to lure walleyes, would not be your first choice for a Trivial Pursuit team.

Being mammals, we primates come with big brains. Being *Homo sapiens*, we come with very big brains. Compared to an adult chimp, our brains are three to four times as large, which is why we get to shoot them into space as test animals instead of the other way around. Chimps are, however, very smart and no doubt possessed of consciousness.

One group of chimps build and use eleven different tools, have elaborate communication skills, and are so highly organized they both plan and execute successful hunts of other primates. Chimps are smart enough to be taught to fish, at least with a simple pole and line.

The battle rages, however, about whether animals, fish and reptiles have minds. In the 17th century, animals were thought to be mere machines and not much more complicated than clocks. By the 18th century, Voltaire had surmised that animals had the ability to learn and to feel pain, distress and grief. By the 19th century, Thomas Henry Huxley had pretty well brought animals beyond the machine and simple feelings to stand a little closer with humans. He attributed them to not only sensations, emotions and ideas, but he made the outrageous suggestion that those principles which apply "to brutes holds equally good of men; and, therefore, that all states of consciousness in us, as in them, are immediately caused by molecular changes in the brain-substance."

As I have said throughout this book, we are all of one life; only our states of consciousness vary.

A Darwinian Theory of Mind

By the time a distinct species called *Homo sapiens* had emerged through eons of natural selection, so had the rudiments of the mind. Once we became our own kind and our brains grew large and cumbersome, we gained something else: all the rights, privileges and prejudices that accompany any creature with the capacity to examine itself, its history and its future. To examine consciousness requires consciousness, putting an even tighter knot in our lines to unravel.

Consciousness is both a great blessing and a great curse, as anyone who worries about how to make a living, how to pay the bills, or how to find the time to go fishing can tell you. Losing consciousness is why sleep is a blessing and why alcohol, a general anesthetic that numbs the cortex, is the most sought after elixir on the planet surface.

"I'd rather have a bottle in front of me than a frontal lobotomy," runs an old gag on the temporary benefits of alcohol on consciousness. A frontal lobotomy removes all worries forever. Consciousness, as with all Darwinian adaptations, follows a cost-benefit formula and is, despite its glory and wonder, not without accompanying pains and sorrows.

Years ago I had occasion to examine a young man who had failed to appreciate the dangers of jumping a motorcycle across a chasm over an Idaho trout stream and launched himself at high speed into midair, à la Evel Knievel. The short flight terminated against a stone cliff. Jim suffered a massive head injury and the equivalent of a prefrontal lobotomy. One of the consequences of this injury was a total loss of short-term memory.

Jim could not remember anything from one day to the next, or from one minute to the next. In the course of my examination and interview, he forgot my name almost as soon as I would repeat it for him. While he could remember events before the accident, he could remember none afterward.

Jim seemed a pleasant, even happy young man, whose sister cared for his every need. With his brain severely and permanently damaged, and any further improvement in function impossible, I asked him what it was like to wake up each morning unencumbered by memories of the night or day or week or month or year before. Jim grinned and said, "Well, doc, it's not so bad. Every day you wake up and, hey, it's a brand new world!"

Chipper and smiling, Jim had lost the capacity to remember the past or imagine a future, and thereby to measure one day against another. He could not even appreciate his injury. With the only organ able to assist his dreams being broken, he could not comprehend his diminishment as a human being and had become, as too often happens to the brain-injured, the most tragic of all the disabled: a physically able person without the capacity to love, work, imagine or suffer.

Still Another Theory of Mind

To enjoy all the benefits of consciousness, one must have memory. Humans have wonderful memories. How we remember, what we remember, and how memories are acquired in the first place, and from what processes this is possible, leads us to yet another theory of mind.

According to Gerald Edelman, winner of the 1972 Nobel Prize for Physiology or Medicine, only the forces and processes of evolution can possibly account for the phenomena of things like memory and consciousness. Consciousness cannot be explained except through natural selection. Picking up where Darwin left off, Edelman's notion of brain and mind are simple on the surface, but complex underneath.

Basically, this developmental biologist sees the brain as an ecosystem of neurons that, like the complex ecology of a trout stream, requires that all the parts and pieces be connected through a complex, interdependent network that sustains life. The brain — like the fingerling trout — is not only resilient, but adapts to the environment in which it finds itself as it matures and develops.

Research has shown that before birth, and for a time thereafter, the brain rapidly organizes itself, sending neurons hither and thither throughout the growing gray matter and as directed by DNA codes. Each individual brain develops, not randomly, but according to rules determined by natural selection.

Neural maps are formed; some maps obviously connect to others, while in others the connections are not so clear. Some connections get made in some people, and some don't. Even identical twins do not have identical brains, in part because so-called "gypsy" neurons are traveling all over the place and no two paths are the same in any two brains. Individual experiences change the topography of our neural maps, thus making each of us even more unique.

In the end, in each of us, a great labyrinthine neural network is established that, unlike a computer, provides a uniquely flexible tool with which to deal with a challenging world of novel environments.

"Sakana," "pescar" and "poisson" are the Japanese, Spanish, and French words for fish. World-traveling fishermen confronted with novel fishing environments need to learn such terms, and to adopt and adapt to them and their local meanings — at least if they hope to be successful anglers in challenging, new environments.

In the complex ecology of the Darwinian brain, how and where does such vital information get handled? Like a trout stream, is there a topography of function? Are there physical areas that have evolved over time to meet the challenges of potential new requirements for adaptation?

According to recent research conducted at McGill University in Montreal, a single neural network on the left and frontal side of your brain handles both your native tongue and any others you need to pick up along the way. When subjects were given words different from their native language to memorize, they all showed evidence of increased brain activity through positron emission tomography (PET) scans during the learning trials in the left side of the brain.

It seems, then, that a single, but extremely complex network of neurons on the left side of your cortex has evolved to handle such important functions as learning not only your first fishing language, but any others. At one time or another in my life I needed to learn Japanese, Spanish, French and German, which may account for all the left-brain headaches I used to get.

The second step in Edelman's theory of mind is that, once we are born, and as our brain begins to experience things, our brain changes. Those neural connections that fit well with the requirements of the environment enhance fitness and become stronger, while those that do not fit well with the adaptive requirements of the environment decrease fitness and become weaker. The brain, like some enormously adaptive fish, *learns* to swim in whatever water it finds itself. It is the brain's immense flexibility to adapt, and to shape itself accordingly, that makes it the most powerful survival tool ever to evolve from stardust.

Language, Intelligence, the Darwinian Brain and American Education

Language is one of the brain's greatest tools for adaptation — my French not included.

Language, intelligence and adaptation are so linked together in the explanation of human survival that whole books have been devoted to these connections. And while great controversies have raged about how all these elements go together, it is clear — at least to me — that the one thing which best distinguishes human beings from all other life forms is our enormous capacity for language and symbols.

Once while fishing with my Army pal Merle in the Sea of Japan, the old Japanese fisherman who took us out in his boat brought along his grandson. The boy was not 5 years old and yet, as Merle pointed out, "Isn't it amazing? That little kid speaks perfect Japanese."

Had the same boy been born into a French-speaking family, he would have spoken perfect French; English, perfect English, and so on and on and on through the millions of languages that have come and gone in the history of mankind — thus the human brain's biological capacity for languages allows each of us to adopt any tongue at birth, and many others thereafter. This adaptive capacity to communicate with one another gives us an unparalleled survival advantage over all other forms of life.

The great controversy in America education is, in large part, being fought over differences of opinion about how the brain works to acquire the information needed to successfully adapt to the requirements of modern life, including how we learn languages.

Do children learn because they naturally love to learn and will do so if given the right setting, or must they be challenged by rigorous learning environments that demand hard work to survive?

Most scholars agree there are biologically built-in capacities for certain functions, language and math among them. At age 4 to 5 years, Asian and American children show no difference in math abilities or on tests of general knowledge, including measures of IQ. But once formal schooling begins, Asian kids start outdistancing American kids on such tests. This difference in performance appears to be due to study habits, school and parental expectations, and homework — just the kind of demanding environment in which a Darwinian brain would change and grow and develop to make sure it not only survived, but excelled.

Perhaps all intelligence, however measured, is more about how a hard-working human brain, properly challenged by a demanding cognitive world, adapts and survives, and not so much about what genetic gifts it inherits, or what kind of rich learning environment it is born into. IQ, an imperfect measure of anything but general intellectual abilities as measured by standard IQ tests, is a poor index of things like specific fishing knowledge and skills required by a particular fishery.

The fishermen I met in the Amazon basin might score poorly on standard IQ tests; however, if a fisherman's IQ test could be constructed for Amazon Basin fishing knowledge and skill requirements, these chaps would blow the socks off all the outside competition. Once again, this would prove Darwin's point that it is successful local adaptation that reflects so-called intelligent behavior.

I'm not sure anyone knows the upper limits to the brain's ability to accept new challenges and adapt accordingly. For the 21st century, our students may need more challenge, not less.

A Final Search

The last part of Edelman's theory is too complicated to understand, or at least for me to understand. This is perhaps because he, like so many others before, tries to lead us to the seep springs which form the braided creeks that lead into the Stream of Consciousness. As best I can sort it out, here's the drill.

Amid all the networks and maps and synapses and chemistry and soft electrical currents in the brain, there are thousands, perhaps millions, of parallel connections going on all at the same time. These firings of neurons are triggered by visual images, sounds and input from such things as muscles, guts, hair follicles and the thought and sound of one hand clapping.

These vast webs of maps and networks are characterized by their constant firing of neurons back and forth, back and forth, around and around, such that the cumulative effect is not so much a *thing* as a process or, as Edelman says, " ... a constant circulation of symbols, back and forth, around and around."

In this idea of mind, there is not so much a single part of the brain responsible for the others — the little fisherman homunculus — but rather, like the ecology of a trout stream in an ancient forest, all parts play an equally important role, and somehow organize themselves into something more than the sum of their parts. Somehow what we call coherent consciousness emerges through a process of self-organization, not unlike the process by which patternless water molecules form into geometric snowflakes while falling through the atmosphere.

Consider the complexity of spotting a single, diving bird that may signal the presence of feeding fish. A simple task for an angler adapted to his local fishing environment, and yet a task so complex as to require a fully enabled consciousness to accomplish it.

The human eye has at least thirty different, functionally separated neural networks scattered throughout the brain, each responsible for the various components that convert light into images. It is only when all these come together that they emerge as a visual system enabling us to see the diving bird, blend that image with a memory of feeding fish, and, integrating that input into our internal mixer for vision and language and memory, utter to ourselves the word, "Fish!"

The true miracle of the mind is this: The brain can put the diving bird together with a particular remembered fish, or several fish, or historical files from fishes past; thumb through the appropriate noun list of what possible fishes might be feeding; and, while telling the knee to push the tiller left so as to put the boat on the only heading that will intercept the target, tell the hands to make ready for that first cast. All of this coordinated assessment, targeting and mental and physical activity is done simultaneously — not in a minute, but in a blinding, seamless millisecond.

Fishing Dreams Interpreted: Five Cents

There isn't room here to explain all the latest developments in understanding the Dreaming Fork of the Stream of Unconsciousness, or exactly how fishermen can catch fish in their dreams, but here's five cents worth.

When fishermen dream their eyes move. This is called REM, which stands for rapid eye movement. Eye movements begin in the womb before you're born and, so long as you are alive, never end. If you wake someone while their eyes are moving, they will report a dream. Try this is on your lover, but not too often.

In the search for the North Fork of the Stream of Consciousness, people have been angling for a satisfactory explanation of dreams since time immemorial. They've caught a few shakers, but the big ones seem to get away.

Currently, there is a popular belief that dreams are examples of the brain's effort to make sense out of the neural nonsense created by chaotic firings among the billions of neurons that make up our gray matter. Dreaming is a state of consciousness with qualitative features that indicate some level of self-organization. Consider this made-up fishing dream:

> "I'm in a boat. It is getting late. I want one more fish, but I'm really hungry and tired. Suddenly, the girl at the drive-through window hands me a bag full of hamburgers. But I wanted a fishwich, not a burger. And how, I ask myself, did a McDonald's get out here on Chapman Lake? The girl doesn't answer, but rather turns into my mother and frowns. I can feel the boat rocking, as if I'm about to be tossed overboard out of the cradle. Suddenly, it is Monday morning and I can see the angry face of my boss. The clock by my bed says I'm late for work."

Many fishermen will recognize this fishing dream turned-to-nightmare. It is one that could easily occur after a Sunday afternoon on the water. It has motion and faces and scenes and needs and desires and frustrations. It is filled with bizarre incongruities and discontinuities, yet makes a sort of internal sense. Since I am not a woman angler who lost her fishing rod over the side, and didn't develop a deep and abiding yearning for another rod, I suppose I wouldn't make a very interesting patient to a Freudian. On the other hand, something semi-logical and symbolic seems to be going on.

The modern theory of dreams is that during REM sleep the higher brain tries to organize a constant cascade of internal neural signals, complete with common symbols and images, that originate from the visual and motor areas, and from deep within the ancient brain. The results are coherent visual images, complete with discontinuities, and what seems like constant motor activity. However, commands to muscle movements are entirely blocked during REM sleep.

But should the eyes stop moving and REM sleep end, we can suddenly find ourselves out of bed after setting the hook or even sleepwalking down to the garage to, say, fix an old spinning reel. Mostly, though, you can't dream and sleepwalk or sleepfish at the same time. Rather, dreams are self-contained mental activities. If you are having a particularly good dream, you will resist being awakened from it.

Do dreams have meaning? Well, yes and no. A dream may appear to organize some critical events of the day, or it may contain a lot of flotsam and jetsam and nonsense. We can attribute all kinds of meanings to our dreams if we like. We can even pay good money to therapists to tell us what our dreams mean, but there is little evidence anywhere that dreams represent much more than the brain's efforts to organize and keep track of its neural activity while the body slumbers. Others disagree entirely and believe dreams are loaded with insights and knowledge.

Perhaps the worst thing about dreams is that some people develop a nasty habit of telling you about theirs every morning at breakfast.

Do dreams foretell the future? Not for some and maybe for others. However, in my case they do; otherwise, I will never catch that huge bass I tried to hook the night my REM sleep skidded to a stop and I twitched myself out of bed.

Dreams — Darwin Style

The Darwinians take a different tack on sleep and the dreaming brain. Selected for through natural slection, sleep is essential for survival and is universal among vertebrates, Darwinians point out. Since they must swim to the surface for air to stay alive, dolphins were once thought not to sleep. But studies have shown that while one half of the dolphin's brain is asleep, the other is wide awake. Clever fishermen, these dolphins.

In analyzing the dreaming state, Darwinians point out that

in recalling dreams, we seldom remember what voices sounded like or how, say, a big fish we caught smelled or felt in our hand. It is as if our senses of sound, smell and touch stop working while we dream. According to adaptation theory, closing some sensory channels while leaving others open should make some survival sense.

To the outside world, and even though our eyes remain closed while we sleep, those senses that might allow us to hear, smell and feel the approach of, say, a dangerous predator, remain operational. Despite how soundly a mother sleeps in or out of REM sleep, she is quickly aroused to her child's cry. Should wolves make it back into the United States in any real numbers, it will be interesting to see how well any of us sleeps in wolf country when the moon is full. In Darwinian terms, dreams are affordable, but only after survival is secured.

Hypnosis, the Middle Fork of the Stream of Consciousness

Since the days of Cartesian Dualism, people have tended to believe that — since our minds only rent space from our bodies — things like thoughts, feelings and ideas could not have a direct impact on, say, heart function, clearly a mechanical operation. Or how much we bleed when cut. Or how vigorously our white cells attack invading bugs. Surely something as wispy and ephemeral as a thought born of consciousness out of a tiny organ deep in the brain could never impact something as real as our experience of physical pain.

And yet, there were stories. Mystics who punctured their skin without apparent feeling. Superhuman feats of strength. Monks who could suspend breathing, even slow their heart rate to a whisper. Fire walking. Fishermen who stood in ice-cold, steelhead rivers until their legs should have turned to wood.

Perhaps the mind *does* overcome matter, at least the matter that makes up our own bodies. But how? Is it magic?

"Magic, schmagic," says the scientist. "Let's test this sucker out." And so, late in the 1900s, another search party set out to find the Middle Fork of the Stream of Consciousness. Among others, the group was led by that intrepid explorer, Sigmund

Freud.

The search for the Middle Fork goes on still, thanks in part to the work of one of my recent graduate students, and many others exploring the nature of hypnosis. While we have not yet found the seep springs from which human consciousness oozes and how altered states arise, we know a great deal more than we did just awhile ago. We know, for example, that any perceived split between mind and body is a phony split and that all things, including trout streams and consciousness, are connected.

Fishing as Self-Hypnosis

Fishing can be a form of self-hypnosis, or at least that is my theory. Fishing has all the right ingredients.

As one of the altered states of consciousness, hypnosis is a trance-like state that, among other utilities, has been used as a method of pain control. First described in the medical literature in the last century, reports from the British physician Eysdale, working in India, described the ability of ordinary Indians to withstand major surgery without pain killers, without screaming and without apparent discomfort. This made no sense to the medical community of that day, and it doesn't make much sense to the medical community of this day.

Despite its limited utilization in modern medicine, hypnosis remains a powerful tool in pain control, including for those steelheaders who insist on standing in freezing, winter rivers. Someone can teach you such methods of pain control, or you can teach yourself.

Patients in pain and steelheaders with freezing legs can be learn to hypnotize themselves; imagine their pain shrinking into a pinpoint, or diminishing into a vanishing pink spot, or whatever journey away from pain fits best with the person's experience of a pleasant sensation. The data are in, hypnosis can not only control pain, but sometimes eliminate it all together.

Very early in my career I studied hypnosis. I learned how to get into a trance myself, and how to help others enter a state of deep relaxation and hyper-suggestibility. In the controlled environment of a professional seminar, I even made a few post-hypnotic suggestions and watched subjects later carry them out. Once, when one of my children burned his arm on the stove, I hypnotized him, suggested his right index finger was now a "magic finger" and that, if he touched the burned spot, it would suddenly chill down and feel good again. He did, and it did.

Hypnosis struck me as real, but spooky. With only two days of training, I felt like someone who had completed just enough flying lessons to get a Piper Cub into the air, but not enough to get it back down again. With insufficient time to explore it further, I gave up hypnosis as a clinical tool.

One winter day, however, I stumbled through a snow bank and, thanks to a hidden drainage ditch and subsequent pratfall, ran the crappie jig I was carrying in one hand through the web between my thumb and finger. The same boy I'd earlier hypnotized said, "Wow! I'll bet that hurts! Dad, why not hypnotize yourself so it won't hurt more when you pull it out?"

I thought about his solid medical advice for a second or two and then, with only a rudimentary knowledge of physics to work with, surreptitiously stuck my hand in the snow bank until it was as numb as a chunk of firewood. Calling the boy back from the crappie hole, I then showed him how to painlessly extract a crappie jig with a pair of fishing pliers. Once again, the lad was amazed at the power of the mind — although this time the mind in question was a deceptive one.

Some kinds of fishing share all the necessary conditions to induce an altered state of consciousness. For hypnosis to be induced in yourself or someone else, here are the ideal conditions: a state of relaxation, a pleasant distraction and optimistic expectations.

Except for combat tournament fishing, most forms of fishing are relaxing. When fishing, both muscular and mental tension slip out of the body, over the reel, through the rod, and down the line into the water where it disappears into nothingness.

On some remote trout streams it is quite possible to focus so completely on the water and the fish and the mayflies and the sound of silence, that entering a trance in which one becomes one with the universe is as easy as pie.

Fishing is also a form of distraction. Even more important, research in hypnosis has shown that pleasant images, especially of the outside environment, are often the quickest route to a hypnotic state. Fluttering aspen leaves, water bubbling over stones, the soft line of green trees waving against blue sky — these are the images into which the mind readily retreats for solace.

For a mind distractor to work well, it helps for it have a rhythmic beat. Hypnotists use watch-fobs or spinning orbs to distract the subject; fly fishermen use fly rods and flies.

Whoosh. Whoosh. Whoosh. Whoosh.

Float. Float. Float. Float.

Whoosh. Whoosh. Whoosh. Whoosh.

Float. Float. Float. Float.

Whoosh. Whoosh. Whoosh ...

There is a highly rhythmic beat to casting, to lifting, loading, drying, and then shooting line and fly. Why, just writing this last paragraph triggered a case of MEGO (my eyes glazed over) and my mind wandered forthwith out to Crab Creek to see if a midge hatch was on.

There, I pinched myself and I'm back.

Hypnosis requires a positive mind set, and fishing is just such a positive mind set, complete with a belief that something good will happen. Nothing describes the fisherman's attitude so well as a state of chronic optimism.

When you put all these necessary hypnotic conditions together, it only makes sense that fishing, and especially flyfishing, ought to allow us to enter altered states, thus enabling us to escape our ordinary lives while our minds rest up and relax.

Anglers skilled at meditation, relaxation and self-hypnosis not only feel less mental, physical and emotional pain when fishing, but when the bite is good and the world and water and sky and mind all come together in the same place at the same time, some are able to pass into a kind of transcendental euphoria. If God has created a better feeling, He's keeping it for Himself.

I've seen these transported anglers, their minds cut loose from the tangles of ordinary life, soaring above and swimming beneath the ripples in the Stream of Consciousness. Fortunately, I've been blessed to be one myself from time to time. Should any angler be so lucky as to die at the peak of such rapture, it would take three morticians a week just to get the smile off his face.

This is Your Brain. This is Your Brain on Natural Selection.

Maturation alone cannot explain how we learn to cast a fly or lure. But if we do learn to cast a fly or lure, the fishing rod is a *novel challenge*. Presented with a long, willowy rod and a length of line, you may now apply the principles of natural selection as they might affect the necessary connections in the brain to make casting a skill.

People who learn to cast well make an evolutionary adaptation because their brains change. Literally. With the brain's enormous elasticity, those neural connections field-tested and found necessary to control muscle and eye movement for proper casting become stronger in the brain, while those neural connections unnecessary for proper casting become weaker. Where inherited abilities and behaviors leave off, adaptation and fitness through learning and conditioning take over.

It is with higher-order brain functions like memory, perception and poetry that all theories of mind begin to come undone. These are the tough challenges. No theory of mind to date explains very much of anything.

Maybe the important thing to remember is something every student of psychology learns early on: While we are all alike in some ways, we are, more importantly, entirely unique and different from one another.

Every human mind is rare, the only one of its kind ever to be produced in the history of the world, and therefore it is to be valued for no other reason than that it exists.

Natural selection has determined that each of us is so much more than our genetic loading that nothing about us can be predetermined or preordained. The variations between us should be treasured, not feared or distrusted. With this theory of mind, each of us has the capacity to become much more than our component parts.

If we have a thing called free will, it must necessarily emerge from the human brain, this one-of-a-kind biological treasure with which we are all blessed. It is our ability to close our eyes and imagine an array of possible futures, and to choose what we shall do from among those futures, that makes us human.

If we *choose* to spend ourselves in a quest for what is worthy and beneficial to our fellow man, our fellow creatures and the Earth herself, and if we are willing to sweat and toil and fight the good fight to achieve what is noble and enduring, we may even lift up the human race and give it dignity. Perhaps then, and only then, can we claim to have something called a spirit.

High in the Headwaters

Like a wild trout stream that is one with the timber standing tall and dark along the slopes of its headwaters, the stream of human consciousness is one with the ferns and frogs and beetles and ants and sky and wind and granite and every blade of grass that bends along its shores and every fish that swims within it. Our consciousness is one with the world from which that consciousness evolved.

The last great journey of man is not out to the stars, but into the mind. Humanity is not yet fully formed, not finally evolved. We have much left to learn. This can be a hopeful journey and I, for one, remain optimistic that one day we will come to understand who we are, where we came from, and where we are going. Perhaps then, if there is a purpose to our being, that purpose will be clear.

Of all the hardware a fisherman carries with to the stream, his timepiece is the least important.
— author

Time, Space and Fishing

'Shouldn't we be heading home?" I ask my old fishing pal again. The sun has been down an hour and the twilight bite is shutting down.

"A couple of more casts," replies R.V., without looking up.

"Haven't you got ... "

"In a minute," he snaps, cutting me off as a bass swirls and misses his surface popper.

At last it is too dark to see and the bass, for reasons known only to bass, switch off.

"Wha ... what happened to the time!?" R.V. gasps, staring at his watch as if returning from a deep coma. "I was supposed to be home two hours ago for Cheri's wedding rehearsal!"

"I tried ... "

"Oh well," the father of bride sighs as he reels in, "at least it's not her first wedding."

Choosing a largemouth feeding frenzy over a daughter's wedding rehearsal is only one of the high crimes for which we angler's are routinely hanged — usually in effigy, but occasionally suffering rope burns.

We are, however, wrongly convicted. Absent a jury of our

peers, too many non-fishermen believe anglers actually make conscious choices about *when* they should be somewhere. This is because people who don't fish don't understand "fishing-time."

Fishing-Time

Fishing-time is not like normal time. In normal time, people are in charge. In fishing-time, fish are. This is where the trouble begins. To a fisherman, a hot bite is like a black hole somewhere in deep space. Time as we know it ceases in black holes. Fishermen swept into such black holes can be favorably compared to some future astronaut who, temporarily sucked into a black hole on her way home from the office, arrives home for supper a couple of centuries late.

You would not blame a well-intended astronaut and mother of two for tardiness due to time distortion, and you shouldn't blame fishermen.

In general, fishing-time tends to be short, not long. A few hours seems to account for most episodes of fishing. Our experience of fishing-time is that it is too limited — which may account for why so many of us spend so much of our non-fishing-time daydreaming about fishing, hanging around tackle shops, tying flies and swapping fishing lies with one another.

Like red wine and white fish, watches and fishing don't go together. A watch tells you when to go home or go to work, not when to go fishing. If you see a fisherman cast, look at his watch, cast, look at his watch, land a fish, look at his watch, cast and look at his watch, you can pretty much figure he's either got a date in court or a bad marriage.

Angling breaks civilization's metronome. It's supposed to. While fishing you should become lost *in* time, and getting lost in time is exactly what some of us need most. Let me explain.

Several years ago I discovered what I call the "Great Outdoor Einstein Effect." The Einstein Effect works like this: The faster you travel through space, the more time slows. At the speed of light, time stops all together. Beyond the speed of light, time runs backward. Therefore, if you can get the old pickup moving faster than the speed of light, you will arrive at the lake as much as an hour before you left home, thus giving you an extra hour of fishing-time — depending, of course, on road conditions.

As a result of testing this theory it will come as no surprise that both my speeding tickets for the past 25 years have been netted on the way *to* some fishing hole, never on my return.

"Makes sense to me," said a county sheriff's deputy when I explained my theory to him. "I like to fish, too. Here's your summons."

The Einstein Effect is very real, or at least as real as a nanosecond. Every fisherman I know drives faster out, slower back. Somewhere in between they lose what the doctors call the "hurry sickness." They get, literally, lost in time.

There are other intriguing possibilities. Perhaps time as we know it ceases to exist on fishing trips. Or maybe there is something about fishing that doesn't love a watch. Having researched this whole subject far more than I ever intended, and in defense of late-arriving fishermen everywhere, I will now spare no horses to explain this curious phenomena.

This will, by the way, be no small feat. No one has heretofore attempted to explain fishing-time. In fact, I'm not even sure I can do it myself. Untrained in physics, cosmology, mathematics, and all sorts of other disciplines that oblige one to understand numbers and equations and such, I'm the sort of person for whom a hand-held calculator is not a convenience but a prosthesis. Fortunately, I am seldom encumbered by a lack of specific knowledge or skill before charging ahead. Like my father before me, I would much rather start fast and flame out, than begin slow and taper off.

Here is my thesis.

Based on a lifetime of fishing, it is my belief that time, space and fishing, like braids of a river, all run together. Having become one, time no longer fits into the neat little package in which we keep it for civilization's sake. Rather, in fishing-time, time takes on a different size and shape. It can move funny, too. A kind of "weird zone" where all the clocks are by Salvador Dali, fishing-time is not at all like ordinary time. In fishing-time, for instance, the fish control the clocks, a subject I will loop around to in due course.

The Disappearance of Fishing-Time

The White Rabbit in *Alice in Wonderland* is always in the hurry mode, trying ever so valiantly to avoid being sucked into the black hole of time escaping as we try to live it. Did we not know better, Lewis Carroll's White Rabbit could have been born and raised in America. Americans, you see, are obsessed with the disappearance of time, and especially time to go fishing.

The only way to escape time-as-we-know-it, and its increasingly corrosive effect on our mental health, is to head for a black hole, slip inside, and pull the lid in behind you. Everyone complains of not enough time. Everyone is running out of it. In a recent survey of fishermen, two out of three reported they are fishing less than just a few years ago. Of these, 80 percent gave "too little time" as the reason.

This simply won't do. When fishermen begin to say they haven't the time to go fishing, time itself needs to be indicted, dragged into court and cross-examined.

What is Time, Anyway?

In a curious way time is and does what we say it is and does. "Time," we say, "is money." "Time waits for no man," we repeat. "Time flies," we complain. Time is an ordinary noun with extraordinary meaning.

Compared to the great expanse of human history, time is now displayed everywhere: big clocks outside, little clocks inside, clocks on our desks, clocks on our walls, clocks in our bedrooms, clocks on the dashboards of our cars, clocks in our computers, clocks in our fishing boats and clocks in our heads. In case we should somehow "forget the time" we strap time to our wrists. We are deeply conditioned not to all measures of time, but to time as metered by our clocks.

One result of all this clock watching is that we've stopped watching nature. In the world of clocks, trains, planes and computers, you don't need nature, you need a Rolex. Once you become a slave to a Rolex, you become a slave to a Tinker Toy god. This seldom produces good results for anglers.

Idea for the day: When your watch starts telling you when

to eat, sleep, make love or go fishing, it's time to reexamine your relationship to time.

We can't, however, afford to be stupid about time or how reliant we have become upon it. Never imagine that something so small as a second is unimportant in a world dependent on carefully minced time. You may not think a second matters much, but if you're a ship at sea and use the latest technology for electronic navigation, a millionth of a second can put you a quarter of a mile off your position. You certainly don't want to fly in a jetliner where the pilot's idea of touching down on a runway is "close enough, give or take a second or two." You can miss whole runways in a half a second. Modern time may be a Tinker Toy god, but he's got us where it wants us.

The Measure of Time

The measurement of time is something new, even for humans. Time never needed keeping until man invented time keepers. Leave it to that upright, uptight, bipedal hominid with low back pain to worry about things like "leap seconds." Before clocks and official time keeping, fishing man kept track of time by things like smelt runs. Or salmon runs. Or white bass runs. The spawning runs of fish were, in ancient times, the best of clocks.

"All is well!" someone would shout, hiking up from the river. "The silver salmon are in!"

"Winter's coming," came the reply. "I'll get the nets ready, if you'll cut some wood. Smoked salmon again this winter!"

Then came sun dials, candles that burned down at a certain rate, and knotted ropes that, lighted on one end, smoldered at so many knots to the day-dark cycle. Finally, the pendulum clock was invented and, swinging away with the help of springs and weights and cogs and such, entire days, weeks and years could be observed, counted and logged. In the early days of clocks, however, synchrony of time was only a dream.

The first uniform time was ordered up in 1370 by King Charles V of France who, annoyed with church bells ringing at random all day and night because no one's time piece agreed with anyone else's, fired off a memo that all church bells in the city of Paris would be rung only at the top of the *same* hour. A rough translation from an annoyed king's original French read, "Synchronize your church bells, or by god heads will roll!" A quick bell-ringer's conference was held and all clocks were duly synchronized. The resulting relief from the constant din of church bells inspired Parisians to foist the idea of synchronized time off on the rest of us, and we've been following King Charles' directive ever since.

Time Is, Time Was and Turtle Time

As it turns out, nobody is too sure what time is. There are all kinds of ways to look at time: the present, the past, the rhythm of time, recollections of times past, imaginations of future time, and all sorts of other interpretations of time depending on where in the cosmos you happen to be casting from. Perceptions of time are easily distorted, by emotional states, for example, including the passions of fishing.

It is very difficult for we humans to get a good handle on the big stretches of time. The Earth was here, spinning round the sun for a couple of billion of years before life emerged. And should all life someday die out, the Earth will go right on spinning around in its orbit as if nothing much had happened. The entire beginning, middle and possible end of the story of life on this planet is but a single hiccup in the existence of our solar system. If the Milky Way had a spokesman, he might say of our fleeting time here, "So what?"

Of all the life forms that have come and gone and are still here, only we humans have evolved to the point where we can begin to grasp some notion of geological time. We have learned to measure it quite well. Consider that wind and rain alone will wear down any given mountain by one-tenth of a millimeter per year. Since we can measure millimeters, heights of mountains and years, we can now calculate that the tallest mountain on Earth could be flattened by wind and rain alone in a mere 10 million years. Since the earth is 4.5 billion years old, you can speed up the video in your mind's eye and imagine the surface of the Earth rising and falling over geological time like those breeze-driven waves undulating over your favorite bass pond.

Had he not first studied geology and imagined the time it takes to, say, raise sea beds into mountains, it is doubtful Charles Darwin would have grasped the idea that only slight variations in life forms from one generation to the next, over vast stretches of time, and when coupled with the engine of natural selection, must *necessarily* lead to the evolution of new and different species.

Darwin's genius is in part due to this humility of perspective. He did not suffer from a boulder-sized ego that placed man at the acme of all life forms. Rather, he saw *us* as *them*, and by them I mean the rest of the living world. Such a long and intelligent perspective on the nature of time enabled his insight into the history of life itself and, into the bargain, he was able to properly place man as a late arrival to the great speciation party.

Darwin's dangerous interpretation of Earth history is that we humans, compared to all the living things that have come and gone, are not so glorious and sublime as we would like to believe. Rather, we may be just another experiment in a long line of failed experiments.

As an example, I invite you to compare yourself to one of those slow, dumb, green turtles you see warming itself on a log in your favorite lake. Try to imagine that that turtle and his kin have survived in essentially the same form for 200 million years, or the equivalent time it would take to wear down twenty Mount Everests with wind and rain power alone.

Turtles have been giving it their best shot about 198.8 million years longer than *Homo sapiens* have been around. According to the fossil record, and comparing our imagined success with other life forms, it is highly doubtful we will survive the next 1 million years, let alone the next 200 million years.

The vast majority of species die out after a few hundred thousand years and are never heard from again. Unlike the turtle, we may already be on the short list for extinction. So, on those mornings when you're feeling fine and cocky and smart as a whip because you're a bigshot human being sitting atop the food chain as you cast lures past turtles to catch fish, show a little respect to Cousin Turtle. Or to Cousin Shark. Or to Cousin Mollusk. Or to Cousin Ant. Or to any number of other ancient, basically unchanged life forms that have proved themselves capable, not of a flashy beginning, but of the long grind, the true marathon of survival.

If we humans have difficulty imagining "Turtle-Time," we haven't had much luck understanding whatever human-time is. We have, however, tried to divide human-time into smaller and smaller fragments, perhaps as a way to dice it up into all its possible component parts for additional study. Each advance we make in the study of time seems to add to our worries about time, not subtract from them.

Not long ago I read that due to the Earth's rotation slowing down, the International Earth Rotation Service in Paris, France has approved that a "leap second" be officially inserted into our clock time on June 30, 1994. It seems those Parisians just can't let go, but I, for one, am glad someone is looking after these things.

Time, Emotions and One Version of Heaven

According to the people who study these things, the experience of time passing is a quite unique and individual thing. Under certain emotionally charged circumstances, the experience of time may even change time itself. To the fisherman who stumbles into one of those twilight zones when the fish are madly feeding, the experience may be that time ceases all together, resulting in such old standbys as, "Holy jumpin' catfish! Where did the time go!?"

Eternity can begin and end in such joyful moments. A string of joyful moments, frozen in time, would make a pretty good rendition of heaven, so allow me to digress from my subject for a minute, or maybe two minutes. Or three. I don't know how long it takes you to read a couple of paragraphs, so right away you can see that your perception of time may differ from my perception of time.

You do have a couple of minutes to spare, don't you?

You don't? Then put this book down immediately, get back to work and make some money!

Just kidding.

Fishermen's Heaven

Because good fishing and heaven ought necessarily to have a lot in common, I've wasted a little time designing an afterlife for anglers. Here's the draft plan.

Over in the "Big Bass and Trout Section" (you can fill in your favorite sport fish), God-fearing anglers would be allotted twelve hours of twilight per day instead of the usual one. This would give the Magic Hour the time it properly deserves. Another six hours would go to the dawn bite. The remaining six hours we'd just waste on things like great food, spirits (and I don't mean celestial ones), sleep and sex.

As most fishermen know, sex doesn't really take all that much time away from fishing, so we'd have plenty of time to take care of boats and tackle and such. I know this to be true about sex and time because one of my high school teachers once asked our social science class if " ... thirty minutes of sex was worth a lifetime of misery?" Given that opportunity, a fishing pal of mine shouted from the back of the room, "How do you make it last *that* long?" This caused Ms. Fox to experience a time warp herself. Judging from her sputtering red face, the next thirty seconds looked to take about three years. Time is, as the experts say, relative to one's emotional state.

Now, if you hadn't taken that extra minute for my digression, you might have missed Ms. Fox's experience of eternity. My pal and I never did, by the way, get an answer to the question.

How Fish Control Time

First, let's get the real culprits to bar. It is fish that cause fishing's black holes, not fishermen. As noted earlier, the perception of time is related to one's state of emotional arousal. Since fish arouse fishermen, it only makes perfect sense that fish cause distortions in time.

For example, a noisy surface-take can delay time for a couple of seconds. A solid hookup several more seconds. A strong running lunker can freeze time for entire minutes. Casting to a school of bait-chasing bluefish can cause time to cease for up to an hour. While the tap of a bluegill may stall time for only a nanosecond, a filibustering blue marlin can lock time down for a whole afternoon.

You see what biting fish do to time. A second here, a second there, a minute on that fish, three on the next, an hour given over to a hot crappie bite and, pretty soon, the angler is nothing more than a cosmic wanderer — lost somewhere in the warp of time and space and pulled hither and yon by finny black holes.

I know this to be true. As a small boy, my father took my brothers and me on high mountain trout trips for up to two weeks. We caught wild trout on dry flies from dawn till dark. It was not at all uncommon on those trips to lose entire days. Like Einstein's space traveler who, traveling beyond the speed of light, returns to Earth without having aged, my family and me came home from the High Sierras younger than when we left. Had I been able to go fishing as much as I'd wanted, I'd still be 14 years old.

Why You Must Defend Your Fishing-Time

Fishing-time is slippery, but if you hope to have any, you must first catch it, keep it, study it and know the face of its enemies. Here are a few of those faces.

Try to imagine a time when there was no little hand and no big hand. No sweep second hand. No quartz crystal clocks. No atomic clocks that, oscillating exactly 9,192,631,771 times inside a cesium atom, defines for the world what one second is. Imagine a time, not 600 years ago, when time was tracked by spring, fall, summer and winter, where hunger alone spelled time to eat, and where we stayed attuned to the natural rhythm of day and dark and twilight and moons and fish runs to keep our appointed rounds.

We have, like Dr. Frankenstein's monster, created time. We've shaped it, built it, laid its foundations, agreed upon its general outline and dimension and now, having sent a bolt of electricity through the monster, the thing stalks and haunts us. Relentlessly. To find time to fish, we must somehow kill the monster.

We are totally preoccupied with time and speed. Kids complain their parents talk too slow. Our faxes are too slow. Our computers are too slow. Our bass boats are too slow. Whatever line you're standing is, the other one is moving faster. Time is being divvied up into smaller and smaller fragments, creating an impending sense of urgency. Whoever the hell invented the nanosecond has, in my view, a lot to answer for.

The Harvard economist, Juliet Schorr, in her book *The Overworked American*, says that since the 1950s Americans are working, on average, six more weeks per year just to keep up the standard of living they enjoyed just thirty years ago.

A marriage counselor these past twenty-five years, I know two-career couples who are so busy they have to make an appointment with each other to make love. And then they get a 20 percent no show. In the last couple of years I've begun to change my practice of marriage counseling. I've stopped treating busy people and started treating their appointment books. "Give me your appointment books," I say early on, "and I'll show what's probably wrong with your marriage."

The most common complaint for too little lovemaking: too tired from working too hard.

The most common complaint for too little fishing: too little time left over from working too hard.

When you are too tired and too busy to make love or go fishing, something ugly is gaining on you.

I saw a highly successful, too-busy, too-tired, Rolex-wearing businessman in my office not long ago. After getting acquainted and sizing up his dilemma, I asked him to take a full minute to think before answering the following question, "What is it you truly want out of life?" He thought a long moment and then said: "A small heart attack. Just enough to have to stop working, but not so bad I couldn't still go fishing."

He had money and success, and lots of both. But he had been so conditioned to the idea that he had to keep running as fast as he could to stay in place, the only way he could take a break was to get sick. The White Rabbit had been after him for a long time. So, therapeutically of course, we shot the White Rabbit. Right through his Rolex.

Fishing in the River of Time

If our wristwatches have become little death reminders that time is always running out then it seems to me that fishing might save us yet. By turning time over to the fishes, we have a chance to return to the slower beat of natural time. In the lingo of time, we might find a way to unwind before our springs snap.

I will grant that my notion of time-distorting, fishy black holes is wacky, but I wage this argument not so much out of some altruistic need to prevent tragedies of misunderstanding between tardy fishermen and their friends and lovers, but to help anglers everywhere take back control of their lives.

I have, quite consciously, allowed rising trout, hungry bass and willing walleyes to interfere with my sense of time passing. I have intentionally ignored my wristwatch. I have headed home only when it was too dark to see, or the bite had died, rather than when the big hand told me to. Despite a few rope burns from arriving late to some damned function or another, you will never hear me complain of too little time to go fishing.

There's an old saying that you can't step into a river in the same place twice. The same is true of time. Most of us believe that you cannot go back in time, and that you cannot go forward in time. But can you? What if, as Einstein said, time is relative and it is the beholder of time that decides its reality?

I was discussing this very point with a fisherman not long ago. When I asked him about his most memorable fish, he instantly closed his eyes, transported himself to a river in Virginia on a snowy Christmas day, cast out a black Rooster Tail, and felt the hit of feisty rainbow trout that, dancing on it's tail through falling snow, pulled the guy across five states and ten years as he spoke to me. "Ohhh," said the fellow, trying to describe his journey through space and time with his eyes closed, "I still get goose bumps when I see that fish."

I checked his skin for goose bumps. He had them. "Do you go there often?" I asked.

"You bet," he said. "Every time something starts going bad on the job, I just close my eyes and I'm gone."

Great fishing memories are living proof that the theory of

relativity is correct; all you have to do to travel backward in time is close your eyes and be there, and that's faster than the speed of light.

So on that evening long ago when my fishing pal was pulled into one bassy black hole after another and missed his daughter's wedding rehearsal, his reality was just as real and valid as, say, the reality of all those people waiting in a church somewhere.

Once you grasp the true nature of fishing-time, it becomes quite clear that, in the case of my friend, he was not actually late at all. Rather, the function was early.

Despite my every effort to describe the quantum physics of time and space and a hot bass bite, the explanation did not play well at the chapel, or so I gathered from the number of purse straps that had been fashioned into nooses.

On the upside, churches are sacred ground and murders are not permitted; otherwise, I might have lost yet another fishing pal to the gross misunderstanding of non-fishermen who, I'm sorry to say, have never zipped through time and space on one of those special magic carpets issued to every true angler.

Time, Money and the Rolex in the Center of the Universe.

I don't know, frankly, if someone somewhere is keeping track of true time, the time by which the universe is kept. They say the Big Bang got us started some 12 billion or so years ago and that, eventually, all matter will reconverge some day into some great black hole from whence it began and then, perhaps, time and space will cease all together.

Today there are other theories of time and space. Do we live in a bubble of time and space, or on the surface of one? Is this the only universe or are there, as some believe, many more, perhaps even an infinity of other universes? If so, maybe we came to this universe, to this time and space, from another universe, from another time and space. We know some of the laws of our universe, and we are living proof that these laws not only work reliably, but are the only immutable, natural laws that would permit life as we understand it.

Consider that if light traveled at only a few miles per second slower than its standard of 186,000 miles per second, or if the laws of gravity were off a few pounds, the universe we evolved in wouldn't even exist. It would have to be a different universe. Not only would there be no sun and no planet Earth complete with its sun-warmed home waters, but there would be no fish or fishing.

If our universe did begin with the Big Bang, and this particular theory proves true, or even if it doesn't, our little planet is still scheduled for renovation when we are finally engulfed by our own exploding sun, at which time all life will perish in a great cataclysm of fire and which will, no doubt, have an adverse effect on the evening bite. That is just one more good reason to stop wasting time, put this book down and go fishing.

If the cosmos do collapse, perhaps the river of time will begin to flow all over again. Or maybe, whoever put the universe inside one of those glass globes with the phony snow will tire of shaking things up to see the white stuff settle and fall throughout the galaxies, and will just put the toy down and go fishing Herself.

We need a river of time. Without a river of time flowing by to fish in and to wade in and to keep us aware that our lifetimes are but a single tick somewhere, we run the risk of letting what time we do have pass unexamined. And this is the greatest tragedy of all.

When you think back over your life all you really get to keep and savor are the "good times." Maybe all the rest is junk. When your popper suddenly disappears in a geyser of exploding water, and you pause to inscribe an indelible memory into your neural networks, is it any wonder the outside clock stops while this most important inside mission is accomplished? I think not.

Question: What if time is *not* money?

What if I said that no amount of money can buy back one single hour of time you could have spent fishing with a son, or a granddaughter, or a brother or best friend? What if I said that what is wrong with money these days is that it costs too much time?

Time to go fishing. Time to be with your family. Time to make love, time to enjoy a sunrise, time to read a book, and time to pause and wonder. There is no meantime, no in-between time, just time.

So go fishing. Now. Often. Kiss your lover, hug your children, and hold on tight while you ask yourself that very serious question: Do I really want a Rolex, and am I willing to spend the only life I have to get it?

Take your time with the answer.

*It's a funny old world — a man's lucky if he
gets out of it alive."*

— **W.C. Fields**

Fish Hard, Live Long

Despite the view that dying is in poor taste these days, ten out of ten anglers persist in doing it. The trick to a long fishing life, then, is to put this dying business off for as many fishing seasons as possible. Since it is patently not true that "Old fishermen never die; they just smell that way," my aim here is to share the secrets of how to fish hard and live long.

So let me make a short cast here about how to extend your life span.

I'll start a slow retrieve.

I think I just felt something.

Was that a pickup?

A tug?

Let me take in the slack and lift the old rod tip.

Like this!

Still reading? Excellent.

One on!

Fishing in the Eye of Death

A couple of summers ago I was consulted by a woman whose father had been diagnosed with terminal cancer. He'd gotten in his four-score-and-ten, but his tippet was frayed and about to part.

"He's gone to Alaska salmon fishing every August for years and years," she began. "Dad loves fishing, but he's wondering if he should go this year. If he has the strength and isn't in too much pain, do you think he should?"

"Does he want to go?"

"Of course he wants to go," said the woman.

"Then he should go," I replied.

"But, what if his doctor doesn't think he should go?"

"Find him another doctor."

Fortunately, I was not involved in her father's case and didn't know beans about his medical status. I explained that my opinion as to whether or not he should go fishing was entirely subjective, entirely biased, and worth just about what she had paid for it: nothing. On the other hand, I could make a reasonably good guess about her father's psychological status and how, if he had much pain, a fishing trip might well offset some of his suffering and even reduce his need for analgesics. A fishing trip might even extend his life a few days or weeks.

More important, chances were very good that he would get tight with one more wild salmon which, in this great human quest to find true purpose and meaning in the cosmos, is about as close to *it* as an angler can ever hope to get.

Before this chapter is out, I will explain why I gave this advice, everything I know about how to fish hard and live long, and even how fishing can be used to control pain. Then, I'll unbutton you and gently release you back into your more natural habitat.

But before I plunge into the many secrets of a long fishing-life, you need to know at the outset that while I am a specialist in geriatric mental health, I am not a physician. Physicians get all sorts of training in anatomy and physiology and biology, whereas psychologists stick pretty much to everything between the ears. We like to know what goes inside the old noodle in terms of thoughts and emotions and attitudes and such, but we don't like to wear rubber gloves to work. If we're Ph.D.s, we live in constant fear that someone in acute cardiac distress might mistake us for R.D.s (real doctors).

My lack of qualifications to make health recommendations hardly carries the weight of the American Medical Society, let alone my mother. I knew I got the wrong kind of graduate degree when I came home from work one night to catch my son answering the phone. "Yes, this is Dr. Quinnett's residence, but he's not the kind of doctor that does anyone any real good."

But we psychologists do know a few things about aging, about mind-body relationships, about the stressors that make people sick, about things that shorten one's allotted span, and something about what people can do to add a few fishing days to this wonderful journey of life. Since this book is entitled *Darwin's Bass*, part of the approach I will take here is from the perspective of the new science of "Darwinian medicine."

Darwinian medicine is a combination of evolutionary biology and modern medical and psychological understanding. The first book of its kind has only just been published, and the ink is hardly dry on *Why We Get Sick*, by Randolph M. Nesse, M.D. and George C. Williams, Ph.D. Their perspective is fresh, fascinating, even revolutionary.

There are a number of things you must know to avoid dying before you really have to. Of all the things you can do to get in an extra fishing season or two or four or ten, the first is to get smart about what makes you sick and why. When you know this, the "to do" part starts to fall into place.

Why We Age

Let me clear something up right away. No one knows exactly why we grow old and die. With some 300 theories of aging kicking around, the gerontologists do not even agree on what "aging" is. Lots of research is going on about how we age and what we can do to avoid getting old or, at least, feeling and acting old. French researchers have recently isolated and are celebrating the synthesis of dehydroepiandrosterone (DHEA), a hormone linked to the onset of aging. If you measure its content in the body, DHEA decreases with advancing years. By taking the drug in replacement doses, the French think they've found the Hormone of Eternal Youth.

Older volunteer subjects who took DHEA for a year in

this country reported increased psychological well-being, improved ability to handle stress, better sleep, less joint pain and, for the men, loss of fat and an increase in lean muscle mass. Still in the testing phase, DHEA apparently does not increase your sex drive.

In this country, strong evidence is building that, when you look at all the data, we are as old as we let ourselves be. Despite the fact we obviously inherit a couple of Grim Reaper genes, there are lots of things we can do to improve our quality of life so that we can get in somewhere between a little and a lot more fishing-time. We may not be able to control the final result of life, but how we live that life can make all the difference. The outer limits of our longevity may have as much to do with our psychology as our physiology.

Death, Numbers and Genes

Most people think of death as something you approach slowly, through gradual aging and increasing vulnerability to disease.

Death happens to old people, not us. No matter our age, we do not see ourselves as old. When we are 20, old is 40. When we are 40, old is 60. And when we are 60, old is 80. When we are 80, old is George Burns. Except for tragic accidents and rare diseases, death is what happens to people older than us. This truth is self-evident until the day we die, at which time the joke is on us.

While advanced years and death go together, lots of people die young, usually of something other than an infection. You can boat without a life preserver, wade too deep, mistake a rattlesnake for your wading staff, and do all sorts of dumb things to get yourself killed before you really needed to check out.

Check-out time for normal, healthy humans is at most 115 years. Only a few make it beyond this mark. Still, if you start fishing in childhood and you take good care of yourself, you could theoretically get in upwards of eighty or ninety fishing seasons, which is a lot better than a sharp hook in the ear.

By age 80, half of us will have reeled in and crossed over that final shoal, and the rest won't be feeling all that well. But a few of us will still be feeling fine and fishing. This is the club you want to join. Interestingly, if you don't die of an accident, heart disease, cancer or Alzheimer's by age 75, the chances begin to improve that you will live well into your 90s and beyond. A few at this advanced age will enjoy quite good health, including the ability to hook and land large trout.

The first thing to do to join this exclusive group is pick parents whose parents were long-lived. Other things being equal, the best predictor of a long life is to be born into a gene pool where natural selection has determined everyone should be a little taller, a little smarter, a little better looking and live at least 100 years. Because natural selection only cares about reproductive fitness, such a gene pool should also be a little sexier.

To underscore the role of genes in lifespan, Michael Rose at the University of California has selectively bred fruit flies, pairing only the most long-lived flies to mate. Over many generations of fruit flies, he has now produced a "Methuselah Fly," one that lives twice as long as ordinary fruit flies. I suppose now that term limits for congressmen has once again gone down to defeat, we can be thankful Michael doesn't breed politicians.

You should pick a gene pool that includes no susceptibility to cancer, heart disease, manic-depression, alcoholism, who-knows-what-all-else and especially myopia. Myopia genes are a very bad choice for fishermen since, by middle age and after all that fly tying, you will find it extremely difficult to slip a 6X leader through the eye of No. 20 trout fly, if you can even see the hole in the eye of a No. 20 hook.

So, to live long, be strong, and have perfect vision at age 50, pick first-rate genes.

You forgot to do this?

Too bad. I certainly hope you didn't compound this oversight by choosing to be male.

Everyone knows females live longer. We'll get to why in a moment. If you've made a couple of poor choices thus far, then you'd better support the hope and promise of genetics research to bail you out of any gene-driven illness that might be gaining on you.

The data on which genes to avoid are still coming in, thanks to what will clearly be the greatest research project of all time, the Human Genome Project. The entire library of the human genome will take years to decipher and read, but we already know enough about some of the less desirable genes and which ones we should, might, must terminate through abortion to avoid premature disease. Testing for sorry genes is already a reality.

This knowledge, by the way, has pitched us neck deep into the greatest cultural, religious, medical, ethical and societal debate in history. In some ways the less you know about genetics research the better you will sleep. In other ways, the future of molecular biology and the promise of 21st century medicine has never been brighter, especially for those who bought their genes off the sales table under the blue light special.

In my first book on the psychology of fishing, *Pavlov's Trout*, I reviewed the typical sources of stress that arise when your problems exceed your resources to cope with them. I tried to make suggestions and recommendations about how the average angler might better deal with the backlashes of life — from major catastrophes to life changes to the daily grind and hassles of life in the harried lane. I will not repeat those recommendations here, but rather begin with some psychological perspectives on living long and well, and then move onto other matters for which I am not qualified to give advice but will give it anyway.

Aging Salmon, Aging Mayflies and Aging Anglers

If growing older increases your risk of death, why bother growing old? Because you have to, that's why. Mother Nature says so.

While no one fully understands all the mechanisms of aging, it is clear that natural selection has shaped most of them. Barring disease or tragedy, the life span of all living things has an outer limit. We humans have only now begun to push that limit for ourselves; that's the reason folks over 65 are the fastest growing age group in America. One in eight of us is now over 65. By the year 2040, there will be somewhere between 1.3 million and 4 million Americans in the 100-year-or-older club, which suggests all of us anglers need to get busy thinking about designing more fishing access for elders.

In the wild, almost nothing dies of old age. I have spent thousands and thousands of hours in the woods and fields and have never seen an old, stumbling, dottering deer. And I doubt you have either. Why? Because you only have to be one step slower than other deer in your herd to be picked off by a hungry predator. The same goes for aging quail, fading foxes and old yellow perch. Predators specialize in slow, sick or aged protein. You enjoy old wine; predators enjoy old protein. Nature has no tolerance for decrepitude, no nursing homes for the infirm.

Humans, on the other hand, enjoy all sorts of protections from natural selection, so many that some have begun to wonder if we haven't defeated the oldest law of nature. Except for the threat of microbes and each other, we humans generally enjoy the opportunity to age well past our reproductive years and join that special Geritol and Supphose self-help group called On-and-on-and-on-and-on.

Even if we manage to avoid predation, viral attack, infection or some other traumatic death early in life, our bodies eventually do wear out; heart, lungs, kidneys, even our casting arms. And when these sundry parts wear out, they tend to wear out as did Oliver Wendell Holmes' "one-hoss shay" that:

Went to pieces all at once,
All at once and nothing first,
Just as bubbles do when they burst.

Salmon and mayflies go to pieces all at once, just as people do, only their journey is speeded up. The greatest part of the mayfly's lifespan is spent waiting for an invitation to dance. When the invitation comes, the mayfly swims to the surface, spreads its wings, grabs its partner, dances, mates, has babies and dies, all on the same day. If a mayfly takes too long to get to know another mayfly before having sex, it spins out of the gene pool at sundown, hits the water and gets kissed by a trout.

Like the mayfly, salmon meet, mate and die in quick time.

The salmon spends its entire life as fry, fingerling, adolescent and young adult aimed at a single function: to return to its birth place, reproduce and die. Both mayfly and salmon age with a vengeance.

Absent a benevolent, all-knowing God, who cares if the salmon ages and dies quickly? When you consider that a salmon is just a salmon egg's way of making more salmon eggs, dying for and right after sex makes perfect sense. Nothing swims faster or jumps higher to navigate swift currents, or is more single-minded of purpose, than an adult salmon on its way home to spawn. Only mature, strong salmon need apply for the mission; all others will be selected out.

Not counting its value as a sport fish, the adult salmon is a kind of all-purpose river vehicle, designed and built to transport the most precious cargo of all: more salmon genes. If the fish doesn't get killed in a turbine or caught by gill nets or hooked, tailed and clubbed by the priest, an adult salmon can be counted on to not only deliver the goods on time, but to the right address.

Humans have a similar program. Our biological programs run out after a hundred years or so, and unless the French researchers are onto something with DHEA, no amount of medicine, spring water or prayer is going to make any difference. Our biological programs start winding down, not at age 50 when all the jokes about hair loss and impotence help cover our fear of aging, but shortly after we peak and pass our sexual prime. After this period we enjoy, thank goodness, a more gentle slope into that dark night.

Unlike salmon, we get to spawn more than once. Or at least a few of us get lucky more than once. But just as with any other physical activity, we pass our prime fairly early and start down the other side of fitness before we're 30. This rule holds true for marathon runners, basketball players and for those who remember spawning three times a day.

Each additional year of life adds to our susceptibility to illness and the body's growing inability to quickly repair itself. Like a post-spawn salmon, we gradually fall victim to the bugs, which is why in the pre-penicillin years, pneumonia was called the "old man's friend." But with modern antibiotics — and providing we don't lose our war with them — we have all kinds of time to take it easy and gradually shift down to dock fishing and storytelling.

Wearing out all at once, or senescence, is not a disease in itself, but with increasing age comes increasing frailty. It's as if our tether to life were sizing down from a 3X to a 4X to a 5X, 6X, 7X, gone. At extreme age, the first little tug from an infection, or a fall, or a failure in our environmental comfort zones can allow us to break off and be gone. It's probably just as well. I've never understood the desire to live forever once your quality of life is gone and you can't go fishing.

How to Keep Your Leader Strong

One way to live long is to fish hard. Exercising, lifting weights, plenty of casting, and fighting bigger and bigger fish are all recommended. Researchers have found that those elders who pumped iron three times a week more than doubled their muscle strength, increased their walking speed and stairclimbing power and, as a result, became less dependent on walkers, canes and such. Older members of running clubs, compared to elders who don't run, have lower mortality rates and less disability.

Exercise not only reduces stress but keeps you from toppling over while hiking down the riprap to the water's edge and breaking something important. Walking alone is not enough to achieve maximum health status, you need to push a little weight around to build muscle tissue and bone mass. The very latest research shows exercise also improves your sex life.

What more do you need to know?

Want better sex, bigger fish and a longer fishing life?

Lift heavy fish, at least three times a week and fish *hard*!

Get to Know the Little Killers

It is important to understand that we are in an arms race with the bugs. It is a race without end. Every living thing is in the same arms race. Right now we humans are in an especially tight arms race with killer viruses, among the most dangerous of which include the microorganisms that cause: AIDS, Lyme disease, Rift Valley fever, Lassa fever, Legionnaire's disease, the hanta virus, dengue fever and who-knows-what-other bugs out there changing themselves into more virulent, more transmittable forms of infection through natural selection.

If one largemouth bass has a little better vision because of a lucky toss of the genetic dice, then some of the perch in his pond had better enjoy some genetic variation in coloration so that at least some of the little perch with this unique and different camouflage will escape detection and being eaten. These hard-to-see perch will be selected *in* while the easy-to-spot perch are selected *out*. This dance, this arms race between predator and prey, goes on and on and on.

The same goes for us. While we have mostly won our race with the big fish, the tiger and the grizzly bear, we still have our hands full with the little guys. Viruses have a tremendous potential to mutate and adapt to new challenges quickly. The HIV virus is changing its genetic coding all the time, improving its methods of transmission and survival.

As I write this, we are on the verge of losing the arms race with the microbes we thought we had won just a few years ago. Cut your finger with a filleting knife, don't get the wound sterilized, cleaned up and closed up, and you could end up cooling out somewhere in a morgue. According to my old friend and one-time county coroner, fishing is very poor in a morgue.

Brainless little bacteria like E. coli consider us lunch. We evolve and create antibiotic toxins like penicillin to kill them, while they fight back, survive and evolve to kill us. This is not revenge, just survival by natural selection.

Biologists call this predator-prey relationship between big bass and small perch, and big humans and small bacteria, the "Red Queen Principle." It was explained to Alice in Lewis Carroll's story as follows, "Now, *here*, you see, it takes all the running you can do, just to keep in the same place."

The "same place" is good health, and that leads to long life and more fishing seasons. Microbiologists and drug companies are working night and day just to keep the human race in the same place. The odds of whether we win or lose our battle with the microbes has recently been said to be no better than fifty-

fifty.

So, avoid hooking or cutting yourself, drink bottled water in foreign countries, follow doctor's orders and take *all* your antibiotics as prescribed when you get an infection. Taking antibiotics for less than the prescribed time only selects out the weak microorganisms and allows the stronger ones to build up, fortify, resist and strike back.

I once met a microorganism as a boy when I fell against a boulder on a fishing trip and broke open the skin on my shin-bone. My father bandaged me up, but after swimming in a public pool some days later, bacteria got through the wound and I ended up with blood poisoning. For a time, I was a very sick boy. Since that painful, leg-threatening episode, I have always held bacteria in high regard and tried to give them the respect they deserve.

Fish Hard, but Don't Be Dumb

Almost everyone reading this book will have known someone who died young, usually in an accident, combat or by their own hand. This will almost always be a boy or young man. The world over, men and boys die earlier than females, by an average of about seven years. Some recent research suggests that while you can fish hard, you need to be careful, cautious and conscientious to live long.

The longest human psychological study still running is on "Termites." These Termites are not a form of sunfish bait, but rather what a study group of 856 boys and 672 girls grew up to call themselves over the more than seventy years since child-hood. They have remained the subjects of the late Lewis Terman, one of Stanford University's most famous psychologists. First gathered together in the 1920s, the Termites are the most studied group of people on the planet surface and they continue to teach the rest of us about life.

By 1991, half of Terman's men had died, while one-third of the women had. A research team at Stanford has studied the psychological data collected decades ago and now contends that dependable, truthful children who think about the consequences of their behavior before they act survive a few years longer as adults than children who are impulsive and unreliable.

This finding was especially true of conscientious boys, who lived two to four years longer than their impulsive counterparts, and more so if they came from steady, non-divorced parents. Interestingly, conscientiousness accounted for greater longevity than systolic blood pressure, cholesterol concentrations, exercise and diet. To once again verify what Grandma said, "For Pete's sake, look before you leap."

We know from all sorts of other data and personal experience that men are dangerous to themselves and engage in more high-risk behaviors, which helps account for why women outlive us. Boys who don't ask how deep the water is before wading in sometimes drown. On average, we males drive faster, drink more and gamble with our lives far more often than women.

Just being male puts you in a high-stakes game. Of those mammals who must compete to sire offspring, males have shorter lives. Young guys in rut not only fight over females and knock each other off in the battle to reproduce, but we fish, fight and fornicate as if there were no tomorrow.

One theory about why males die younger is that, since you can't get into the gene pool without a date, we fellas wear ourselves out competing for access to females. Money, feathers, huge antlers — all these go into the cost/benefit equation. If your costs run too high, you may end up with too few reserves to fight off things like bacteria, infections and young whippersnappers. For every male there comes a time when even old age and treachery cannot overcome youth and skill.

Perhaps we males should take the advice of the old fisherman, "Son, don't spend yourself entirely on women. Find one good one and stick by her."

Suicide, Sex and the Single Fisherman

An expert on suicide, I should also point out that with only a couple of exceptions, men the world over kill themselves at four times the rate of the fairer sex. We do this for all sorts of reasons, but the most common ones are those associated with reproductive success, untreated depression and getting ourselves into situations from which there is no escape.

Women tend to marry up in class and status — anthropologists call this hypergamy — and tend to avoid men without prospects, big antlers or on their way down the status ladder. As my wife says of this observation, "Why waste time with a loser?"

Young men tend to become suicidal when they lose the girl, the job, the money and the hope of ever getting some — in about that order. Without a girl, job or money, one's prospects for swimming in the gene pool are nil.

By far the most common dynamic for male suicide is this: Woman leaves man, man leaves planet. It is mostly young men and, in America, old white guys who are in the highest risk groups for suicide. While the most complicated of all human behavior to understand, suicide is usually too much a solution to any problem or set of problems. But in the minds of too many men, the answer to the following questions cannot be found: What is a fellow to do when he has no woman, no job, no money, no fun, no purpose, no meaning, no pride, no health, no joy, no duty, no sense of humor, no hope and no one to go fishing with?

The answer too many come up with is to stop the pain and suffering with a bullet.

I've worked with many depressed, alcoholic, miserable, suicidal, older men. Those that had once been fishermen all had one thing in common: They had stopped fishing. Into the bargain, they had lost touch with their old fishing buddies. If you lose touch with your fishing pals and stop fishing, you give up hope. If you give up hope, you stop living. To live long and well, you must never give up hope and fishing. This is a subject I will detail more thoroughly in the last chapter.

Women have things to worry about, too. But killing yourself over a man isn't usually one of them. The best protection against suicide for a woman is — despite the suicidal behavior of young girls jilted by their boyfriends — not a man to look after her, but responsibility for children. "If having one child protects a woman against suicide, what would ten do?" asked a Scandinavian research team recently. You guessed it, the more children you have the less likely you are to kill yourself, or as I prefer to interpret the data, "The little old woman who lived in the shoe had so many children she didn't have time to even think about suicide."

Longevity numbers worldwide do not lie. Women outlive men. That means they end up with not only the fishing boat but all the money. As I have long been suspicious, the female vessel is the better built of the two, both physically and psychologically. Perhaps the reason Mother Nature favors females is that she is, after all, a female.

I could be wrong. Men might live longer if, for example, they were better fathers. And I don't mean donating a few sperm to the cause, I mean being a father for the long haul. If women benefit from caring for children, couldn't men as well? What if men — rather than abandoning their young like some members of the lizard family — stayed with them, cared for them, raised them, and took them in their arms once in a while and loved them? Would this not help protect men from premature death by suicide? From alcoholism? From one damned thing or another?

Of course it could.

Alone? Isolated? Depressed?

Wondering if life is worth living?

Consider this. What if I told you that by taking a kid fishing you could live a little longer? The research on death and dying shows that people with duties, obligations and responsibilities to others put off dying until their chores are done. By taking a kid fishing, you'd have to put off getting sick. By taking a kid fishing you have put off dying for another day, or week or season. By taking a kid fishing you could be taking the psychological equivalent of a hope pill.

It can be your kid, someone's else's kid, or a whole bunch of kids from a group home or from some inner city. Kids are not merely the hope of the world, they are the future of fishing. There is nothing wrong with a little enlightened self-interest, so be selfish and live a little longer. Go ahead, take a kid fishing.

Save Your Skin and Other Important Parts

Cancer is a collective term that describes all sorts of renegade cells that your body creates everyday. Any part of your body has the potential to produce abnormal cells, but depending on diet and lifestyle, some parts have more potential than others. Mostly these abnormal cells get eaten up, and that's the last you hear of them. But when your immune systems fails, these renegades can go to work in their own interest, divide and get bigger and stronger. If something doesn't stop them, they can kill you off. As my father said of his last battle with cancer, "I'm fighting a war here, Paul, a war." Not a medical man, Dad was right on in his description.

The best way to avoid cancer is to die young, before you get it. In Stone Age times not many fishermen died of cancer because not many people made it to 60 years, and most never made it to 40. When you consider that the human body is composed of 10 trillion cells, that these cells are exposed to all sorts of radiation, toxins, air-born particulates, abnormal diets, high and unnatural concentrations of things like nicotine and alcohol and fat, it's amazing that we don't get cancer earlier and more often. The price of youth and vigor in our century is often bought at the price of cancer later on. All things considered, though, this is still a good deal.

To get in more fishing, every angler can take the usual and customary precautions to delay cancer as long as possible. Avoid heavy drinking, give up tobacco, skip the heavy fats, pass on the charbroiled burgers, and don't hang around x-ray machines unless you're wearing your lead waders. But perhaps the most important thing fishermen need to do is cover up.

Because our lifestyles as fishermen put us out in the sun more than most, anglers suffer a high incidence of skin cancer, especially if we're light-skinned. Even though it is curable if caught in the early stages, skin cancer kills one American every hour, and according to recent reports, skin cancer is killing more Americans than lung cancer, breast cancer and prostate cancer. To save your skin, it helps to have a lot of pigment in the outer skin to protect the underlying tissue. A suntan is nothing more than an inducible defense against the sun's radiation.

Evolutionary biologists point to a loss of melanin, or pigment, in those humans who moved out of our birth place in sunny Africa to the northern climes of Europe and Asia. Thanks to cloudy skies and having to cover up with animal skins to stay warm in the colder climates, darker, protective skin gradually bleached out like those pink, colorless catfish you find in the bowels of subterranean caves.

Had a European living in a cave returned to Africa at the end of the Stone Age to go fishing with a cousin, he might have been met with, "Holy cow, man! What the hell happened to your skin?"

Pale Europeans and young trout are especially vulnerable to strong light rays. Organisms unaccustomed to bright light have no natural defense against it, as many a fish biologist learned in the early days of trout hatcheries when exposing fertilized trout eggs to fluorescent lights caused massive mortality. Trout eggs are supposed to mature among layers of rocks and pebbles in shady trout streams, not under the bright light of an artificial sun. Similarly, we are now experiencing rapidly increasing rates of the worst kind of skin cancers among fair-skinned Europeans, not all that long out of their caves and furs.

Think about it. We work five long days in artificially lighted caves, otherwise known as factories and office buildings. Then we rush outdoors on the weekends to fish. Absorbing high, intense doses of solar radiation for hours and hours, we hammer our unprotected skin cells with ultraviolet light that depletes the skin's immune response. Burning holes in the only skin you'll ever have puts you in a special class of stupid, and possibly in a cancer ward.

The majority of skin cancers are quite common, and most are not the malignant little bastards called melanomas. These little killers start out as tiny black moles, oozing dark spots and such. Dangerous beasties, you don't want to get even a little one, let alone give it a little time to develop. Malignant melanomas can seed themselves all over the body and are on the rise everywhere in fair-skinned folks. The sunnier the climate, the higher rate. Australian fishermen have five times the rate of Scottish fishermen. Since these suckers move fast and kill quick, the best thing to do if you are in the least suspicious of something on your skin, is to run, not walk, to your nearest doctor.

According to dermatologists, it's a good idea to have family members check each other's skin for changes in moles, splotches or anything unusual, the same way you look for ticks after an outing in tick country. As sun worshipers have known for centuries, you must not only honor the orb that gives you life, but you must respect it. So cover up.

Attitude is All

We now know from a great deal of new research in how the mind, body and environment all work together that any perceived split between these entities is a phony split. All things are connected. Since you cannot have an illness or accident without an attitude toward it, perhaps now you can see why conscientious kids live longer, and why those fishermen who take care of and maintain their bodies like fine fishing reels end up fishing a little longer than the rest.

Life is risky, but risk is always manageable. As the Buddha said, life is suffering, but suffering passes, and so too does the need to kill oneself or engage in dangerous, life-threatening behavior. Life is growing older, but *how* we grow old is up to us. And when the end comes, *and it will come*, the best way to meet death is with an attitude — one that grins and says, "Screw you. I fished hard!"

Perhaps now you can see that the advice I gave to the woman about her dying father was not without merit. He did go fishing one last time to his beloved salmon river. He experienced little enough pain, had a wonderful time, and returned home in good humor the first day in September. He died together with the last of the run of king salmon.

You have to be smart to fish long, and in my view you have to have a sense of humor as well. If you don't have a sense of humor you should probably go right out and buy one before it's too late. A light perspective on living and dying is at least as essential as food, water and fishing.

One of the oldest-lived women in the world, Jeanne Calment of France, recently celebrated her 120th birthday. Unable to walk due to a broken hip and blind by her own choice to not have cataract surgery, when asked what kind of future she expected, she quipped, "A very short one."

Her secret to a long life, "I took pleasure when I could."

Translation: Don't take yourself seriously, keep laughing and fish often.

Now, then, I'll just remove this hook so you can swim away and rest up. Maybe I'll hook you again in the next chapter.

And the end of all our exploring
Will be to arrive where we started
And to know the place for the first time.
— T. S. Eliot, *Four Quartets*

Sex, Hope and the
Psychology of Fishing

Actually, there is not much sex in this last chapter. I just wanted to make sure I could hook you one last time and keep you hooked. Sometimes when I have a really good fish on, I will pull up on the rod one last time to make sure the steel is well set. Consider the mention of sex in the title here as that extra jerk you just felt.

Actually, I learned the value of putting a little sex in your title way back in 1983 when I wrote a little story for *Sports Afield* entitled, "Sex and the Single Fisherman." There wasn't much sex in that story either, but according to the folks who analyze magazine readership, "Sex and the Single Fisherman" was the most read outdoor story in the summer of 1983. I don't know what this says about fishermen and their sex lives, but it helps explain why bass plugs in the shape of hula girls are among the most sought after fishing collectibles.

There is, however, a relationship between sex, hope and fishing, and also a relationship between fishing and love, fishing and passion, and especially fishing and hope. When you put all these together and learn how to make sex, hope and fishing work for you, then you have the most powerful formula for the good life ever devised.

So, with the hook well set, let me guide you through the lily pads toward a new understanding of the evolutionary psychology of angling.

You may be thinking, "Hey, can this guy really deliver?"

Well, of course not. I promise you this final integration with the full knowledge that I'm not at all sure what the hell I'm talking about. Ph.D. stands for Piled Higher and Deeper, not Powerfully Helpful Director. I don't take myself very seriously, and neither should you. On the other hand, I have read an awful pile of books, listened to thousands of lectures, and am old enough to know that despite their credentials, no one else knows what the hell they are talking about either. Somehow this truth is both frightening and strangely comforting.

But you're hooked now, so you'll just have to come along for the ride.

I do promise you this: If you listen up you may find a bit more time to go fishing, a few more reasons to hope and a few more seasons to fish. With all this going for you, even your sex life could improve.

Sex and Fishing

Let's get the gratuitous sex and fishing stuff cleared up right away. First, good sex and good fishing both require passion. The only thing worse than passionless sex is passionless fishing. Passion expands our allotted time and can consume us into the bargain. For a time when I was young I was so passionate about fishing I paid little attention to other sports. I didn't know ball scores. I didn't know ball players. I didn't know which team played which in the World Series. When a guy asked me what I thought of the Indianapolis 500, I said I thought they were all guilty.

Unless you married someone who is as crazy about fishing as you are, then you already know how sex and fishing can come to conflict and grief. Too many couples get married with a secret agenda. That agenda is to wait a decent interval after the ceremony and then start trying to change the person they fell in love with. In the case of fishing, the first chill that officially ends the honeymoon can be summed up with this question, "You're not going fishing *again?*"

If you're one of the rare smart ones, you had this agenda on the table and worked it through before you bought the rings. Love means loving all of a person, not just a piece. For the fisherman, *all* includes his or her passion for fishing.

One groom I know should have known he was in trouble when, on his wedding day, he found his bride-to-be standing in her waders casting caddis flies to rising trout instead of waiting for him at the altar. "I told you, Harold," she said without looking over her shoulder, "after the hatch. *After* the hatch!"

A perfect understanding between lovers includes knowledge of each other's passions. Tolerance, compassion, timing and priorities are important if you hope to enjoy both sex and fishing. To get it all to work together correctly, you must develop perfect timing.

Three fishermen are standing in a trout stream. It's late afternoon and time to go home. One of them says, "I hate to go home. My wife will be waiting for me. She'll book me on one of her guilt trips about how I love fishing more than her. I'll pay and pay and pay. Sometimes I wonder if fishing is worth it."

The next guy says, "I hate to go home, too. All the time we've been gone my wife has been working on a honey-do list. It'll take me a month of chores to work off this trip. At least we could have caught something."

And the third guy says, "Boys, you obviously don't know anything about the psychology of fishing and suffer from bad timing. When I get up at five in the morning to go fishing, I wake my wife up and ask, 'What'll it be dear, sex or fishing?' And she says, 'Don't forget your waders.' "

After about age 30, the reply "Don't forget your waders" becomes more and more desirable for both sexes until, by the time you reach retirement years, you finally understand when life truly begins. Life begins not at the instant of conception, or at the moment of birth, or on the day you catch the biggest fish of your life: Life begins when the dogs die, the kids move away, and you start fishing in the middle of the week.

Fishing can be favorably compared to sex in still another way. Just as the need to fish waxes and wanes, so does the need for sex. Full moons affect both. Hot bites and hot dates inspire equal passions. Both desires can be sated, but not for long. When still a young man I made the greatest discovery of all about sex and fishing: The only thing equal to actually enjoying sex and fishing is the yearning that soon follows the fulfillment.

There is a serious side to the conflicts that can surround sex and fishing. These conflicts are real, not imagined. Jealousy is the green-eyed monster. Without understanding your lover's love of fishing, you the jealous spouse, run great risks of wrecking everything.

You and Me and the Fishy Makes Three

I have been privileged to counsel hundreds of couples down through the years. They have taught me a great deal. For the cheapest consult you will ever get, here is the single best rule for a happy relationship: Never ask your lover to give up that which he or she is most passionate about. It could be fishing, or it could be the theater, painting, bull-roping, antique hunting, reading, you-name-it.

It is fine to introduce the man or woman you love to fishing, but he or she is not obliged to love it as you do. Whatever your passion, it is your passion, not necessarily your lover's passion. No one should be asked to give up the thing they love most. If you ask this and you win, the person you love will be miserable. If you ask and lose, and then make a nag of yourself, you will both be miserable.

We who want to be in relationships must ask ourselves a very important question: Do I envy my lover's passion for something other than me?

If the answer to this question is yes, then the solution is not to make the person we love choose us over something they also love, but to ask ourselves two questions: Why am I not equally passionate about something? What is missing in my life that I have no passion?

Answer these two questions and you will step into a whole

new world of sex, hope and fishing. Love does not get ahead by getting even; love gets ahead by helping, by hoping and by charity.

Here is an old and favorite story of mine that illustrates this modest truth. It is about an old and spiteful fisherman's wife who, on her death bed, is surrounded by her three daughters. She hasn't much time left and her daughters ask, "Mom, we have a question we want you to answer."

"Go ahead," says the old woman.

"Well, we know you were married to Dad for fifty years before he died, and it seemed to us that you were unhappy with him about his fishing for at least forty-five of those years."

"So?"

"So, we've wondered why you stayed with him?"

The old woman leaned up on one elbow and growled, "Because I wasn't finished with the son-of-a-bitch!"

As the old fisherman said, "Hatred can keep a marriage together as long as love."

Remember the old Sicilian's saying, "He who would seek revenge should dig two graves."

Hope and Fishing

Hope is the yearning for new possibilities, for one more chance. Hope is to dream we might yet become the master of our fate. Hope is not only the wellspring of our humanity, but it is the single most important ingredient not only in fishing, but in life. Hope is the source of an angler's optimism and our good will toward others. It is the impetus for our greatest achievements as human beings. Without hope there would be no fishing, and without fishing there would be no hope.

"These hooks are really dull," I said, checking a young angler's lure after he missed a strike.

"Oh, it doesn't matter," he said. "I never catch anything anyway."

Pessimists catch less fish because pessimists won't invest in sharp hooks and the hope it takes to hone them.

If hope is the necessary condition to go fishing at all, then mastery is where hope begins. If you ever learned to ride a bicycle, you may remember the first time you peddled that unlikely machine around the block on two wheels.

Remember the feeling of power? Even defiance? You had just spit in the eye of the laws of gravity and now controlled a whole new physical world. Remember the first time your fly line shot out over the water in a perfect rolling loop? Or your bass plug splashed down one inch from the lily pad you were actually aiming at? This feeling, this good, inside feeling of power and control, is what psychologists call mastery.

Mastery is the one thing we all want to feel. We want to feel that we are able, powerful and competent. Whether it be solving for X, memorizing a poem, or tying a Royal Coachmen, all humans seek mastery. First you hope, then you master, and so it has always been.

When I was just starting out as a young student psychologist, I hoped to be a good clinician, master the counseling skills I'd been taught, and somehow help people. All counselors remember their first real patient. Mine told me an awful story of loss, suffering, broken dreams, abuse, depression, alcoholism and suicide. She ended her story of pain with tears in her eyes and the comment, "So, you see, I'm doomed and might as well kill myself." And I remember thinking, "Holy cow! This lady needs professional help!"

But of course I *was* the professional, and while I did my best to feign the mastery I would someday feel, I learned that while hope must run ahead of mastery, it must never disappear from view.

If hope is the vision, mastery is the only true reality. We in the healing professions are, more than anything else, in the hope business. No matter our specialty, without an offer of hope through mastery, no one would seek our services.

Hope is also the fisherman's main reliance, yet he, too, needs skill and mastery to feel competent and at one with his sport.

The Meanings of Hope

In Greek mythology, Pandora opened the box the gods forbade her to open. Pandora's box contained all the ills and ailments that are to plague man down through the ages. Evils flew from the box before she clamped down the lid, thus saving for man one of the few good things in the casket: hope. Was hope a cruel illusion, as Euripides said, or was hope the one thing we most needed to deal with all the rest?

I've read a little Euripides. A tragedian and pessimist, he was the kind of fellow who believed nothing turns out well. For Euripides, the bite was always off. Today, we professional psychologists would say a fellow like Euripides was probably suffering from a condition known as "optical rectitus." This is a neurological condition in which the nerves to your eyes and your rectum somehow grow together, and you end up with a shitty outlook on life. Any right-minded angler would have thought twice before inviting a guy like Euripides on a fishing trip.

From the Latin, "*Dum spiro, spero*," meaning "While I breathe, I hope," we know that hope stands front and center with the forces of life. Saint Paul ranked hope right up there with faith and charity. From the national anthem of Israel, "*Ha Tikva*," means "the hope." "Hope," wrote Alexander Pope, "springs eternal in the human breast."

From ancient times to modern, listen to how often the word hope appears in common language — in newspapers, in speeches, and especially in fishing talk. Hope is in such common usage, almost no one has noticed how the word's usage has changed in recent years.

Which phrase is the stronger?

"Hopefully, we will have a good bite and catch some fish."

Or, "I hope we will have a good bite and catch some fish."

In which statement does the speaker's action count? In which statement is the speaker not the actor, but the acted upon?

The phrase "I hope" is strong. The adverb "hopefully" is weak. "I hope" can be followed by, "I will! I can! I shall!" "Hopefully" is tentative and pitiable. Speakers, writers and fishermen of serious resolve never use an adverb when heavy lifting by a verb is required.

You will never hear a successful fisherman say, "Well, gee, hopefully the perch are biting." The successful fisherman says, "I hope the perch are on the bite. But if they're not, we will catch them anyway!"

The locus of control for successful anglers is not "out there," but "in here."

Locus of Control and Catching Fish.

Locus of control is a term we psychologists thought up to explain how people view the whereabouts of power in their lives: out there, or in here. If what causes things to happen is perceived as "out there" and beyond our personal control, then the power behind events is located outside of ourselves, and we can't do much about them.

But if we see the cause of things as inside ourselves, and that we are the power behind events, then we are responsible for the things that happen in life, in which case the locus of control is inside us.

Our view of how life works is everything. If the locus of control is out there, then mastery of ourselves matters little, since we are but pawns in some great and unknowable game. But if the locus of control is in us, then mastery of ourselves becomes the only goal to living a full and rewarding life.

Someone once said there are three kinds of people in the world: those who make things happen, those who watch things happen, and those who say, "What happened?" Those who make things happen catch more fish because they see the locus of control inside themselves.

Those who watch things happen see the locus of control outside themselves and say things like, "Shoot, those guys are having all the luck."

Fisherman who wonder "What happened?" haven't got a clue, do not rely on science, hope or mastery, and trust the outcome of any fishing trip entirely to chance. Such anglers become accustomed to getting skunked.

Fishing luck, by the way, is of no value to anglers whose locus of control is inside themselves. But even the most hopeful, master fisherman needs luck — not to explain *his* catch, but to explain the *other guy's* catch.

When we masterful anglers catch a big fish, it is because of skill, intelligence, lightening fast reflexes, our vast knowledge of fish behavior, lure selection and presentation. When the other guy catches a big fish it is because of, you guessed it, not intelligent luck, but pure, unadulterated *dumb* luck.

The children of hope are leadership, success, catching fish and a long life. I say a long life because a study in the July 1993 *Journal of Epidemiology* found that those people who reported severe hopelessness had four times the death rate due to coronary heart disease than those people who saw their lives as hopeful. Starting with the same level of health, and when controlled for sex, age, cigarette and alcohol use, blood pressure and other factors associated with heart disease, those people with even mild to moderate levels of hopelessness had higher rates of coronary heart disease than the hopeful travelers. The findings of this 12-year scientific study seem to support an older version of Biblical wisdom, "Hope deferred maketh the heart sick."

If you see the locus of control inside you, you are more likely to be hopeful not only about catching fish, but about how your life will turn out. This trait, called dispositional optimism, is a persistent belief that good things will eventually happen, that things tend to work out for the best. As a quick test, you might answer the following questions true or false:

In an uncertain bite, I still expect to catch fish.
No matter the weather, I always look on the bright side.
With the right lure, I don't need luck.
If something can go wrong on a fishing trip, it will.
When I go fishing, the fish stop biting.
The fishing trips I plan never work out.

People who answer "true" to the first three and "false" to the last three score high on dispositional optimism and have high hopes. People who answered "false" on the first three, and "true" on the last three, score low on dispositional optimism and are more hopeless. It doesn't take a Ph.D. to figure out which type of person you want to take fishing or which type of person we might all strive to be.

People with high hopes have been found to engage in

more adaptive coping strategies, which is psychobabble for they try harder. They try harder because they believe in positive outcomes. They enjoy higher self-esteem and less depression. Being more outgoing and prosocial, they tend to make good salespeople and have more friends. Because they imagine a long life for themselves, they eat the right foods, brush their teeth and floss. They recover more quickly and with better final health status from coronary bypass surgery. And, although no one has done the most critical research of all, they catch more fish.

Why?

Because an optimist doesn't know when to quit. Long after the pessimist has gone home, the optimist still has a line in the water. Positive anticipation, coupled with an unyielding belief that the bite will start at any moment and that, when it does, "I'll be ready!" keeps hope alive. And as long as hope thrives so the does the vessel in which it is kept.

Make no mistake, there is nothing so toxic to the mind and body as hopelessness and no medicine so powerful as hope. If despair is wrong, hope is right. One of the first hopeful anglers, Father Izaak Walton, lived to 94 years in a time when even the best food and health care couldn't get you much more than 50 years. If you want to live a long and healthy life, learn to be chronically optimistic, hopeful and never leave town without a travel rod.

Oscar Wilde wrote:

We did not dare to breathe a prayer
or give our anguish scope ...
For something had died in each of us
and what had died was hope.

While sitting in an airplane flying to some far fishing adventure, I wrote the following counterpoint:

We flew high and fast
and soared above death ...
Lifting and lofting
on a single molecule of hope.

Now, who would you rather go fishing with, Oscar Wilde or me?

Anglers as Hopeful Travelers

To travel hopefully is to deny the devil his due. There's a reason for that sign over Dante's inferno that reads, "Abandon all hope ye who enter here." Because if you could smuggle a single molecule of hope into hell, it wouldn't be hell anymore. I have it on good authority, by the way, that while golfers are welcomed into hell, fisherman are banned. The reason is obvious: Satan can't stand our optimism.

According to polls taken of high school students, the senior classes of 1957 and 1958 rated their hopes for the future higher than any other graduating class before or since. I was in the class of '57. We were hopeful travelers, perhaps because we lived in more hopeful times. Suffer me this brief retrospective on an era of hope.

We had a chronic optimist and fly fisherman in the White House, Dwight "Ike" Eisenhower. We had won World War II and stopped communism in Korea. Chuck Berry had just invented rock 'n' roll. General Motors had just cooked up the overhead cam engine and put it in the '57 Chevrolet, now the most collectible car in America. People really did see Elvis in the supermarket and all of our heroes, Bobby, John and Martin were still very much alive. John F. Kennedy was elected, in part, on a rewrite of Frank Sinatra's popular song of era, "High Hopes." Perhaps because the class of '57 had such high hopes, America enjoyed its lowest teen suicide rate in its history.

Maybe the old fisherman was right when he said, "Hope is not just a state of mind, it's the place you want to live."

I'll admit I have little tolerance for dispositional hopelessness, pessimism, cynicism and for those who want to quit fishing before we absolutely have to. Those who place the locus for control outside themselves and thereby attempt to avoid personal responsibility for their lives are not only pathetic, but dangerous.

Consider that we currently live in a cultural climate of excuse-seeking and victimhood. The "Laugh-In" comic Flip

Wilson started it all when, to explain his outrageous behavior, he joked, "The devil made me do it." Some people in my profession encouraged us to avoid personal responsibility, place the locus of control out there so that we could blame our mothers, then our fathers, and then the both of them. And if that wasn't enough, we could blame our grandparents, or adoptive parents, rap music, or, in case we killed someone, too much sugar in our Twinkies.

In case you forgot to file your tax return, I can probably help you. I can write the IRS and explain that due to the trauma triggered by the terrifying spectacle of a U.S. Government tax return form, you now suffer from a "Failure to File Syndrome."

The price of placing the locus of control outside ourselves is the loss of personal power, self-control, and the forfeiture of that wonderful sense of mastery that is so essential to being a happy human being. If everything happens to you, you cannot be held accountable. In turn, you get to be a victim, and a victim needs someone to blame. Blamers are losers, and losers don't catch fish. The worst outcome of all is that such psychological excuse-seeking paralyses hope, thus making us physically, mentally and spiritually weak.

So be careful around psychologists like me. Some of us are trained to help you find excuses, excuses which can stall your life and confound your natural tendency to rise above conflict and adversity.

Ernest Hemingway once said that "Life breaks us all, but some of us are stronger in the broken places." This is true of bones, and it can be true of hearts and minds as well. We all earn purple hearts for suffering through life's usual and customary conflicts, battles and losses; however, wearing them is optional.

The Species that Hopes

Perhaps it is our built-in, shock-proof dispositional optimism that best defines us as a species. If so, then optimism must have been selected for and must, therefore, have survival value. Recent research shows that optimism is associated with elevated mood and a sense of well-being. In turn optimism leads to more resilience under adversity, a greater capacity for persistence and decreased vulnerability to stress. By nature human beings are hopeful travelers.

Some have taken the view that the theory of evolution strips us of our hope; that such a scientific explanation of humanity diminishes us to a deterministic, if interestingly complex, electrochemical, biological experiment. What we call mind or soul can't be much more than an ephemeral wisp, the epiphenomenon of an admittedly complicated mammalian brain.

Hope defined in this biological, deterministic context seems a silly notion. But silly to whom? To us. We are definers of what things mean, not the other way around. If we need and value hope, then we will have it. Compared to our ancient ancestors, we ought to have more of whatever hope is than any prior generation of humans ever dreamed possible. Hope is our ace-in-the-hole and our royal flush.

Compared to the anglers of old, we are speeding into the light. Scientific knowledge is piling up at an unbelievable pace. We are learning how the world works, and how other worlds work. Our understanding of all things leaps forward, while hope climbs on strong legs.

Hope and the Girl Next Door

Consider the hope and promise of the brave new world of genetics. By accident more than plan, we humans are heading into an era of unprecedented genetic diversity and good health. No longer are we obliged to marry the girl next door, or our cousin, as did Charles Darwin. Understanding blood lines as well as he did, Mr. Darwin worried his whole life that his children's health was jeopardized by his marriage to a cousin. Outbreeding keeps any species strong, more adaptive and more resilient. It is well-worth the reminder that two-thirds of the people reading this will die for reasons connected to the genes they carry. This is due, in part, to the limited gene pool from which each of us has had to choose a mate.

As an aside, one of the reasons boys and girls find that

boys and girls from the neighboring tribe, the next town down the road, or the from any far land are strangely alluring, sexy and attractive, may be due to our natural inclination to take a dip in a gene pool other than our own. This love story theme covers every romance from *Romeo and Juliet* to *West Side Story* to *The Bridges of Madison County*.

Consider, now, that the distance between what were considered separate gene pools has never been shorter. The distance between the birthplaces of our grandparents was less than 20 miles. Today it is now several hundred miles, and for most couples their respective gene pools are so far apart as to be completely unrelated. You can catch an airplane in any direction, meet and marry an African, a Russian, a Japanese, a Brazilian or an Alaskan native, and many of my fishing friends have. There are good biological reasons to do so.

If an African carrying the gene responsible for sickle-cell anemia marries a European carrying the gene for cystic fibrosis, any children born of the union will be protected against both diseases. If you want your child to be born without some life-limiting genetic illness, then marry someone from a different gene pool. It is the blending of our diversity, both physical and cultural, that gives us reason to hope and a strength we have never before enjoyed.

The Fishing Gods Can Go to Hell

Last spring, several young fishermen and I opened the early trout season with a trip to a place called Twin Lakes. By age comparison I was the geezer, the old fisherman. One young angler in the group could not catch a brook trout despite a steady bite. Using the same lures and flies as the rest of us, he was still fishless toward the end of the day. As the shadows lengthened, efforts to tease him out of a darkening mood met with a set jaw.

Landing yet another nice trout and releasing it, I turned to him and said, "Good grief, Kevin, you didn't have sex with your wife last night, did you?" The young man smiled sheepishly.

"No wonder!" I said "The fishing gods are angry with you. Here, take my rod, you can probably catch one before they find out." Within three minutes he hooked and landed his first fish of the day.

Before the discovery of the scientific method, we fishermen needed taboos and moody fishing gods to explain such fishless days. We needed to make sacrifices, observe ritual and be pure of heart. We gave up sex for what we hoped would be better fishing.

Except for the case just cited, we now know such beliefs to be false beliefs. What we want now are good theories, testable hypotheses, facts and researched-based protocols for, say, lure presentation. All of these — plug choice for type of bass, delivery of that plug for given water and light conditions, structure and time of year, together with proper scents and laser-sharpened hooks — are the gifts of science. With science as our ally, the fishing gods can go to hell.

Some say scientific naturalism diminishes our dreams, not only for this life but for whatever comes after that final voyage over the far shoal. I do not believe this. Every day science gives us fresh hopes and new dreams — even new universes we didn't have a week ago.

Science prods our imagination and stimulates our creativity. Science has taken us to Jules Verne's moon and back again. And while we did not find little green men on the moon — or more important, a single trout stream — the bass back here on *terra firma* still hunt by its light, the grunion still run when its face is full, and we still write songs and make love by its soft and enchanting glow. Knowing the moon through science does not destroy its magic, but gives us richer moon stories to tell.

Back to the Beginning

From that sterile moon in whose beams the big bass search the lily pads, we humans can look back down on our little blue planet and wonder at the only known experiment in this miracle called life. It is an awesome view, a privileged view and a humbling one.

Every last fisherman is connected to every last living thing, and every last non-living thing. A stone in the river has no life as we know it, and yet it is shelter to the trout, home to the caddis pupa and the rock upon which we stand to cast the fly. We — the river, the stone in the river, the caddis fly and the trout — are one, and all have equal standing.

Natural selection is not a theory about rankings or improvement or progress, or who is the more intelligent, deserving or righteous; natural selection is a theory about how we're doing today. This month. This year. This generation. Here and now.

All living things adapt to the places in which they find themselves, or they die out. With no place to go and no place to grow, you must necessarily die out. Fish, foul, frog or fisherman — either you find a friendly place in the cosmos and remain a Darwin's bass, or you start sucking pond water and follow the millions of other life forms to join the largest club in the world: the extinct.

A stone in a river is but a particle of cosmic dust, but so am I. And so are you. We move and cast and laugh today, but tomorrow we are as the stone in the river, still and silent. "Ashes to ashes," the Bible says. Stardust to stardust. To grasp our true meaning and realize our duties, we fishermen must never forget our equal station in the great web of life. Today we catch the worm that catches the bass; tomorrow the worm catches us.

Saint Thomas Aquinas wrote that it is not possible to be ignorant of the end of the things if we know their beginning. The journey back to the origins of life, of our life, and of our life of consciousness may be no more than a fisherman's dream of a big bass in the night on Chapman Lake, but it is still one wondrous dream. It is still something to sing about.

Now, let's circle all the way round to the beginning of this book one last time.

Looking to the 21st century, we will surely find a new humanity, a new beginning or a new species at the head of the food chain. The future depends entirely on us. We have the tools and the knowledge to change not only the very nature of mankind, but the world and all the living things therein. The question is: Do we have the wisdom?

We cannot turn back, no more than the Greek gods could

turn back. Behind us lies darkness, dogma, disillusion, ignorance and catch-and-kill every damn last one of them. Ahead of us lies the unknown, but not the unknowable. Already we can catch-and-release or catch-and-kill according to our intelligence, knowledge, restraint and the needs of a fishery. There is every hope we can become the good fisherds before we kill them all, maybe even become the kind of humans we dream to be.

To explore this unknown future we will rely as never before on the spirit of science and its self-correcting powers. Our understanding of nature, and of human nature, may never be complete, but wisdom through science can inch us forward toward greater creativity, greater understanding and greater liberty.

This late June night I am camped alone, finishing this book, at a place called Breakfast Creek, a little stream in North Idaho that works its way down through the Rocky Mountains and eventually finds the Clearwater River, the Snake, the Columbia and the Pacific Ocean.

The fishing was not spectacular this morning, but it was plenty good enough. I enjoyed a long hike upstream and listened to the rush of snowmelt and felt the first summer wind blow down the canyon. Rising to the fly, a dozen rainbows and a few wild cutthroat trout were hooked. They are trying to adapt to a logged-over drainage. There was the promise of a big bull trout when I dredged the deep holes with Muddler Minnows, but as with most fishing dreams, this one remains a dream.

As I finish this writing by the campfire, the embers burn low. I can hear the high water, running wild and free beside me. It will be a good sound to sleep by. Soon I will go to bed per chance, as Shakespeare said, to dream. I might even dream of catching a fish, maybe a bull trout, or maybe that big bass from Chapman Lake.

The Greeks believed in fire as truth. A bold Titan, Prometheus, brought fire and truth to us. Prometheus caused we mortals to stop seeing doom in the forecast and start seeing hope. When the folks asked Prometheus how he managed to lift man up, he said, "I placed in them blind hopes."

Prometheus was a fisherman; I'd stake my reputation on it.

If he were here with me tonight, I'd offer him some coffee, maybe with a splash of bourbon in it for a nightcap. Then, in the morning, I'd take him fishing with me. A hopeful traveler, he'd catch a trout, too. You could bet on it.

May hope be with you.

There, now, let me remove the hook so that you can swim free.

About the Author

In the two years that have elapsed since the publication of his first-ever psychology of fishing, *Pavlov's Trout*, Dr. Paul Quinnett has held true to his own advice to go fishing often, with excursions to Alaska, Canada, Christmas Island and his own home waters around eastern Washington and northern Idaho. When not on the water, he is Director of Greentree Behavioral Health in Spokane, Washington. He also serves as Clinical Assistant Professor in the Department of Psychiatry and Behavioral Science at the University of Washington School of Medicine. Quinnett is a nationally recognized authority on suicide prevention, about which he has written several books, including *When Self-Help Fails* and *Suicide: The Forever Decision*. He also created "QPR, CPR for Suicide Prevention," a national program for the prevention of suicide.

Dr. Quinnett likes to say he's been a fisherman all his life, but a psychologist for only the last 27 fishing seasons. He uses his frequent outdoor pursuits as grist for a prolific writing avocation that has included publication in hundreds of national magazines, including *Gray's Sporting Journal*, *Sporting Classics*, *Field & Stream*, *Sports Afield*, *Audubon* and others.

To Order More Copies of
Darwin's Bass

Send $14.95 for each softbound copy ordered, or $24.95 for each hardbound, plus $3 shipping to:

Keokee Co. Publishing, Inc.

P.O. Box 722

Sandpoint, ID 83864

Visa and Mastercard orders by phone accepted at: 208/263-3573 from Monday through Friday 8:30 a.m. to 5:30 p.m. (Pacific Time).

Also Available:
Pavlov's Trout: The Incompleat Psychology of Everyday Fishing

If you enjoyed *Darwin's Bass*, you'll love its predecessor *Pavlov's Trout*, Paul Quinnett's first exploration of fishing psychology. In its fourth printing after only two years, *Pavlov's Trout* is poised to become a classic of fishing literature. Order from Keokee Publishing, above.

224 pages • Hardbound, $24.95 • Softbound, $14.95